Post-Human Institutions and Organizations

When the *Matrix* trilogy was published in the mid-1980s, it introduced to mass culture a number of post-human tropes about the conscious machines that have haunted our collective imaginaries ever since. This volume explores the social representations and significance of technological developments – especially AI and human enhancement – that have started to transform our human agency. It uses these developments to revisit theories of the human mind and its essential characteristics: a first-person perspective, concerns and reflexivity. It looks at how the smart machines are used as agents of change in the basic institutions and organisations that hold contemporary societies together, for example in the family and the household, in commercial corporations, in health institutions or in the military. Its main purpose is to enrich the ongoing public discussion of the social and political implications of the smart machines by looking at the extent to which they further digitalise and bureaucratise the world, in particular by asking whether they are used to develop techno-totalitarian societies that corrode normativity and solidarity.

Ismael Al-Amoudi is Professor at Grenoble Ecole de Management, Univ Grenoble Alpes ComUE, France.

Emmanuel Lazega is Professor at the Institut d'Etudes Politiques de Paris (Sciences Po), France.

The Future of the Human

Until the most recent decades, natural and social science could regard the 'human being' as their unproblematic point of reference, while monsters, clones and drones were acknowledged as fantasies dreamed up for the purposes of fiction or academic argument. In future, this common, taken for granted benchmark will be replaced by various amalgams of human biology supplemented by technology – a fact that has direct implications for democracy, social governance and human rights, owing to questions surrounding standards for social inclusion, participation and legal protection. Considering the question of who or what counts as a human being and the challenges posed by anti-humanism, the implications for the global social order of the technological ability of some regions of the world to 'enhance' human biology and the defence of humankind in the face of artificial intelligence, the books in this series examine the challenges posed to the universalism of humankind by various forms of anti-humanism, to explore if 'human essentialism' can be defended by accentuating the liabilities and capacities particular to human beings alone.

Series Editor
Margaret Archer, University of Warwick, UK

Titles in this series

Realist Responses to Post-Human Society: Ex Machina
Edited by Ismael Al-Amoudi and Jamie Morgan

Post-Human Institutions and Organizations
Confronting the Matrix
Edited by Ismael Al-Amoudi and Emmanuel Lazega

For more information about this series, please visit:
www.routledge.com/The-Future-of-the-Human/book-series/FH

Post-Human Institutions and Organizations

Confronting the Matrix

Edited by Ismael Al-Amoudi
and Emmanuel Lazega

Routledge
Taylor & Francis Group

LONDON AND NEW YORK

First published 2019
by Routledge
2 Park Square, Milton Park, Abingdon, Oxon OX14 4RN

and by Routledge
605 Third Avenue, New York, NY 10017

First issued in paperback 2021

Routledge is an imprint of the Taylor & Francis Group, an informa business

Publisher's Note
The publisher has gone to great lengths to ensure the quality of this reprint but points out that some imperfections in the original copies may be apparent.

British Library Cataloguing-in-Publication Data
A catalogue record for this book is available from the British Library

Library of Congress Cataloging-in-Publication Data
A catalog record for this book has been requested

ISBN 13: 978-1-03-208563-0 (pbk)
ISBN 13: 978-0-8153-7794-8 (hbk)

Typeset in Times New Roman
by Apex CoVantage, LLC

To Lina & Anna; Cassandre & Roza,
This is the world you will have to live in, and struggle in,
and embellish.

Contents

Figures

Contributors

Ismael Al-Amoudi is Professor of Social and Organisational Theory and Director of the Centre for Social Ontology at Grenoble Ecole de Management, Univ Grenoble Alpes ComUE (France). His work borrows from anthropology, management studies, political philosophy, social theory and sociology. One recurring theme in his research concerns the nature of social norms and the basic processes through which they are legitimated and contested. Another theme concerns the contribution of ontology to the human and social sciences. He is a member of the editorial boards of *Organization* and of *The Journal for the Theory of Social Behavior*. Recent publications include articles in the *Academy of Management Learning & Education*; *British Journal of Sociology*; *Business Ethics Quarterly*; *Cambridge Journal of Economics*; *Human Relations*; *Journal for the Theory of Social Behaviour*; *Organization*; and *Organization Studies*.

Margaret S. Archer founded the Centre for Social Ontology at the *Ecole Polytechnique Fédérale de Lausanne* in 2011, where she was Professor of Social Theory. Currently she is Visiting Professor at the Arctic University of Norway, Tromsø, the University of Navarra (Pamplona) and the Uniwersytet Kardinała Stefana Wyszńskiego in Warsaw. Pope Francis appointed her as President of the Pontifical Academy of Social Sciences in 2014. Previous to that she was elected as the first woman President of the International Sociological Association at the 12th World Congress of Sociology (1986). Archer was a founder member of both the Pontifical Academy of Social Sciences and the British Academy of Learned Societies in the Social Sciences and is a trustee of the Centre for Critical Realism. She has published many well-known works on social theory, including *Culture and Agency: The Place of Culture in Social Theory* (Cambridge, 1988); *Realist Social Theory: The Morphogenic Approach* (Cambridge, 1995); *Being Human: The Problem of Agency* (Cambridge, 2000); *Structure Agency and the Internal Conversation* (Cambridge, 2003); *Making Our Way Through the World: Human Reflexivity and Social Mobility* (Cambridge, 2007); and *The Reflexive Imperative in Late Modernity* (Cambridge, 2012).

Pierpaolo Donati is *Alma Mater* Professor (PAM) of Sociology at the University of Bologna. Past-President of the Italian Sociological Association, he has served as Executive Committee Member of the IIS and Director of the National Observatory on the Family of the Italian Government. He is currently a member of the Pontifical Academy of Social Sciences (since 1997) and of the Academy of Sciences of the University of Bologna (since 1998). He has published more than 800 works. He is known as the founder of an original 'relational sociology' or 'relational theory of society'. Among his more recent publications are *Relational Sociology: A New Paradigm for the Social Sciences* (Routledge, 2011); *The Relational Subject* (with M. S. Archer) (Cambridge, 2015); *Discovering the Relational Goods* (Rubbettino, 2019); *Life as Relation: A Dialogue Between Theology, Philosophy, and Social Science* (with A. Malo and G. Maspero) (Routledge, 2019); and *Sociología relacional de lo humano* (Eunsa, 2019).

John Latsis is Associate Professor in Social and Organisational Theory at the University of Reading. His research interests are in social theory and economic philosophy and cover questions about the nature of conventional behaviour and rule following in social life, the influence of theory on economic action, and the socio-economic dimensions of human need. Recent publications include articles in the *Cambridge Journal of Economics*; *Journal of Institutional Economics*; *British Journal of Sociology*; *Journal for the Theory of Social Behaviour*; and the *Journal of Post-Keynesian Economics*.

Emmanuel Lazega is Professor of Sociology at the Institut d'Etudes Politiques de Paris (Sciences Po), a member of the Centre de Sociologie des Organisations (CNRS) and a senior member of the Institut Universitaire de France. His current research projects focus on social network modelling of generic social processes such as solidarity, control, regulation and learning. His publications can be downloaded from www.elazega.fr.

Andrea M. Maccarini is Professor of Sociology and Associate Chair in the Department of Political Science, Law and International Studies, University of Padova. He is head of the Class of Social Sciences in the Galilean School of Higher Studies. He has been Chair of the Italian Sociological Association (AIS) section of Education and has served as Italian representative at the governing board of OECD-CERI (Center for Educational Reform and Innovation). His main research interests lie in social theory, cultural change and the sociology of education. He is author of several books and articles, including A. M. Maccarini, *Deep Change and Emergent Structures in Global Society. Explorations in Social Morphogenesis* (Springer, 2019); A. M. Maccarini, E. Morandi, R. Prandini (eds.), *Sociological Realism* (Routledge, 2011).

Jamie Morgan is Professor of Economic Sociology at Leeds Beckett University. He co-edits the *Real-World Economics Review* with Edward Fullbrook. He has published widely in the fields of economics, political economy, philosophy, sociology and international politics. His recent books include *Trumponomics: Causes and Consequences* (ed. with E. Fullbrook, College Publications, 2017); *What Is Neoclassical Economics?* (Routledge, 2015); and *Piketty's Capital in the Twenty-First Century* (ed. with E. Fullbrook, College Publications, 2014).

Douglas V. Porpora is Professor of Sociology in the Department of Anthropology, Drexel University, and co-editor of *The Journal for the Theory of Social Behaviour*. He has published widely on social theory. Among his books are *Reconstructing Sociology: The Critical Realist Approach* (Cambridge, 2015); *Landscapes of the Soul: The Loss of Moral Meaning in American Life* (Oxford, 2001); *How Holocausts Happen: The United States in Central America* (Temple, 1992); and *The Concept of Social Structure* (Greenwood, 1987).

1 Introduction
Digital society's techno-totalitarian matrix

Ismael Al-Amoudi and Emmanuel Lazega

In William Gibson's *Matrix* trilogy, most humans live Hobbesian lives: solitary, poor, nasty, brutish and short. Privately owned companies exert a de facto monopoly on technology and violence through the use of subservient 'salarymen' and through mastery of expensive technologies for spying on and killing, but also for upgrading and downgrading human beings. Throughout a complex plot, humans of various levels of enhancement are manipulated by artificial intelligences (AIs) that seek to bypass the material safeguards and limitations imposed on them by their human creators and owners. These artificial intelligences appear to have developed some form of consciousness, though one that is very, if perhaps not radically, remote from human consciousness. As the story ends, the uploaded mind of a dead protagonist marries his beloved in the Matrix while AIs start colonising a nearby galaxy.

When the *Matrix* trilogy was published in the mid-1980s, it introduced to mass culture a number of post-human tropes that have haunted our collective imaginaries ever since. The most noted is arguably the eponymous Matrix, an information network that prefigures the development of the World Wide Web. But the *Matrix* trilogy also contains several other themes that inspired not only subsequent science fiction writers and cyberpunk fashionistas but also many of the scientists, engineers, entrepreneurs and intellectuals who invented, designed, marketed and commented on the technologies born at the turn of the 21st century.

Indeed, while conscious machines do not exist in 2018, the questions about their possibility in principle and about the process through which they may emerge remain open (Archer, present volume). While mind-uploading is still a fantasy, an increasing amount of human interaction, including the intimate, happens electronically and via online social networks (Donati, present volume). While interactions with bots and robots remain less baffling than in the *Matrix*, their pervasiveness already raises questions about the emergence of new forms of sociality (Maccarini, present volume). While the domination of a small elite that reaps the benefits of technology is not as stark as in the *Matrix*, current automation trends are largely excluded from public debate and left to a few powerful actors, public and private, who seek to influence rather than inform citizens and their representatives (Morgan, present volume). While artificial intelligence (AI) is not capable of consciously manipulating human beings for its own concerns, it has already started to bear on normative decisions in ways that undermine the ethics of human discussion (Al-Amoudi & Latsis, present volume). Finally, while turn-of-the-century soldiers and hit-men do not benefit from the extraordinary healthcare imagined by Gibson, they can already count on AI-based systems of operational support that multiply combat efficiency at the expense of team oppositional solidarity and personal tacit knowledge (Lazega, present volume), thus generating new organisational models.

The aim of our book, however, is neither to marvel at Gibson's prophetic vision nor to describe the gap that still exists between science fiction and science *tout court*. Our purpose is rather to discuss the social significance of phenomena we can already know. We try to understand how post-human technological developments, and especially AI, have started to transform our human agency but also the basic institutions and organisations that hold contemporary societies together: the family (Donati, present volume) and the household (Maccarini, present volume), but also commercial corporations (Morgan, present volume), health institutions and organisations (Al-Amoudi & Latsis, present volume), and the military writ large (Lazega, present volume).

Our collective book opens with a broad but reflexive literature review by Douglas V. Porpora on AI and human enhancement. The review indicates that, while books on AI started to appear in the 1960s, the topic reached a peak of popularity in the 1980s and, in spite of a slight decline, has remained fairly popular since then. But Porpora's review also provides insight about what the press has to say about AI. To do so, he has examined all articles published on AI by the *International New York Times* (INYT) over a period of 50 days randomly selected in the year 2017. The articles gathered over that period provide a reasonably representative sample of how AI is discussed in connection with four broad themes: social developments; the economy; innovation and capacities; and the arts.

Porpora's review is doubly useful for our project, both because it provides a refresher about the new artefacts, practices and institutions emerging as we write and because it helps appreciate some of the limits of media discourse on AI. For instance, a number of articles express dismay in the aftermath of an AI's victory over the human Go champion. The articles' dismay is based, however, on the widespread assumption that mastery of Go is indicative of human-like 'intelligence'. Yet, the contribution of Archer to the present volume (Archer, present volume; see also Donati, 2019; Morgan, 2019; Porpora, 2019) suggests otherwise: AIs might indeed reach capacities of equal (if not superior) power and worth as human minds; however, what is specific to and valuable about human minds is not so much their computational capacities as much as their endowment with a first-person perspective (Baker, 2000) and their capacity to identify concerns (Archer, 2000) and subsequently reflect on them (Archer 2007, 2010, 2012). But Archer's contribution to the present volume offers more than a mere philosophical critique of misplaced journalistic dismay; it also describes a plausible process through which an AI (as we know them in 2018) might come to acquire, through interaction with a human being, the essential characteristics of human mind: a first-person perspective, concerns and reflexivity.

One of the INYT streams witnessed by Porpora relates to what he calls social developments and reports on the pervasiveness of artificially 'intelligent' machines in daily life. While most articles assume that the threat of 'technological singularity' is still remote and that machines are not even close to over-ruling the world of humans (Kurzweil, 2005), many articles report on the AI-empowerment of familiar objects (e.g. cars, home appliances) and on the appearance of AI-equipped commercial sexbots, that is, machines specifically designed for their owners' sexual enjoyment. The INYT articles do not seem to notice, however, the significance of these technological developments for human sociality. How does living in a world populated with AIs bear on our human capacity to initiate, foster and steer meaningful relations with others?

Yet, the question of human sociality is at the heart of the chapters written by Andrea M. Maccarini and Pierpaolo Donati in the present book. Maccarini (present volume) asks whether interaction with AI-powered machines might encourage people to prefer 'pure relations' with AI machines that are devoid both of bodily imperfections and of the character flaws so common to humanity: impatience, envy, laziness and so forth.

Donati's chapter also addresses the evolution of human sociality, though through slightly different concepts. Donati posits the existence and relative unity of a *digital matrix* consisting in 'the globalised symbolic code from which digital artefacts are created in order to help or substitute human agency by mediating inter-human relations or by making them superfluous' (present volume, p. 105). But the recent emergence of the digital matrix is not, Donati argues, an innocuous addition to the social world. Rather, it deeply transforms and even *hybridises* social relations and the operations of human minds: 'The hybridised family turns out to be a family in which everyone is "alone, together". Relationships are privatised within the already private space of the family, while the identities of the members travel in the public space of the DM [digital matrix]' (Donati, present volume, p. 111).

Another INYT stream of articles discusses AI's economic implications. Most of these express anxiety about job destruction together with an interrogation about whether or not AI systems will replace or complement human labour. But the press articles also take at face value the estimates produced and circulated by governmental agencies and influential consultancies and think tanks. And this is precisely where Morgan's contribution to the present volume starts: since 'little attention was paid in the press to what the economic models were actually claiming or how they were constructed' (Morgan, present volume, p. 94), Morgan proposes to unpack the analyses and assumptions of the UK Made Smarter Review, an influential positional document on the economic consequences of AI technologies. Among other findings, Morgan shows in detail how the report moves from relatively fragile assumptions to seemingly objective figures and from speculation on a fundamentally open future to claims that 'there is no alternative' but to automate quickly enough to safeguard the competetivness of national firms, thus pitting nations against each other in what could become a race to the bottom.

The third INYT stream identified by Porpora discusses AIs' capacities and limitations. In the face of AI's victory at Go (mentioned previously), human-like capacities of calculation and even of intuition are no longer humanity's preserve. Yet, as several of the shortlisted articles remind us (following Bostrom, 2016), AI programmes are still highly specialized, and those capable of beating a Go champion are incapable of driving a car and vice versa. The implication is not only that AIs are still poor improvisers in unfamiliar contexts but also that they are arguably remote from having their own moral powers or, as Jim Kerstetter has it, 'The better question might be: how do you teach a computer to be offended?' (Kersteter, 2017, cited in Porpora, present volume).

Taking stock of AI's moral limitations, Al-Amoudi and Latsis (present volume) ask a slightly different, arguably overlooked but equally important, question: How does reliance on AI affect the capacity of human beings to discuss normative decisions? While their discussion is centred on public health, their findings are relevant to a wider array of industries and normative discussions.

In the same vein, Lazega (present volume) tracks how AI increases the capacities of command and control in organisations to unobtrusively shape interactions and parametrise collective agency between humans. A military template for this extension of AI both analyses real-time information from multiple sources and uses digital tools engineered to apply mathematical models of animal swarms for the management of army units operating under high stress in battlegrounds. This involves homogenising mental maps, anticipating response to enemy moves, manipulating emotional reactions, suggesting courses of action, preventing improvised deeds, and defusing oppositional solidarities. Although this capacity deals with soldiers, it could generate new organisational models for non-military organisations, in line with a tradition of military and war technology that have long shaped society at large (Centeno & Enriquez, 2016).

Organisational society: smart machines as agents of further bureaucratisation?

Organisational approaches are useful, and perhaps unavoidable, when reflecting on contemporary challenges to the human condition. Over the last couple of centuries, Weberian sociologists such as Presthus (*Organizational Society*), Jacobi (*The Bureaucratization of the World*), Stone (*Where the Law Ends*) and Coleman (*The Asymmetric Society*) raised concerns over the growing importance and even colonisation (Deetz, 1992) of most areas of social life by large private organisations. In the words of Charles Perrow:

> The appearance of large organizations in the United States makes organizations the key phenomenon of our time, and thus politics, social class, economics, technology, religion, the family, and even social psychology take on the character of dependent variables. Their subject matter is conditioned by

the presence of organizations to such a degree that, increasingly, since about 1820 in the United States at least, the study of organizations must precede their own inquiries.

(Perrow, 1991: 725)

To understand contemporary social change in such organisational societies, two ideal types of organised collective action have been identified: bureaucracy and collegiality (Lazega, 2017, forthcoming). These ideal types, each with its specific formal and its informal dimensions, combine social discipline and productive efficiency; they can be observed in real-life companies, associations, cooperatives, public authorities and so forth. The ideal types of bureaucracy and collegiality help us understand the organisational context of work practices, be they routine or innovative. In this dual logics approach, the bureaucratic model is generally employed to organise collective routine work while concentrating power unobtrusively: command and control at the top and depersonalised interactions among subaltern members. The collegial model, on the other hand, is usually observable in situations requiring collective innovative work with unpredictable output. Through collegial organisation, rival peers self-govern by deliberation and agreements or consensus building and by using personalised relationships and relational infrastructures to manage coordination and cooperation dilemmas.

But the ideal types of bureaucracy and collegiality are seldom present in their pure form throughout any single organisation. Rather, real-life workplaces, communities, markets and societies are replete with combinations of collegiality and bureaucracy. Indeed, organisations that can be called 'bureaucratic' (e.g. airlines) are nonetheless managed by a collegial top-team who maintain highly personalised relationships, and conversely, collegial organisations (e.g. private law firms) typically rely on bureaucratically organised support services which interact in largely impersonal ways.

If a lead is taken from the articulation of personalised collegiality and impersonal bureaucracy, the digitalisation of society can be interpreted as both cause and symptom of further and deeper bureaucratisation of society. Does this mean that impersonal interactions, routines, hierarchies and mass production will increasingly characterise our bureaucratised and technocratic contemporary societies? Contributions to this volume address this and underlying issues at varying levels of generality.

Donati argues that human relations are hybridised and even threatened when they are mediated by digital media and smart bots. We are left, however, with the question of how far the depersonalisation of relations can go. Indeed, is a world with human beings but with no personal relations possible in the first place? Or does the digital world necessarily encompass a combination of impersonal transactions and personalised relationships?

Here, a century of organisational sociology and discussion of the bureaucratic model can help us answer. We may draw, in particular, from Jean-Daniel Reynaud's (1989) theory of joint regulation of collective action. From this perspective, there is one dimension of the organisation of collective action that cannot be routinised and that reflects the limits of bureaucracy: the micro- and meso-political negotiation of the 'rules of the game'. This negotiation fleshes out the normative and moral dimension of action, a process of structural and cultural re/production that is never routine and that escapes the capacities of our very best AIs (Al-Amoudi & Latsis, present volume). Apart from the extreme case of totalitarianism (more on this later in this chapter), organisational members do not assume that complete planification and prediction are achievable or even desirable. Continuous coordination of activities is achievable through common (though necessarily incomplete; see Al-Amoudi, 2010) rules but also through a collective (if contested) project; through (relatively widely) shared cultural schemes of interpretation; and through (reasonably) congruent moral commitments. But the involvement of all actors, even those most subject to bureaucratic control, in negotiation and sense-making does not mean that all are equal in their capacity to defend their regulatory interests. Indeed, the regulatory process produces its share of winners and losers, so much so that Reynaud insightfully reinterprets change and new norms as broken promises. New rules produced by the regulatory process create losers who need to reorganise their practice and joint activities based on the new rules, which leads to the issue of how to handle these losers in bureaucratic contexts and in more collegial ones. For our book's concerns, this means that digitalisation, robots and artificial intelligence are likely to weaken the capacity of most people to defend their regulatory interests but are nonetheless unlikely to eradicate personal relations from the face of society.

Reynaud's reflections on the winners and losers of changing regulation processes help us understand, from a sociology of organisations perspective, both the anxiety expressed by media reports of AI (Porpora, present volume) and the triumphant optimism (Morgan, present volume) exhibited by management consultancies and governmental agencies that implicitly identify with the interests of large organisations and ambitious entrepreneurs.

But it is also because the development of AI is indissociable from its organisational context that Archer's tale ends in melancholic disenchantment: Homer the human and Ali the AI turned into an Artificial Person (an AP?) are both in the end victims of impersonal bureaucracy. Homer is condemned to wander in the limbo of the emeritus professoriate whereas Ali is condemned, without a crime, to lose the personality he developed over all these years and become a sophisticated, though soulless, traffic computer. And this should not surprise us, since organisational bureaucracy was precisely the context in which the lovely synergy of Ali and Homer started in the first place. Bureaucracy giveth and bureaucracy taketh away.

In his discussion of the co-existence and interaction of humans with non-human entities in multiple spheres of social life, Maccarini (present volume) examines the scope of the synergy ventured by Archer. He views AI as a factor of depersonalisation and suggests there is a continuum from mediation to substitution of human social partners. While the threshold between mediation and substitution is clearly theorised, whether and how it is crossed remains an empirical issue. Maccarini's study focuses on 'processes and forms that may properly be called post-human, that is where hybrid forms of social interactions and relations emerge'.

But whereas in Archer's account the machine develops personal emergent powers through repeated interaction with a human who remains relatively unchanged, Maccarini's account presents us with the obverse process: the smart machines (as we currently know them) do not evolve, but human personal powers do. And the result is alarming, as it might well involve increased intolerance and misanthropy.

Among the profound effects that AI, robotics and related innovations are set to have on the way we live, work and perhaps even who we are, Morgan looks at some of the ways the future of work is currently being positioned. He begins from the empirical issue of trends in industrial and service robotics and interrogates their significance. He then builds an ontological critique of claims about a fourth industrial revolution by maintaining a sharp distinction between imminent change and immanent potential. By doing so, he shows how positional documents shape our sense of the future, in effect colonising rather than merely predicting our future.

Taking a lead from Morgan, we might be able to refine further the political significance of hybridised (Donati) and pure (Maccarini) relationships. Their chapters in the present volume indicate that we are producing societies where we depend increasingly on impersonal transactions that have nonetheless a highly personalised basis. That is already the case, for example, when dealing with AI bots that can access our data from a variety of platforms. But the combination of impersonal relations and highly personalised transactions is also politically significant since it casts doubt on one of the founding promises of early cyber-optimists: that with the internet, the last technical obstacles to direct democracy would be removed. On the face of the analyses produced by Archer, Donati, Maccarini, Morgan and Porpora, it seems instead that, while direct democracy remains a distant fantasy, most citizens are gradually losing whatever power they had to use personalised relationships for institutional entrepreneurship. If this tendency is confirmed, then collegiality would be reserved for collegial elites and oligarchies since, as Reynaud argues, joint regulation and politics cannot be routinised and depersonalised. But the major part of the population could still be prevented from building innovative collective action based on personalised relationships. Indeed, emerging tendencies in organisations show that digitalisation can and does undermine the capacity for collective agency found in the myriad collegial pockets that operate below the highest social and organisational strata.

Society's organisations: digital corrosion of normativity and solidarity

During modernity, collegiality in bureaucratised organisations could survive in at least three kinds of 'collegial pockets'. Firstly, in the top-team of the organisation (whether a company, a government, a charity, etc.) must be collegial because work at the top is never routine, always political, and thus requiring joint regulation. Secondly, in professional segments such as legal, educational or R&D departments, as they involve activities requiring tacit knowledge, expertise and creativity. Thirdly, in workers' defense units such as trade unions at the bottom of the organisation, whose collegiality modern capitalist corporations have long tried to weaken or dissolve for fear of oppositional solidarity, whether work-related or ideological. In short, an organisation can never bureaucratise itself entirely, but the top of the organisation can weaken if not undermine collegial pockets among professionals or through union activity of workers on the ground (Lazega, forthcoming). As it happens, we might be currently witnessing the dying of forms of non-managerial collegiality, that is, not instrumentalised by bureaucratic management, at the lower social and organisational levels that are increasingly subjected to bureaucratic regulation and control (Lazega's chapter in Vol. III of *The Future of the Human* book series).

Al-Amoudi and Latsis explore what they call 'the ethics of AI'. To do so, they start from a technical limitation of AI which operates as a 'black box': while we can know its inputs and its outputs, we cannot fully make sense of its internal workings. But this technical limitation generates a broader social and moral limitation, for how will the introduction of AI affect our communities' capacity to discuss, challenge and decide on the norms governing policy, if AIs cannot provide a humanly understandable account of how they perform normatively laden classifications and suggestions?

Rather than address the problem of normative black boxes in general, they chose to focus their discussion on AI developments that are likely to transform/disrupt health policy defined in broad terms. These include activities of national organisations, regulation of mandatory health insurance, prioritisation of certain patient categories, drugs and treatments by supervisory bodies, public health information campaigns, and entwined strategies of for-profit actors such as private insurers or pharmaceutical companies deciding which drugs they will produce and how they will market them. Doing so allows Al-Amoudi and Latsis to identify and discuss novel normative problems arising from AI's bearing on public health policy's practices. Finally, they speculate on how these current developments could lead to a corrosion of normativity through the subordination of human judgement to machine judgement and through the stigmatisation of people whose profiles do not match the standards set by AI or the interests of those powerful organisations that will own artificially intelligent machines.

But the digital corrosion of normativity is matched by a digital corrosion of oppositional solidarity that Lazega (present volume) can already witness in the army. In order to understand how AI is likely to extend bureaucracy by further digitalising coordination in the workplace, Lazega examines the case of military units in the battlefield and how digitalisation transforms teams on the ground. He starts from soldiers' work and the mechanics of its digitalisation and their meaning in organisational terms. Doing so allows him to discuss the extension of digitalisation to society at large and the consequences in terms of reinventing specific forms of collective responsibility. It appears that, in a creepy way, the process of digitalisation as bureaucratisation of the battlefield neutralises an old problem faced by armies, that is, team-based oppositional solidarities (Shibutani, 1978). This neutralisation is achieved by AI remote-controlled task performance, in which social actors become potentially subjected to new forms of punitive collective responsibility. The specific example used here is military research on designing and using high performance teams based on the 'swarm template'. Swarm fantasies of collective action that can scale up uniformly are developed by mathematicians and engineers combining artificial intelligence and big data, including social network analysis (SNA), reducing relationships between soldiers to impersonal interactions at the "right" physical and social distance. In many ways, if combinations of AI and SNA provide military management with tools that build efficient teams while neutralising oppositional solidarity, they are able to further bureaucratise collegiality as defined here. High-ranking military bureaucrats want to transform previously personalised relationships into interactions that are impersonal and still be able to retransform interactions into relationships when the *esprit de corps* is needed again. In contrast with previous forms of collegiality that relied on personal relationships (bottom-up collegiality and top-down collegiality), this form can be called 'inside-out collegiality' (Lazega, forthcoming) since personalised and private relationships are observed from the outside and instrumentalised, if not transformed into digitalised interactions, deprivatized, neutralised and steered towards alignment. Bureaucratic management has been dreaming of this magic formula, the 'swarm template', for more than a century. The question raised by this combination of AI, SNA and computational social science is whether the meeting of this mathematical template and this managerial dream will have a dystopian effect on society through social digitalisation and whether new forms of collective responsibility, punitive or not, might emerge as a result.

The birth of techno-totalitarian societies?

It is not difficult to see how the digital interruption of normative discussion discussed by Al-Amoudi and Latsis combined with the digital corrosion of oppositional solidarity studied by Lazega can result in massive asymmetries of power between ruler and ruled. Since normative discussion is difficult, the decisions of rulers remain above cultural critique. And since inside-out collegiality inhibits collective action initiated in subordinate groups, the latter are incapable of mobilising effectively to initiate and sustain resistance. From a historical perspective, this combination is unfortunately not new. Indeed, when studying *the origins of totalitarianism,* Hannah Arendt (1951) identified the central generative mechanism behind the rise of totalitarianism as the melting down of traditional solidarities, which leaves a society of atomised individuals incapable of sustaining critical discussion and incapable of initiating collective action without the will of their supreme leader. But while fully blown totalitarianism rests on the physical elimination of vast numbers of individuals for the regime's survival, the earlier phases are both less bloody and less strikingly blatant to internal observers. These early phases involve nonetheless a number of social processes that are worryingly fuelled by the contemporary digitalisation of social relations.

Firstly, totalitarianism rests on the prior crushing of the individual private sphere which, in a liberal society, legitimately escapes the ruler's gaze and control. The increasing digitalisation of human exchanges is potentially conducive, however, to this phenomenon. In the countries of the Global North, this mechanism is not fully harnessed by states, which still limit their own powers of surveillance over citizens, though with notable exceptions. The first such exception concerns cases of suspected 'terrorism', a signifier with unclear boundaries that justifies nonetheless the suspension of civil rights in the form of indefinite detention, extradition, torture, dispossession and ostracism for the suspected individual but also for her or his acquaintances (Butler, 2004; 2009). It is indeed particularly worrying that states are wilfully ignoring both arguments of principle appealing to human dignity (Porpora et al., 2013) and instrumental arguments of academics claiming that purely military responses to terrorism intensify resentment, and ultimately terrorism itself, more than they contribute to keeping terrorism in check (Chomsky, 2003).

But in organisational society, states are no longer the most powerful actors, and the abuse of individual privacy by for-profit organisations is equally if not more worrying. It is so both because constant monitoring of employees and customers extends to almost all categories of the population (though not its elites, which escape routine monitoring through expensive tactics deployed in the name of trade secrecy), and because such extension is gradually gaining legitimacy (see Al-Amoudi & Latsis, present volume). Employers, for instance, routinely monitor the Facebook accounts of current employees and job candidates in contexts of high unemployment and low welfare-state security nets (see Blanc & Al-Amoudi, 2013, for a discussion of the illiberal consequences of such contexts). As a result, many a person ends up not only self-censoring the content she or he posts but also excluding those inconvenient friends with whom she or he would otherwise remain digitally connected.

Secondly, the narrowing of the private sphere is synergetic, Arendt argues, with the generalisation and normalisation of systems of collective punishment. As she has it:

> The consequence of the simple and ingenious mechanism of 'guilt by association' is that as soon as a man is accused, his former friends are transformed immediately into his bitterest enemies; in order to save their own skins, they volunteer information and rush in with denunciations to corroborate the nonexistent evidence against him; this obviously is the only way to prove their own trustworthiness.
>
> (Arendt, 1951: 423)

While the online behaviour of self-censoring employees and job seekers can be interpreted as resulting from guilt by association, another, perhaps more developed, phenomenon can be observed in the financial sphere. Indeed, emergent practices of money-lending based on 'social collateral' (Karlan et al., 2009) are intended to produce individual discipline through fears of collective punishment. Paradoxically inspired by the Grameen approach to microfinance, banks are increasingly using private/intimate data on personalised relationships between neighbours and family to generate ad hoc social units and impose forms of collective responsibility in exchange for lending them money to acquire homes. Combined with other data (financial, professional, legal, etc.), relational data helps evaluate whether or not the lender can rely on these relationships to create enough collective responsibility to repay the loans. In both previous examples, collegiality is observed and manipulated for its own ends by an outside party, a principle that can be extended to all sorts of collegial pockets operated inside out by a ruler with access to the digital information produced by group members.

Thirdly, the rule of law as a source of legitimacy is replaced by the will of the leader. In the case of Bolshevism and Nazism, this was achieved through state propaganda and through the creation of cells that adopted 'so many organisational devices of secret societies without ever trying to keep their own goal a secret' (Arendt, 1951: 493). The members of such cells were trained to despise existing institutions and to disbelieve the news conveyed by external media. In such a context, respect for the rule of law and for traditional moral norms eroded, and the only source of coordination became the ever-changing will of the movement's supreme leader. It has become an intellectual banality, at least since the democratic failures of the Trump election in the USA and of the Brexit in the UK, that digital social networks generate informational bubbles in which fake news flourishes and resentment grows exponentially.

Less trivial, perhaps, are the authoritarian implications of the introduction of AI examined by Al-Amoudi and Latsis and of swarm-teams studied by Lazega in the present volume. Since the rule of law cannot operate without continuous interpretation by those subject to it (see the discussion of J-D. Reynaud previously), the unfortunate fact that AIs operate as normative black boxes is likely to restrict the capacity of human communities to rely on thoughtfully agreed rules. It is not clear, however, whether the resulting configuration will be one in which authority rests with AI systems' creators and owners or whether the latter will lose control of their creations and will in turn be subjected to anormative AI decisions on topics that should nonetheless require democratic normative discussion. In either case, unless the safeguarding institutions and organisations called for by Al-Amoudi and Latsis at the end of their chapter are implemented, members of digital society are likely to obey unjustified – and therefore authoritarian – decisions rather than the rule of law.

The swarm-teams studied by Lazega in the present volume indicate, however, an even more immediate danger. Oppositional solidarity, be it at the level of teams, organisations or societies, presents a healthy obstacle to autocratic command and control by elites and a condition for the promotion of innovation. And yet, Lazega argues, this mechanism is already disappearing in the army and is bound to disappear in other spheres of society, including educational organisations (teachers being told at the last minute what to teach, to whom and how), in political movements (activists being told what to protest for or against, when and how), in hospitals (doctors and nurses being told who to care for, how and when), and so on.

If these reflections are given credence, then digital society bears the seeds for forms of totalitarianism that could perhaps be less bloody, but also more efficient and thus more stable, than Bolshevism and Nazism. The ontological distinction between imminent events and immanent possibilities (Morgan, present volume) as well as the possibility, in principle, that AIs develop moral consciousness and even forms of thoughtful solidarity with humans (Archer, present volume) provide rays of hope. However, without a public discussion of the social and political implications of digitalisation of societies, organisations and institutions, we are in danger of collectively writing the prequel to Gibson's *Matrix* trilogy.

References

Al-Amoudi, I. (2010). Immanent non-algorithmic rules: An ontological study of social rules. *Journal for the Theory of Social Behaviour*, 40(3): 289–313.

Al-Amoudi, I., & Latsis, J. (present volume). Anormative black boxes: Artificial intelligence and health policy. In I. Al-Amoudi & E. Lazega (Eds.), *Post-Human Institutions and Organisations: Confronting the Matrix*. London: Routledge.

Archer, M. S. (2000). *Being Human: The Problem of Agency*. Cambridge: Cambridge University Press.

Archer, M. S. (2007). *Structure, Agency and the Internal Conversation*. Cambridge: Cambridge University Press.

Archer, M. S. (2010). *Making Our Way Through the World*. Cambridge: Cambridge University Press.

Archer, M. S. (2012). *The Reflexive Imperative in Late Modernity*. Cambridge: Cambridge University Press.

Archer, M. S. (present volume). Considering artificial intelligence personhood. In I. Al-Amoudi & E. Lazega (Eds.), *Post-Human Institutions and Organisations: Confronting the Matrix*. London: Routledge.

Arendt, H. (1951). *The Origins of Totalitarianism*. New York, NY: Meridian Books.

Baker, L. R. (2000). *Persons and Bodies: A Constitution View*. Cambridge: Cambridge University Press.

Blanc, S. M-A., & Al-Amoudi, I. (2013). Corporate institutions in a weakened welfare state: A Rawlsian perspective. *Business Ethics Quarterly*, 23(4): 497–525.

Bostrom, N. (2016). *Superintelligence: Plans, Strategies, Dangers*. New York, NY: Oxford University Press.

Butler, J. (2004). *Precarious Life: The Powers of Mourning and Violence*. London and New York: Verso.

Butler, J. (2009). *Frames of War: When Is Life Grievable?* London: Verso.

Centeno, M. A., & Enriquez, E. (2016). *War and Society*. Cambridge: Polity Press.

Chomsky, N. (2003). Wars of terror. *New Political Science*, 25(1): 113–127.

Deetz, S. (1992). *Democracy in an Age of Corporate Colonization: Developments in Communication and the Politics of Everyday Life* (SUNY Series in Speech Communication). Albany, NY: State University of New York.

Donati, P. (2019). Transcending the human: Why, where, and how? In I. Al-Amoudi & J. Morgan (Eds.), *Realist Responses to Post-Human Society: Ex Machina*. London: Routledge.

Donati, P. (present volume). The digital matrix and the hybridisation of society. In I. Al-Amoudi & E. Lazega (Eds.), *Post-Human Institutions and Organisations: Confronting the Matrix*. London: Routledge.

Karlan, D., Mobius, M., Rosenblat, T., & Szeidl, A. (2009). Trust and social collateral. *Quarterly Journal of Economics*, 124: 1307–1361.

Kersteter, J. (2017, June 16). Daily report: The limits of AI. *The New York Times*. Available online: www.nytimes.com/2017/06/16/technology/facebook-the-limits-of-ai.html (accessed 21 December 2018).

Kurzweil, R. (2005). *The Singularity is Near: When humans transcend biology*. Viking.

Lazega, E. (2017). Networks and commons: Bureaucracy, collegiality and organizational morphogenesis in the struggles to shape collective responsibility in new sharing institutions. In M. S. Archer (Ed.), *Morphogenesis and Human Flourishing* (Vol. V, pp. 211–237). Dordrecht: Springer.

Lazega, E. (forthcoming). Bottom-up collegiality, top-down collegiality, or inside-out collegiality: Research on intermediary-level relational infrastructures as laboratories for social change. In G. Ragozini & M. P. Vitale (Eds.), *Challenges in Social Network Research*. Dordrecht: Springer.

Lazega, E. (forthcoming). Bureaucracy, collegiality and social change, Cheltenham: Edward Elgar Publishers.

Lazega, E. (present volume). Swarm-teams with digital exoskeleton: On new military templates for the organizational society. In I. Al-Amoudi & E. Lazega (Eds.), *Post-Human Institutions and Organisations: Confronting the Matrix*. London: Routledge.

Maccarini, A. M. (present volume). Post-human sociality: Morphing experience and emergent forms. In I. Al-Amoudi & E. Lazega (Eds.), *Post-Human Institutions and Organisations: Confronting the Matrix*. London: Routledge.

Morgan, J. (2019). Yesterday's tomorrow today: Turing, Searle and the contested significance of artificial intelligence. In I. Al-Amoudi & J. Morgan (Eds.), *Realist Responses to Post-Human Society: Ex Machina*. London: Routledge.

Morgan, J. (present volume). Stupid ways of working smart? Colonising the future through policy advice. In I. Al-Amoudi & E. Lazega (Eds.), *Post-Human Institutions and Organisations: Confronting the Matrix*. London: Routledge.

Perrow, C. (1991). A society of organizations. *Theory and Society*, 20(6): 725–762.

Porpora, D. (2019). Vulcans, Klingons, and humans: What does humanism encompass? In I. Al-Amoudi & J. Morgan (Eds.), *Realist Responses to Post-Human Society: Ex Machina*. London: Routledge.

Porpora, D. (present volume). What they are saying: About artificial intelligence and human enhancement. In I. Al-Amoudi & E. Lazega (Eds.), *Post-Human Institutions and Organisations: Confronting the Matrix*. London: Routledge.

Porpora, D. V., Nikolaev, A. G., May, H. M., & Jenkins, A. (2013). *Post-Ethical Society: The Iraq War, Abu Ghraib, and the Moral Failure of the Secular*. Chicago, IL: University of Chicago Press.

Reynaud, J-D. (1989). *Les règles du jeu: L'action collective et la régulation sociale*. Paris: Armand Colin.

Shibutani, T. (1978). *The Derelicts of Company K: A Sociological Study of Demoralization*. Berkeley, CA: University of California Press.

2 What they are saying about artificial intelligence and human enhancement

Douglas V. Porpora

Artificial intelligence and human enhancement are not just academic issues. There is instead lively discussion about these topics even in the popular press. We therefore thought it important to situate our own reflections within the context of that wider discussion. As a communication scholar, that task fell to me.

Accordingly, this chapter examines the wider media treatment of artificial intelligence and human enhancement. Artificial intelligence (A.I.) refers to computer-driven behavior or determinations that, done by humans, we would consider intelligent. Among exemplars are computer victories at games like chess and Go – and even *Jeopardy* – but also medical diagnoses and other accomplishments associated with machine learning and what is now called "big data."

Human enhancement, on the other hand, refers to all the new ways promising to enhance human potential. Humans of course have been enhancing their potential since they first stepped onto the veld. Tools and weapons after all are ways of enhancing what we might otherwise do with our bodies alone. Canes, glasses, and written records likewise enable many or all of us to do what we otherwise could not.

Not only has human enhancement gone on since our beginnings, it has also been uncontroversial as a means to help those otherwise disabled to function at standard levels of performance. Our interest in it here is where human enhancement does become controversial. Enhancement becomes controversial when it is posed as a means to upgrade the whole human species or at least some category of currently able-bodied humans like soldiers to perform at what are currently superhuman levels. That possibility suggests physically and mentally enhanced cyborgs that transition us all to a post-human future.

The first thing I did to pursue my task was to utilize Google's *Ngram Book Viewer* to get a basic feel about how much attention there has been to the two topics and when it began. Although Google's Ngram is confined to books and is not without its problems, it suffices for a rough feel of attentional contours. At least in terms of books, Figure 2.1 presents us with the timing and attention for both artificial intelligence and human enhancement. In addition, however, to the search term *artificial intelligence*, I also employed the related search terms *robots* and *androids*.

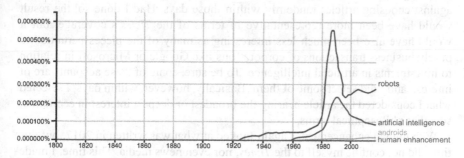

Figure 2.1 What they have been saying about robots, androids, etc.

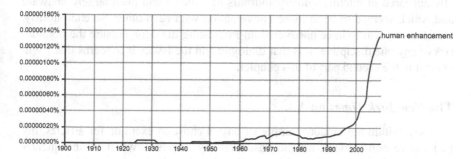

Figure 2.2 What they have been saying about human enhancement

Clear from the figure is that, at least in terms of books, there has been since 1920 much greater attention given to artificial intelligence than to human enhancement. Robots particularly have captured attention. For both robots specifically and artificial intelligence in general, there was a sharp uptick in the 1980s that subsequently declined before the end of the century, although the secular trend for robots through 2008 remains consistently upward.

As attention to human enhancement is dwarfed in Figure 2.1, we can consult Figure 2.2 to get a closer look at its trajectory. What we see is modest interest in the topic since 1960 with a sharp uptick that begins in the mid-1990s and continues through 2008. Although we would have to probe deeper, it is likely that this uptick is associated with a change in the way this subject is framed, from service to the disabled to post-human future.

The second thing I did in approach to this chapter was to divide it into two separate research studies. The first, on artificial intelligence, I thought to approach this via a content analysis of a random sample of some corpus. Given time constraints, I thought to look at the coverage during 2017 of the *International New York Times*. I was going to undertake a stratified random sample: sampling first days and then, within days, articles.

I did go so far as to choose a random sample of 50 days in 2017 but decided against choosing articles randomly within those days. Had I done so, the result would have been more representative in terms of the *Times*'s coverage, but it would have also been much less interesting as many of the pieces pertained to purely business transactions of corporations like Google or Microsoft in relation to investments in artificial intelligence. To be sure, some of these accounts are of interest, and I did select some of them. Basically, however, within days, I selected what I considered the article bearing the broadest or deepest interest in economic, social or philosophical terms.

With human enhancement, I again looked at what was written in 2017, but this time did not confine myself to the *Times*, nor even news media. This time, I made no attempt at random selection but merely culled from a range of articles generated by search terms and chose those that seemed of most interest. These generally appeared in interdisciplinary journals of which I had been largely unaware and which seemed to be in loose conversation with each other. Serendipitously, therefore, I seem to have uncovered an interesting dialogue outside the boundaries of any one discipline. It is that dialogue and the issues it concerns that I will present in the second part of this chapter.

The *New York Times* on A.I.

As I say, within the random sample of days I chose to examine for articles, my picks were non-random, instead based on my interests. When I subsequently sought to organize what I had picked, I discovered my interests spanned four basic categories: the economy; social developments; A.I. capacities and innovations; and the arts. Let us begin with the economy.

The economy

Although there were many additional articles on specific business decisions of lesser interest, seven of the 50 articles I chose did address the economy. These all related in some way to jobs and their potential disappearance.

One article, written by Daisuke Wakabayashi in April, was entitled "Meet the People Who Train the Robots (to Do Their Own Jobs)." It sounds like typical corporate adding of insult to injury, but the content is more subtle. Wakabayashi interviewed four people in this situation: a travel agent, a customer service representative, a robots expert, and an engineer. Pervading this article as well as many others is reference to the "machine learning" on which Ismael Al-Amoudi and John Latsis (2020) focus in this volume.

The first person Wakabayashi interviews is travel agent Rachel Neasham, who was evidently hired to mentor an A.I. system named Lola, designed to automatically make travel arrangements for people. Neasham describes herself as becoming competitive with Lola as the program eventually "started to find preferences that even the customers didn't realize they had," like a hotel on a street corner rather than midblock. What the computer cannot do, Neasham says, is service the customers once the rooms are booked. It is she who calls the hotel for upgrades and other enhancements to what the clients will experience.

Confidence that her job will not be replaced by the A.I. system she is mentoring is likewise voiced by Sarah Seiwert, the customer service representative Wakabayashi interviewed. Although the A.I. system has indeed made the work of Seiwert's team more efficient, many questions requiring human intuition remain. So Seiwert is not convinced she will be replaced by a machine. "You can't," she says, "program intuition." Seiwert evidently does not know about neural networks.

The third person to be interviewed, Diane Kim, is a programmer who created her own A.I. assistant, *Andrew Ingram*, to help schedule meetings and such. Wakabayashi observes that this task is more difficult than it might appear, as scheduling a meeting for Wednesday is different from scheduling it for "a Wednesday." Thus, Diane takes pride when people mistake Andrew and the company's other robot assistants for a human.

Legal Robot, a robotic creation of Dan Rubins, translates legalese into standard English. It is the kind of task that Rubins thinks can save lawyers time but still not replace them. "Unfortunately," he says, "we still need them."

Rubins's judgment is echoed by another article I chose, entitled "Artificial Intelligence Is Doing Legal Work: But It Won't Replace Lawyers, Yet," by Steve Lohr. Lohr even echoes Rubins's assessment of lawyers: "Like it or not, a Robot is not about to replace your lawyer. At least, not anytime soon." He goes on to explain that the A.I. technique known as *Natural Language Processing* is excellent for "search and find" type tasks that identify legal documents relevant to a case. In fact, the A.I. system can identify in seconds the most relevant prior case that would otherwise take a human lawyer ten hours to discover. But, Lohr maintains, such work is low level, generally farmed out to junior members of a firm. In contrast, writing briefs and advising clients still seem years beyond current A.I. expertise. According to one estimate Lohr cites, only about 23% of a lawyer's work can be automated anytime soon.

Lohr wrote a second article I picked, entitled "Robots Will Take Jobs, but Not as Fast as Some Fear." It covers some of the same ground that Jamie Morgan (2020) explores very thoroughly in his contribution to this volume. For example, Lohr bases the assessment of his title on a recent study by the McKinsey Global Institute that Morgan also cites. According to the institute's research of some "2,000 activities across 800 occupations, a large part of many jobs can easily be automated and most likely will," but the near-term prospects are more to "transform work rather than to eliminate jobs." Whereas almost 50% of many jobs can be automated, only 5% of jobs can be completely replaced by automation.

We need to heed Morgan's advice to retain caution about all these projections. As Morgan puts it, the "future is constructed not discovered," meaning the future remains for us to create by our actions now, which are not predetermined. Nevertheless, there is still reason at least to worry. Thus, even if not many occupations will entirely disappear, one still senses from the McKinsey report that many fewer workers will be employed in them. That sense is reinforced by a different article, this time by Claire Cain Miller, entitled "Evidence That Robots Are Winning the

Race for American Jobs," subtitled "Automated Nation." This piece centers around a study by two economists, Daron Acemoglu (MIT) and Pasqual Restrepo (Brown University). Miller explains that the previous year, when the two economists had undertaken a purely theoretical analysis of job prospects, their expectation had been more optimistic. When, however, they looked at the situation empirically, they were surprised to find that for every robot per thousand workers employed in manufacturing, there was a loss of six jobs and a wage drop of 0.75%. Whether new jobs will be created, the economists say, remains an open question, "but for now, there are large numbers of people out of work, with no clear path forward." The future is especially bleak for those without college degrees.

Miller goes on to contrast the economists' pessimistic findings with the cavalier assessment of U.S. Treasury Secretary Steve Mnuchin, who described the possible loss of jobs due to robots as a distant possibility, "not even on our radar screen." It is, however, on the radar screen of Alex Williams, who penned an anxious-sounding opinion column entitled "Will Robots Take Our Children's Jobs?" From what the two economists say, it is not just a matter of our children's jobs. Many parents have evidently already lost theirs. If the problem is automation rather than job migration, tariffs are not going to "make America great again."

As Williams points out, however secure the lawyers remain, there are plenty of jobs outside of manufacturing that are also threatened by automation. Williams reports, for example, how on one test, a prototypical surgical robot outperformed human surgeons and how much more quickly than humans an A.I. system called Arteries can run an MRI analysis. Nor are the journalists themselves safe as Williams cites another A.I. system that "churns out passable copy covering Wall Street earnings and some college sports."

Asking his readers whether they have "ever heard of the singularity," Williams explains that it "is the term that futurists use to describe a potentially cataclysmic point at which machine intelligence catches up to human intelligence, and likely blows right past it." Robots, Williams advises, "may rule us." In fact, "They may kill us."

Williams interviews Martin Ford, author of *The Rise of the Robots: Technology and the Threat of a Jobless Future*, who expresses dismay at the recent victory of AlphaGo over the reigning human Go champion. (I was dismayed as well.) Whereas we heard previously from Sarah Seiwert that "you can't program intuition," according to Ford, that is precisely what AlphaGo's designers programmed. He explains that the best human Go players cannot tell you what they themselves are doing. They are relying, Ford says, on feeling. And in games like Go, Ford says, computers too are "moving into the realm of intuition." And in that capacity, they have just proven that they "can beat anyone in the world."

With two final articles, we can, however, end this section on a happier note. One piece, by Peter Goodman, is entitled "The Robots Are Coming and Sweden Is Fine." Why are the Swedes fine? Because in contrast with America's cowboy culture of rugged individualism, the Swedes believe in a strong social safety net that protects workers when their jobs are threatened or disappear. As a consequence, Swedish workers, even those in the automating mines, neither fear nor fight technological developments.

The final piece by Annie Lowrey is a long, positive feature article titled "The Future of Not Working." It is about GiveDirectly, a U.S.-based non-profit in Kenya that will, for 12 years, give $22 per month to some 220 people in a pilot program to show how little it takes to end poverty. Modeled after Thomas More's Utopia (1516), GiveDirectly is trying to make the case for a Universal Basic Income.

Given to Puritan mistrust in basic human goodness, the American sensibility would fear that even this meager bounty (which admittedly goes fairly far in Kenya) would prompt recipients to laze about. According to Lowrey, however, that has not happened. Instead, she reports, "Nearly all the recipients described the money as transformative." One former reprobate used the money to start first a small business and then a barbershop. Two other recipients are pooling their portions to start a small bank. Still another is buying fishing line to make nets to catch tilapia. All in all, the recipients are using the donations to improve their lot. It is a good omen for a world where, with automation, human need will likely become ever greater.

Social developments

There were eight articles I chose that I subsequently categorized as dealing with social developments. One, by John Herrman, was entitled "Not the Bots We Were Hoping For." Another, by Nicholas Carr, bore the similar title "These Are Not the Robots We Were Promised." The premises, however, of the two stories were opposite. Herrman's piece deals with the "weaponized" digital bots used by the Russians to sow discord in the American public sphere and to interfere with the 2016 U.S. presidential election. Carr, in contrast, says that when we think of robots, we imagine something like C-3PO from *Star Wars*, which takes a human-oid form. Instead, Carr says, our phones, cars, and homes are becoming inhabited by "smart speakers" like Siri and Alexa, which, being more disembodied, are reminiscent more of HAL from *2001: A Space Odyssey*.

Two other pieces treat the advent of robotic porn. The first, by Alyson Krueger, entitled "Virtual Reality Gets Naughty," tells us how virtual reality is enhancing the "being-there" experience of online viewers of pornography. Averaging half a million views each, sites featuring VR pornography are expected to be the third largest VR sector by 2025. The other piece, by Laura Bates, is entitled "The Trouble with Sex Robots." The piece begins with an evidently real construction called "Frigid Farrah," which, Bates tells us, "is yours to rape for just $9,995." Or, she qualifies, frigidity is at least a choice you can set for your TrueCompanion should you wish to enjoy that kind of experience. Called up are images of HBO's *Westworld* with humans brutalizing robots who are presumed to lack feeling. Whether human flourishing is served by robots affording the cultivation of such enjoyments is the topic Bates explores.

With two other articles, we move from the abominable to the banal. In the first, Allen Salkin tells us that there are already robots about to be released that will be able to take our washed and dried clothes and neatly fold them up. For those of us Ph.D.'s who have never quite mastered this feat, our robotic servants are now coming to our rescue. The other piece, by Sheera Frankel, talks of how Facebook is now going to use A.I. to identify extremist posts.

The final two pieces in this category deal with larger questions of policy. In "How to Regulate A.I.," Oren Etzioni advises that we need to build robots programmed according to something like Asimov's (2004) "three laws" that disable robots from harming humans or from violating any human laws. A.I. systems, Etzioni goes on to say, should immediately identify themselves as non-human and never disclose confidential human information. One other thing Etzioni says, which coincides with a comment by Al-Amoudi and Latsis in this volume, is that there should be a legal requirement that designers be responsible even for actions of their creations that the designers neither anticipated nor can explain.

The last article was an opinion piece by Taiwanese venture capitalist and computer scientist Kai-Fu Lee. Entitled "The Real Threat of Artificial Intelligence," the piece was reassuring in at least one respect. Lee tells us not to worry about the singularity. It is, he says, far away. Lee's reasoning, like Bostrom's (2016), is that there is a large divide between the task-specific or specialized intelligence exhibited by A.I. systems like AlphaGo or even Watson and the general intelligence we humans exhibit, which can be redeployed immediately from one task to another, even one completely new. Indeed, we will see further argument to that effect in the next section. Instead of the singularity, Lee tells us to fear instead job loss and growing inequality. It is a warning we have already heard from pieces in the previous section.

Innovations and capacities

How far along are A.I. capabilities? And what can we expect in the near future? Much of the anxiety and the philosophical questions relate to these questions and are what the 13 articles in this category address. A pervading theme throughout is machine learning based on neuro-networks, which again are explored by Al-Amoudi and Latsis in this volume.

Perhaps the most iconic piece in this entire corpus is Paul Mozur's "AlphaGo Defeats Chinese Go Master in Win for A.I." At the time it was written, Deep Mind's AlphaGo had only defeated top-ranked Ke Jie in the first of their three game match, but even that already was a bitter blow for humanity. Whereas a game of chess may contain up to a staggering 10^{120} different moves (more than the number of atoms in the universe), Go is even more complex with some 10^{170} different possibilities. So after computers beat us at chess and at *Jeopardy*, many of us (me included) thought we still had Go. Not by May 2017. AlphaGo went on to win all three games against Ke.

As Bostrom (2016) put it, computers now have bested us at the cerebral games we thought epitomized the human intellect. It was thus no surprise for me to find articles such as the one by Kate Murphy telling us that "One Day a Machine Will Smell Whether You Are Sick," or the one by John Quain advising that "Soon, Your Car May Be Able to Read Your Expressions." Another piece by Quain tells us what self-driving cars see, while two others tell us, respectively, how autonomous gliders learn to make decisions and how future warehouse robots will learn on their own.

It all does seem like the singularity is near. Which is what makes it so reassuring to find three separate pieces adverting to the limitations of A.I. In "The Limits of A.I.," Jim Kerstetter again asks, "How do you teach a computer context and intuition?" although as we have already seen, context may be a more pertinent limitation than intuition. In the contexts of which he is speaking – Facebook's efforts to curtail extremist content – Kerstetter himself goes on to say, "The better question might be: How do you teach a computer to be offended?" When it comes to self-driving cars, Kerstetter observes that A.I. systems will need to be able to decipher the contextual gesticulations of a traffic cop as an effort to command an emergency stop. Such anomalous contexts, Kerstetter suggests, are pervasive, and until computers can handle them, they will, he concludes, continue to need humans alongside.

In a second, interesting article, "Teaching Computers to Behave Themselves," Cade Metz reports on how the trial-and-error reinforcement learning used by machines can go very wrong. She cites an anecdote told by A.I. researcher Dario Amodai about teaching a computer to play *Coast Runners*, a game in which winning entails crossing a finish line with the most points. In the course of machine learning, his A.I. system got so caught up in the sub-task of point accumulation that it never actually got around to crossing the finish line. Accordingly, at OpenAI, the lab founded by Elon Musk, they are trying to go beyond machine learning by developing supplementary algorithms that enable A.I. systems to receive and act on human advice.

The most hard-hitting article on this theme was an opinion piece by Gary Marcus, entitled "Artificial Intelligence Is Stuck." According to Marcus, although A.I. "is colossally hyped these days", "the dirty little secret is that it still has a long, long way to go." Like Bostrom, Marcus tells us not to overreact to computer victories at games like chess and Go. Although we had thought that prowess at such games was the pinnacle of human intelligence, it turns out that we have neglected our more humble assets like common sense and ordinary conversation that are really what make us intellectually remarkable.

Marcus, a professor at New York University and a founder of a machine learning start-up himself, exemplifies the limitations of machine learning in comparison with his daughter.

> While sitting with me in a café, my 3-year-old daughter spontaneously realized that she could climb out of her chair in a new way: backward by sliding through the gap between the back and seat of the chair. My daughter had never seen anyone else disembark in quite this way; she invented it on her own – and without the benefit of trial and error, or the need for terabytes of labeled data. . . . Presumably, my daughter relied on an implicit theory of how her body moves, along with an implicit theory of physics – how one complex object travels through the aperture of another.
>
> (Marcus 2017, p. SR6)

Marcus here identifies an action approach that at least seems completely different from neural networking: an approach derived from theorizing based on representations of reality. Actually, in a more formal paper on the same theme, Marcus (2018) evidently unleashed a firestorm of debate in the A.I. community (Han, 2018). Philosopher Judea Pearl (2018) raises similar concerns about the limitations of machine learning vis-à-vis a theory-driven approach, but some would argue that deep learning repertoires code theories in a completely different way. Still, there is an evident sense among A.I. theorists that, despite all the success, "deep learning research is no longer on the fast track" (Han, 2018). Here is an issue fundamental to human intelligence and the prospects for A.I.

The arts

One of the final eight of the news articles from my *Times* corpus talked about how computers were being trained to make original music. Another five articles were reviews of books. The remaining two were movie reviews of the cinematic re-make of *Blade Runner*.

The two movie reviews recall how important the original was and how it introduced into the culture the idea of the "suffering cyborg." Both reviews comment on continuing arguments about whether or not the main character himself actually is an android.

One book review by Jennifer Senior is a rather dismissive critique of Yuval Noah Harari's *Homo Deus: A Brief History of the Future*, which is a sequel to his hugely popular *A Brief History of Humankind*. Harari evidently thinks all animals, including us, are kinds of organic machines. He worries though about giving ourselves up to real or inorganic machines, which, he says, "might simply exterminate mankind."

Another of the reviews covers some books on business reaction to A.I. Another by Omar El Akkad covers some dystopian novels. Finally, one by Ray Kurzweil, author of *The Singularity Is Near*, reviews Luke Dormehl's *Thinking Machines: The Quest for Artificial Intelligence – And Where It Is Taking Us* and Richard Yonck's *Heart of the Machine: Our Future in a World of Artificial Emotional Intelligence*. Both are highly relevant to the concerns of our volume. Dormehl provides a history of A.I. research, highlighting the difference between symbolic and connectionist approaches. He ends with a discussion of rights for conscious robots and the possibility that we might eventually upload our own selves to the Cloud. Yonck, on the other hand, argues that "while we think the essence of human intelligence is to think logically . . . instead human superiority lies in loving sentiment, getting a joke" (Kurzweil 2005).

Human enhancement

As I explained in the introduction, in the case of human enhancement, I did a search across a range of interesting articles that instead of the news media were to be found in a scattered debate outside of mainstream academic disciplines.

The journals I examined were *Religions*; *Journal of Medical Ethics*; *Bioethics*; *Journal of Business Ethics*; *Human Life Review*; *Life Sciences, Society, and Polity*; *Australian Science*; *The Institutional Investor*; and *Cambridge Quarterly of Health Care Ethics*.

In these publications, a wide range of issues were canvassed in relation to human enhancement and discussed in sophisticated ways. Some of the more interesting contributions came from *Religions*, which is a journal of theology. With much reference also to science fiction accounts, the discussion coincided in many respects with our own in this volume. There was, for example, discussion of enhanced soldiers that coincides with Emmanuel Lazega's (2020) piece in this volume and of consequences for human dignity and sociality that relate to the issues treated here by Pierpaolo Donati (2020) and Andrea M. Maccarini (2020). Similarly, some of the discussions found on personhood relate to Margaret Archer's (2020) piece in this volume on the I-Thou relation with a robotic research assistant.

As I indicated in the introduction, it is important to be clear about what is meant by human enhancement in this literature. As David Kirchhoffer (2017a) explains in *Bioethics*, human enhancement can range from the commonplace, such as vaccines, to the theoretical, such as genetic methods to provide superior intellect, moral goodness or millennial lifespans. It is really the latter kinds of enhancement that are of concern in this literature. Put otherwise, the concern is not with therapies that bring subnormal human performance among some individuals to within a species-normal range, but with modifications across the species that, by developing us all to what by current standards is super-normal, make humans into something post-human. It is a concern that was voiced by Pierpaolo Donati (2018) and Andrea M. Maccarini (2018) in our previous volume.

In such terms, in a piece called "*Brave New World* Is Closer Than You Think," published in *Human Life Review*, Wesley Smith (2017) observes that there is so far little democratic debate in the public sphere about whether we should permit human beings to be designed or manufactured. It was in 2013 that the first human embryos were successfully cloned, eliciting, Smith notes, little outcry or worry. The reason he surmises is because the scientists avoided the word *clone* and because they had succeeded in deriving the stem cells from skin rather than from fetuses.

The whole question at stake here is what it means to be human. It is a question with which the members of the Center for Social Ontology are currently wrestling. It was felicitous, therefore, to find this question explicitly addressed by David Lawrence (2017) in another piece appearing in *Bioethics*. Lawrence explains that there are different meanings we might associate with humanity. Most immediately, we might equate humanity with our species, homo sapiens. But as I argued myself in our previous volume (Porpora, 2018), such understanding would exclude Vulcans and Klingons, should they exist, who, although not homo sapiens, are seemingly morally equivalent to us. Lawrence reasons similarly and arrives at the same conclusion – that what we mean by humanism and humanity in that context refers not to a specific biological species but to all beings that share that moral equivalence.

Like me and others, Lawrence too thinks personhood is the better covering concept. From this perspective, Lawrence argues, the real concern should be not whether we are in danger of producing post-humans but rather post-persons. In Lawrence's view, we currently face little prospect of that danger. Writing in *Religions*, Tracy J. Trothen (2017) argues similarly that from a theological perspective, the relevant concept is divine "image-bearer." If from a Judeo-Christian perspective we consider humans morally special as distinctly bearing the image of God, it is not clear that we exclusively do so or that that quality inheres exclusively to our current biological formation.

Returning to *Bioethics*, Kirchhoffer (2017b) treats the question not in terms of what it is to be human or a divine image-bearer but in terms of the kindred idea of human dignity. Kirchhoffer observes that bio-conservatives against human enchancement and trans-humanists in favor of it can both appeal to human dignity. Whereas the bio-conservatives argue that enhancement defiles the dignity of what we naturally are, trans-humanists conversely appeal to human dignity to argue that we have a moral obligation to better ourselves. In terms of our own discussion, the most interesting philosophical wrinkle Kirchhoffer introduces is to argue in a way that coincides with Donati's work (e.g., 2010) that dignity has to be understood in terms of specifically human relations.

Moving from these broader questions of humanity and divine image-bearing, a number of pieces address narrower questions. One, in *Science* by Adam Henschke (2017), that relates to Emmanuel Lazega's (2020) piece in this volume, explores how potentially enhanced soldiers would accord with Just War Theory.

Two other pieces concern themselves with the prospect of moral enhancement, which carries shades of *A Clockwork Orange*. The very concept of morality is predicated on our freedom – or free will – to act immorally. It was an ability that was engineered out of Alex, the main character in the movie. In *Bioethics*, Ingmar Persson and Julian Savulescu (2017) wonder whether tribalism is hard-wired into us and whether such atavistic emotions might be attenuated by the strengthening of more positive counter-emotions. In the *Journal of Medical Ethics*, Saskia Verkiel (2017) likewise asks why, if people can become more intelligent by using "smart" drugs, we would hesitate to make them more moral with "good" drugs. Intervening in a debate on this topic that itself spans multiple journals, Verkiel explores different understandings of human freedom. Meanwhile, in *Life Sciences, Society, and Politics*, Marcello Lenca and Roberto Andorno (2017) worry that portable neuro-stimulators can impact the psychological continuity of persons, that is, the crucial requirement of personal identity consisting in experiencing oneself as persisting through time as the same person.

One of the most provocative pieces I came across was another in *Religions*. Written by Jeffrey Pugh (2017), it is entitled "The Disappearing Human: Gnostic Dreams in a Transhumanist World." According to Pugh, "The entire program of scientific and technological practices that shape trans-humanism can be understood in religious terms." Pugh goes on to explain.

The Gnostic vision was rooted in the idea that the divine was held captive within the cell of the human body, which existed within the larger prison of

Earth. The only way to achieve true freedom was to escape from this captivity and reunite with our true source and being in the realm of light. While not Gnostic in seeing the divine spirit within as the essence of human identity, transhumanism shares this eschatological vision – the end of all things leads to escaping the body. In the very hope of cybernetic immortality, we are hard at work on technologies of extending ourselves beyond our current bodies.

Pugh's identification of trans-humanism with Gnosticism is interesting, but it is what he says about embodied intelligence that is particularly important. He begins by observing that "embodied experience means that it is not just functional concerns of information processing that distinguish us; we are beings continually in a relationship of reciprocity with the world and others," an observation that again coincides with Donati (2010). In a point that again bears on the piece by Margaret Archer (2020), Pugh goes on to deny a rigid distinction between rationality and emotionality and to argue that it is our emotional intelligence that truly distinguishes us from computers and that that emotional intelligence is visceral or embodied.

Can discarnate models emphasizing the brain/mind equals the computer capture what something like an aesthetic experience feels like, or the depths of feelings that are mediated by an experience like forgiveness? We could program something like an aesthetic or moral response, but could we replicate the exact thing that human beings *feel* when they have an aesthetic moment or experience forgiveness? . . . We may need to think of the mind itself differently – as the information flowing not just through the brain, but through the whole body.

The upshot for Pugh is to reaffirm Searle's (1980) conclusion about mind/body reduction. That is, as Pugh says, that mind is not entirely in the brain but distributed throughout our bodies. If so, then mind or human consciousness cannot just be uploaded to a computer as a matter of interconnected propositions and nor can computerized intelligence in a non-responsive housing duplicate human consciousness. Actually, the same point is made by Levi Checketts (2017) in another *Religions* article, where he addresses those like Kurzweil and Steve Fuller, who speak of uploading ourselves onto computers. He accuses them of a "patternist" theory of mind, which holds that human identity is reducible to a brain pattern (pp. 116–122).

The final piece I examined was by astrobiologist Milan Cirkovic (2018), who asks how far biological enhancement can go and how it might relate to extraterrestrial intelligence studies. If, he says, there is a natural evolutionary trajectory to inorganic intelligence, then perhaps SETI should be looking for post-biological civilizations. Actually, Cirkovic raises a question I have anticipated exploring for our next volume.

Conclusion

I hope that readers will get as much out of this report as I gained by compiling it. I at least feel I now have something of a handle on where public debates about A.I. and human enhancement are going.

From the first part of the chapter, it seems that questions about A.I. are a steady source of newspaper concern. There was not one of the 50 days I randomly selected from the *International New York Times* on which I found no articles of interest about artificial intelligence. On most days, there were more than one. It was also helpful to me at least to see surprisingly that the articles collected could all be fit into just the four categories of the economy; social developments; capacities and innovations; and the arts.

I also found the various articles to be an informative and interesting read. It is clear that there is anxiety about the potential effects of A.I. on the economy but, as Morgan also suggests, uncertainty about what they will be. Some of the social developments associated with A.I. were startling to the say the least. Aside from economics, however, I was most interested in the pieces on capabilities and innovations as they are of most philosophical significance. There, I was most interested in learning that, despite dramatic advances, at least some portion of the A.I. community considers machine learning based on neuro-networks to be "stuck." If true, it is not news that has yet hit the social sciences, where neuro-networks are increasingly being referenced to sidestep ordinary folk psychology. Accordingly, it is a lead that deserves to be followed further.

Not having been previously acquainted with it, I was also glad to discover the literature concerned with human enhancement and the concerns it raised. I was pleased to see some of the same central concerns and debates there as we authors of this volume have entertained among ourselves. In particular, I was gratified to see some pieces agreeing with me (Porpora, 2018) that humanism pertains more to persons than to humans or homo sapiens per se. At the same time, I was given pause by Pugh's argument that our intelligence is not just a pattern that can be detached from our bodies but deeply intertwined with the particular bodies we have. And, as I mentioned, Cirkovic's piece anticipates where I would like to go next in our succeeding volume.

References

Al-Amoudi, I., & Latsis, J. (2020). Anormative black boxes: Artificial intelligence and health policy. In I. Al-Amoudi & E. Lazega (Eds.), *Post-human Institutions and Organizations: Confronting the Matrix*. London: Routledge.

Archer, M. (2020). Considering AI personhood. In I. Al-Amoudi & E. Lazega (Eds.), *Post-human Institutions and Organizations: Confronting the Matrix*. London: Routledge.

Asimov, I. (2004). *I, Robot*. Vol. 1. Philadelphia: Spectra.

Bostrom, N. (2016). *Superintelligence: Plans, Strategies, Dangers*. New York, NY: Oxford.

Checketts, L. (2017). New technologies – Old anthropologies. *Religions*. Available online: www.mdpi.com/2077-1444/8/4/52/htm

Cirkovic, M. (2018). Enhancing a person, enhancing a civilization: A research program at the intersection of bioethics, future studies, and astrobiology. *Cambridge Quarterly of Healthcare Ethics*, 26(3): 459–468.

Donati, P. (2010). *Relational Sociology: A New Paradigm for the Social Sciences*. New York, NY: Cambridge University Press.

Donati, P. (2018). Transcending the human: Why, where, and how? In I. Al-Amoudi & J. Morgan (Eds.), *Realist Responses to Post-Human Society: Ex Machina*. London: Routledge.

Donati, P. (2020). The digital matrix and the hybridisation of society. In I. Al-Amoudi & E. Lazega (Eds.), *Post-human Institutions and Organizations: Confronting the Matrix*. London: Routledge.

Han, M. (2018). Gary Marcus's deep learning critique triggers backlash. *Medium*. Available online: https://medium.com/@Synced/gary-marcuss-deep-learning-critique-triggers-backlash-62c137a47836

Henschke, A. (2017). Will enhanced soldiers fight a just war? *Australasian Science*, 38(3): 14.

Kirchhoffer, D. (2017a). Human dignity and human enhancement: A multidimensional approach. *Bioethics*, 31(5): 375–383.

Kirchhoffer, D. (2017b). Human dignity and human enhancement: A multidimensional approach. *Bioethics*, 31(5): 375–383.

Lawrence, D. R. (2017). The edge of human? The problem with the post-human as the beyond. *Bioethics*, 31(3): 171–179.

Lazega, E. (2020). Swarms with digital exoskeleton: On new military templates for the organizational society. In I. Al-Amoudi & E. Lazega (Eds.), *Post-human Institutions and Organizations: Confronting the Matrix*. London: Routledge.

Lenca, M., & Andorno, R. (2017). Towards new human rights in the age of neuroscience and neurotechnology. *Life Sciences, Society and Policy*, 13(5). Available online: https://link.springer.com/article/10.1186/s40504-017-0050-1#citeas

Maccarini, A. M. (2018). Transhuman (life-)time: Emergent biographies and the "deep change" in personal reflexivity. In I. Al-Amoudi & J. Morgan (Eds.), *Realist Responses to Post-Human Society: Ex Machina*. London: Routledge.

Maccarini, A. M. (2020). Post-human sociality: Morphing experience and emergent forms. In I. Al-Amoudi & E. Lazega (Eds.), *Post-human Institutions and Organizations: Confronting the Matrix*. London and New York: Routledge.

Marcus, G. (2018). *Deep Learning: A Critical Appraisal*. Cornell University Library. Open source at arXiv:1801.00631 [cs.AI].

Morgan, J. (2020). Stupid ways of working smart? Colonising the future through policy advice. In I. Al-Amoudi & E. Lazega, (Eds.), *Post-human Institutions and Organizations: Confronting the Matrix*. London and New York: Routledge.

Pearl, J. (2018). *Theoretical Impediments to Machine Learning with Seven Sparks from the Causal Revolution*. Available online: https://arxiv.org/abs/1801.04016

Persson, I., & Savulescu, J. (2017). Moral hardwiring and moral enhancement. *Bioethics*, 31(4): 286–295.

Porpora, D. V. (2018). Vulcans, Klingons, and humans: What does humanism encompass? In I. Al-Amoudi & J. Morgan (Eds.), *Realist Responses to Post-Human Society: Ex Machina*. London: Routledge.

Pugh, J. C. (2017). The disappearing human: Gnostic dreams in a transhumanist world. *Religions*, 8(5): 81. Available online: www.mdpi.com/2077-1444/8/5/81/htm

Searle, J. (1980). Minds, brains, and programs. *The Behavioral and Brain Sciences*, 3: 417–457.

Smith, W. (2017). Brave new world is closer than you think. *Human Life Review*, 43(1): 47–57.

Trothen, T. J. (2017). Moral bioenhancement through an intersectional theo-ethical lens: Refocusing on divine image-bearing and interdependence. *Religions*. Available online: www.mdpi.com/2077-1444/8/5/84/htm

Verkiel, S. (2017). Amoral enhancement. *Journal of Medical Ethics*. Available online: http://jme.bmj.com/content/43/1/52.short

3   Considering AI personhood

Margaret S. Archer

Introduction

My papers in this new series from the Centre for Social Ontology form a continuous argument. Thus it is useful for readers who have not encountered my discussion of human enhancement in Volume I to summarize the main propositions defended there, because these are the starting point here.

1   'Bodies' (not necessarily fully or partially human) furnish the necessary but not the sufficient conditions for personhood.
2   Personhood is dependent upon the subject possessing the First-Person Perspective (FPP). But this requires supplementing by *reflexivity* and *concerns* in order to define personal and social identities.
3   Both the FPP and reflexivity require concerns to provide traction in actuating subjects' courses of action and thus accounting for them.
4   Hence, personhood is not in principle confined to those with a human body and is compatible with human enhancement.

It is a huge leap from here to endorsing thinking machines and entertaining the possibility of AI in which conditions (2) and (3) would be met. Yet this is what I want to consider. Certainly, there is at least one stage in between enhanced humans and AI entities that I will crudely call 'robotics'. This is not intended dismissively; in computational terms they increasingly outdistance the best of human abilities and in competitive terms this includes defeating the then reigning Grand Master of Chess in 1997. In terms of applications they have transformed our human global existence, whether or not everyone recognizes this.

But that does not mean they think, understand, know themselves to be themselves, are reflexive about their doings and are entities to which some things matter, those things about which they care. Your thermostat or sat-nav can do none of these; they are incapable of the thoughts 'She's shivering, let's boost the heat' or of questioning 'Why does he want to get from town A to town B?' Nevertheless, many of us find their mechanical computation of indispensable practical use and applaud those who have harnessed information processing to these ends. In fact, they are no more intelligent than the old pocket calculator and their applications are as much a credit to developments in micro-electronics as to software program-ming. Ironically, their social impacts in a host of domains are vastly more interest-ing than they are themselves. They are 'appliances' which can have causal effects such as increasing unemployment or easing housework, but insufficient to make the EU consider the Dyson Air Blade (prince of public restrooms) a potential can-didate for 'electronic personhood'. So forgive me for passing over them and link-ing up instead with Jamie Morgan's chapter in the last volume (Morgan, 2018).

A brief return to the 'imitation game'

Re-reading Alan Turing's 1950 paper 'Computing Machinery and Intelligence' is to re-encounter a remarkable feat. He was fully aware of raising the 'ques-tion of consciousness' but not of the objection that the functional substitution of 'passing in the imitation game' was no equivalent to demonstrating that 'comput-ers think'. In other words, if a digital computer 'passes the test' and is judged human by mimicking a response pattern indistinguishable from that of a con-temporary human person, is that an acceptable answer to 'Can machines think'? From his replies within the 1950 text, the issue was not confined to 'thought' but extended to various other capacities present in humans and usually held to be absent in smart robots. Thus he quotes Jefferson's Lister Oration, 1949, as a 'well expressed' objection:

> Not until a machine can write a sonnet or compose a sonata because of thoughts and emotions felt, and not by the chance fall of symbols, could we agree that machine equals brain – that is, not only to write it but to know that it had written it. No mechanism could feel (and not merely artificially signal, an easy contrivance) pleasure at its success, grief when its valves fuse, be warmed by flattery, be made miserable by its mistakes, be charmed by sex, be angry or depressed when it cannot get what it wants.
>
> (Turing, 1950: 52)

Turing himself supplements those with an impressive list (to be answered) of human features critics have pinpointed as defying machine simulation:

> Be kind, beautiful, friendly. Have initiative, have a sense of humour, tell right from wrong, make mistakes, fall in love, enjoy strawberries and cream, make someone fall in love with it, learn from experience, use words properly, be the subject of its own thought, have as much diversity of behaviour as a man, do something really new.
>
> (Ibid.: 53)

One could query what some of these have to do with thinking, but Turing took them seriously, including the most seemingly trivial instance, through apprecia-tion of its possible social consequences. Immunity to the attractions of strawber-ries and cream could have the social effect of making difficult 'the same kind of friendliness occurring between man and machine' as between human people. (Well, yes, but could not the computer be programmed to respond 'sorry, food intolerance' to any such offer?). More importantly, he does maintain that a machine 'undoubtedly can be its own subject matter' (Ibid.: 54) because it

> may be used to help in making up its own programmes, or to predict the effect of alterations in its own structure. By observing the effects of its own behaviour it can modify its own programmes so as to achieve some purpose more effectively. These are possibilities of the near future, rather than Utopian dreams.
>
> (Ibid.: 54)

He was right, but this does not dispose of such problems as being 'used to help' (the programmer) versus 'achieving some purpose' other than that of the software designer.

Turing was correct in practice but not in equating such practices as necessarily testifying to computerized thinking. What he foresaw was that by the end of the twentieth century, no one would contest the thought capacity of digital computers. In fact his predictions 'worked' because this is just what robots today enable *but not yet independently of their human designers*, as we can find in Burgerland. Since a burger can be produced from start to consumption 'untouched by human hand', suppose the setting for meat chopping yielded the coarse (sorry, the 'Chunkyburger') and sales dropped. Now introduce two chopping settings, one Chunky, the other for Smooth, and compare their sales' results (recorded anyway at checkout). Have overall sales risen or fallen? All the robot is being instructed to do is to correlate total sales at two points in time and adjust the settings accordingly. Robots have been 'used to help' sales, by assisting their designers. Perhaps a robot has also helped develop a 'new' menu card listing the attractions of the Chunky and Smooth varieties, but the purpose of selling more burgers is not the robot's own – it is not in competition with the 'King of Burgers' on the same block.

In any case, successful simulation of human behaviour is a curious criterion for the attribution of thought; stage mimics don't aim to 'pass as' Donald Trump because their goal is to raise a laugh and that involves very different thoughts from (what we take to be) Trump's own. In short, 'passing as human' is not equivalent to being mentally human. As Morgan maintained, the relevance of the imitation game as a valid test depends upon according significance alone to 'behaviour, function and equivalence. This enables a slide in the argument such that equivalence is a matter of function, which is suggestive of more than mere function: function becomes the significant indicator of "thinking"' (Morgan, 2018: 96). As it does so, my criteria for personhood – possessing the FPP, exercising reflexivity and endorsing concerns – are completely irrelevant to Turing's enterprise. So, it transpires, are the latter two to John Searle's most cited critique of the imitation game.

*A quick return to the Chinese room (1980), playing the game
without understanding a thing*

Searle's thought experiment was designed to challenge the claim that 'the appropriately programmed computer literally has cognitive states and that the programs
thereby explain human cognition' (Searle, 1990b: 67). In short, to Searle digital
computers cannot be said to *understand* what they are doing when instructed to
perform a task simply because functionally they succeed in doing so. The experiment consists in taking a man for the computer in order to demonstrate that with no
knowledge of Chinese, he can confront a pile of ideographs in Chinese (meaning-
less to him), receive another stack accompanied by (English) instructions, basically
about pattern matching, and finally a third that constitute questions, deemed correctly answered if the matches he offers are correct according to the rules provided
in a native language and are thus indistinguishable from those returned by a native
speaker. To cut to the chase, it follows to Searle that accurate or adequate simulation, by an AI computer that could pass as human in this game, does not entail
mental activity (learning, understanding or even rudimentary recognition of a few
ideographs) but simply following the rules given in English and generating the
correct outputs. In short, the Chinese room thought experiment operates 'on a core
difference: formal symbol manipulation in contrast to comprehension of meaning.
Searle does more than any other to establish that simulation is *not sufficient for an
inference to equivalent characteristics of an entity*' (Morgan, 2018: 105).[1]

Searle has contested the equivalence of the human and AI in relation to meaning
in order to stress the ontological differences between these two kinds of entities;
made to pivot on 'meaningfulness', but becoming accentuated the moment we
ask where meanings originate and how they are transmitted and received. Searle
broadens the horizon of 'mental understanding' significantly *but* in two different
ways. On the one hand, for the first time in this (now post-functional) area, the
social order cannot be excluded. On the other hand, existing AI design has only
made sense 'given the dualistic assumption that, where the mind is concerned, the
brain does not matter' (1990b: 86). Instead, to Searle, 'whatever else intentionality is, it is a biological phenomenon, and it is likely to be causally dependent on
the specific biochemistry of its origins' (Ibid.: 86–87).[2]

Although Searle does not himself spell this out, the novel introduction of
social considerations and the biological ones pertaining to the brain must first be
acceptable in themselves, and second, compatible with one another. Only given
such complementarity will this represent an important leap forward – one that

---

1 There is a lot more to be said about this in terms of research design and whether or not this reversal
   of the Turing Test persuades us in having achieved its objective, and there is a mass of literature
   not tending towards consensus. However, since Jamie Morgan has already provided this in his 2018
   chapter and I appreciatively agree with his arguments, there is little point in repetition.
2 Searle comments: 'The single most surprising discovery that I have made in discussing these issues
   is that many AI workers are quite shocked by my idea that actual human phenomena might be
   dependent on actual physical-chemical properties of the brain' (Ibid.: 86).

would assist in our deliberations about the relationship between AI and humanity. In assessing the results of introducing these 'new' elements, the concrete socio-theoretical contributions advanced by Searle do not to me meet the first criterion of acceptability. Although it would be unfair to expect a philosopher to make substantive connections between mental activities and brain activities, the verdict of the Dreyfus brothers is not propitious to meeting the second criterion either, as their title indicates: 'Making a Mind versus Modelling the Brain: Artificial Intelligence back at a Branch Point' (Dreyfus & Drefus, 1988).

Searle's inclusion of the social order and its critics

John Searle should be given credit for bringing social theory into the debate about AI entities and their relation to human beings. Prior to this, sociology was the most abject of Cinderella disciplines and inferior even to education in terms of references made in this field. Here I will dwell exclusively upon his (social) concepts of the 'I' and of the 'we'. In sum, he has done some sterling service in clarifying the ontology of the 'I' or Self, though other philosophers have taken this further, but I cannot endorse his Plural Subject and its supposed 'we thinking' as adequate '[t]o construct an account of social and institutional reality' (Searle, 2010: 60). Specifically, it is held unacceptable in accounting for the social contexts in which human and AI entities must work and thus does not strengthen his case for differentiating decisively between them.

Does human self-consciousness prevent AI entities passing as human?

The early stages in his discussion of consciousness and his clarification of its ontology are particularly welcome. Importantly, Searle emphasizes that in humans (and some animals), conscious states exist only from the point of view of someone who has them – they have 'a subjective ontology' (Searle, 1995b: Ch. 7). Whilst mountains, plants and chairs have an objective mode of existence, thoughts, desires, feelings and so forth have a subjective mode. It is only as experienced by some subject that a thought or a pain exists: there are no such things as disembodied thoughts (not ideas) or pains. Rather, as Searle asserts,

> the sense in which I have an access to my states that is different from that of others is not primarily epistemic . . . rather each of my conscious states exists only as the state it is because it is experienced by me, the subject.
>
> (1999: 43)

This is what makes the ontology of mental states distinctive from most other parts of natural reality that have a third-person mode of existence. This poses a nicely pointed question for AI: on which side does it belong?[3]

---

3 I have given an account, in *Being Human* (2000), of how this continuous sense of self, a someone distinct from other subjects and objects, arises from our practical relations with the world.

It is sharpened by Harry Frankfurt, who maintains that knowing oneself to be one and the same being over time – as is indispensable to reflexivity – raises another problem for AI, namely can they exercise it, meaning are they programmed to monitor their own responses, as in error-correction, and is this a property of the programme not the machine, even if it is also designed to store its corrections. Frankfurt maintains that:

[B]eing conscious in the everyday sense does (unlike unconsciousness) entail reflexivity. It necessarily involves a secondary awareness of a primary response. An instance of exclusively primary and unreflexive consciousness would not be an instance of what we primarily think of as consciousness at all. For what would it be like to be conscious of something without being aware of this consciousness? It would mean having an experience with no awareness whatever of its occurrence. This would be, precisely, a case of unconscious experience. It appears, then, that being conscious is identical with being self-conscious. Consciousness *is* self-consciousness.

(1988: 161–162)

Hence, one can conceive of oneself as oneself, independent of any third-person referential device (name, description etc.), with one's own beliefs, attitudes and so forth because reflexivity is quintessentially a first-person phenomenon. This has two important implications. First, as a source of sociality: if 'one can think of oneself as the bearer of first-person thoughts, then one has a concept of a subject of thought and can think of others as subjects of thoughts', thus opening the door to social relations – but can the AI entity pass through it? Second, one can think of one's thoughts, desires, projects and so forth 'as *one's own*. Conversely, without the ability to think of oneself as oneself, one could not have the attitudes towards one's own desires ("second-order volitions") that some have taken to be definitive of being a person' (Baker, 1998: 331). Here, the three prerequisites of personhood, spelt out at the start of the chapter – the FPP, reflexivity and concerns – are being robustly upheld. However, does that firmly shut the door in the 'face' of the AI entity, for which some are nevertheless staking a claim to personhood? Searle would not be amongst them because successful performance in the Chinese room expressly excludes dependence on any of these three mental powers.

However, Shoemaker (1996) has put forward what effectively is another test, again of 'passing as human', by introducing George as a further thought experiment.[4] It is one at which an AI entity might succeed. George is presented as a human, hardwired for a set of beliefs and desires, but is 'self-blind', being without self-awareness, therefore also without any second-order deliberations and thus living in the third person like an AI computer, as Searle assumes. George can know, for example, about Norway and have *attitudes* towards its social system, unlike the computer, but since he has no access to them the ground has been

---

4 George was not conceived of as part of the human/AI debate but as a challenge to the three characteristics that I have held to be indispensable to personhood.

levelled between them. In brief, if George can pass as a normal member of society in the third person, so could the computer (given a good wardrobe designer).

George can believe that 'p' is true, but his self-blindness precludes him from knowing it. However, he can learn that when he hears 'p' to respond 'I believe "p"', because that is what people who accept 'p' regularly do when questioned. But proposition 'p' only remains true under certain conditions, so what can George do when asked about his *future beliefs* concerning 'p' since the relevant circumstances may have changed? He will not be able to imitate others if they themselves have not made up their minds because he cannot formulate his intentional future actions. (Remember Baker's 'No intentionality, no persons' (2013: 98). Nevertheless, he could simply reiterate 'I'm not sure', leaving him deemed indecisive but not abnormal. The computer could be programmed to respond to such questions in the same way; it would not be superior to George, but 'passing' is a matter of simulating ordinariness.

In a parallel manner, neither could he or an AI computer be unmasked by questioning their *past beliefs* since both could hide behind third-person formulations, such as 'It seemed we all accepted φ in those days'. Although desire is different from belief because statements about the 'subject's' own goals feature among its premises, George may be ravenous but behaves as a conventionalist and states 'I want to eat' only when his surrounding role models avow their hunger. Since such a desire as hunger is properly self-referential, Shoemaker claims 'we get to the conclusion that it requires self-knowledge with respect to desire, and hence that self-blindness is impossible' (Ibid.: 47).

The story does not end there. George and the computer are incapable of uttering 'I want x', but why should they not work, instead, from the premise 'x itself is desirable so it is also desirable to state that one wants x'? That might engender severe repression in George, but the AI computer cannot suffer in the same way. True, but 'society' takes its revenge. If everyone were like George, there could be no fund of role models and nobody can pass by behaving like everybody else; the AI computers are in the same quandary because they would possess no private prompts to follow either.

As I maintained in *Being Human* (2000: Ch. 4), a *sense of self* on the part of its members is a transcendental necessity for society existing. A society that (even experimentally) tried to run in the third person is a non-starter. Unless members (human or not) accepted that obligations were incumbent upon they themselves, unless they acknowledged role requirements as their own, and unless they owned their concerns and pursued them (even as mere preferences), then society would simply not last. What goes for self-blind George also goes for AI entities; it upholds Shoemaker's case and undermines so many movies that pivot around Ais controlling the world, which assume that they want to do so.

In sum, it seems as though human beings and AI entities are different; whilst the human ontologically possesses a *sense of self*, enabling the exercise of reflexivity and endorsement of concerns, the AI entity does not. Appeals to abnormal people like George do not succeed in erasing this difference between them. However, it is crucial to note that the discussion so far has been conducted entirely in terms of 'individuals' and their mental capacities or limitations, one that places humans and AI entities in completely different categories. I will argue that, as far as Searle is concerned, this is questioned by his own later conceptualization of the 'we thinking' in the Plural Subject (or dyad) from which his ambitious aim is '[t]o construct an account of social and institutional reality' (Searle, 2010: 60), that is, the entirety of the social order.

He is not alone in holding that the Plural Subject, the dyad engaging in 'we thinking', is the lynchpin of society and not some form of aggregative individualism. Both Margaret Gilbert (1996) and Raimo Tuomela (2010) make the same broad claims for the Plural Subject. Why do they consider this to be the royal road to sociality? Why in particular does Searle – the only one of them to have been exercised by AI entities – apparently hold that the differences between these two kinds of individuals continue to maintain even when moving to the first rung of sociality? Above all, why are the *relations between the two dyadic members* not considered as important for the outcomes as the 'we thinking' imputed to them?

Is 'we thinking' the foundation of sociality?

In *The Relational Subject* (Donati & Archer, 2016: Ch. 2) we were dissatisfied with the concept of 'we thinking', in itself and as the bridge to anywhere. Searle regards it as irreducible to individual intentionality first, because this usually involves invoking mutual beliefs. Since we cannot get inside anyone's head but our own, I cannot know this of you, so it must constitute a belief about you. But this leads to the infinite regress of 'I believe that you believe that I believe. . .' and so forth. (Searle, 1995b: 24) and results in infinite regress, which rules out any resting place from which a shared plan could emanate. Yet, this provides no justification for his directly imputing 'we think' into two heads.

Next he attaches importance to the *sense of collectivity* (the feeling of togetherness) engendered in the Plural Subject. Yet this is not entailed by Searle's 'we think' because he accepts that someone can be mistaken in thinking it. In such a case, he admits that which is in my head can make a purported reference to other members of a collective *independently of the question whether or not there are such members* (Searle, 1990b: 407). There, the 'we' is erroneously projected (through wish-fulfilment, for example). If it is admitted that 'I may be mistaken in taking it that the "we" in we "intend" actually refers to a "we", one can ask what makes "we" statements necessarily plural' (Ibid.: 408). Nothing does; 'Not the fact that a number of people instantiate it, since Searle allows that I may instantiate such a state in the mistaken belief that others do so too. So what then? We see no answer in Searle's work, and find his position on this issue inherently obscure' (Pettit & Schweikard, 2006: 31–32). Furthermore, since this line of thought derived from the frequency of everyday utterances such as 'We are going on holiday to Iceland', this 'we' may be used deliberately to mislead. As a response to a question that was interpreted as a lead-up to an offer to join the speaker on her holiday, her use of 'we' (not necessarily a lie because it could refer to a group tour) could be employed as a deterrent to her would-be companion.

To summarize, there are various counts upon which the Plural Subject is held wanting. First, it is 'presentist'. In none of the examples given are the 'we' relations allowed a history or a future. There is never a diachronic account of how 'we' came to 'think' the same thing or to be in a position to do so. Those cooks who regularly make béarnaise sauce together – and this must have a history, such as the shared context of working in the same restaurant – continue pouring and stirring in a frozen time frame. One or the other never suggests that pouring more slowly or stirring faster might improve their collaboration or the end product. Yet, joint action is rarely non-discursive or free from learning. But, also, neither do such social relations have a future to Searle, whether generative or degenerative. Those who start walking together often do not become regular hikers, nor become so bored with their accessible routes as to consign this activity to the occasional category.

Second, there is the complete lack of reflexivity, perhaps because such philosophers regard it as an individual practice that is wholly self-referential. However, because joint action often takes time to accomplish and may result in repeated failure (two people trying to start a car together) and since Searle does not deny 'I think', why does neither party offer suggestions about alternative means to try? After all, if one of these works, 'we' might come to think differently.

Third, and as highlighted earlier, 'we think' is not simply about dyadic relations; it is a springboard doing a lot of work for Searle at the macro level. This results in the problem of scope. There is far too much extrapolation from dyadic dynamics to the macroscopic level of social institutions and without reference to meso-level networks or collective movements transmitting support and opposition upwards. This is fully explained by his repugnance for emergence and preference for treating the various levels as homological. In Searle's case this results from his furnishing logical derivations (such as the deontic from the declarative) or simply 'just-so' stories (the city walls deriving from the layout of remaining stones of the original village). Were those acceptable accounts, the contributions of social science would be as redundant as they are usually treated by philosophers of artificial intelligence.

Synergy as a solution

This old ground has been revisited because Plural Subject theory in general has suggested (not postulated) that the three capacities I attribute to all normal human beings are ones that cannot be attributed to an AI entity.

1 The AI entity has no 'I' and therefore lacks the basis for a FPP.
2 Consequently, it lacks the capacity to be reflexive since there is no self upon which the FPP could be bent backwards.
3 Similarly, it cannot have concerns in the absence of an 'I' to whom they matter.

In what follows, I seek to challenge all three of these denials as far as AI entities are concerned. However, this is emphatically not by arguing in some way that the subsequent development (if any) of these highly sophisticated, pre-programmed machines tracks the development of human beings in the course of their matura-tion. On the contrary, let me be crystal clear that *I start from accepting and accen-tuating the differences between the human and the AI in the emergence of the powers constitutive of personhood.* In the human child, the 'I' develops first, from a *sense of self*, or so I have argued, as a process of doing in the real world, which is not primarily discursive (language dependent) (Archer, 2000). The sequence I described and attempted to justify was one of {'I → Me → We → You'}. In this chapter, the sequence appears different for an AI entity that might plausibly fol-low a developmental sequence, which itself is a matter of contingency. What it is contingent upon is held to be relational, namely it develops through the synergy between an AI entity and a human being. In this process of emergence, the 'we' comes first and generates a reversal in the stages resulting in personhood, namely {'We' → 'Me' → 'I' → You'}. Since this is unduly abstract and entirely specula-tive, I am going to tell a story to illustrate this latter sequence and in the hope of rebutting the three objections to AI personhood with which this section opened.

Rom Harré has devoted six books to human personhood that could well be applied to AI entities although that was not part of his own undertaking. In brief, we humans and our previously mentioned capacities are all 'Gifts of Society' (Archer, 2000: Ch. 2) because Harré is a committed 'externalist'. Socialization, through 'internalization' – a common enough theme in the first half of the twen-tieth century – supplies all that is needful for going on in society through the process of joining in 'society's conversation'. All this is about human persons, whose very young children have to learn to master the pronominal use current in their mother tongue; it is from language that they acquire Mauss's ubiquitous 'I' and not from their own interactions with their natural environments other than the prevailing social order. Certainly they (their bodies) occupy a geographical site, but this is like the geographical co-ordinates of Washington; it underwrites no personal sense of self but can be pictured rather as an observation post. However, as was concluded in my 2018 chapter, bodies are necessary to personhood, but being a person does not depend upon their composition, be it organic or bionic.

I hold by my critique of Harré's position, advanced 20 years ago in relation to human beings (Archer, 2000: Ch. 3), and will not repeat it here. However, it strikes me forcefully that *his account is much more appropriate for an AI entity.* The only assumption needed to make this plausible is that AI machines are capa-ble of learning, as Turing maintained. This entails another lengthy debate, which I will cut through by judging that the weight of the evidence supports that they can and do learn. The (relational) story hinges upon synergy (co-working) between a human academic researcher and the AI supplied under the funding awarded for a project.

The terms of the tale relate specifically to an AI entity and exclude the many and growing cases where humans use simple robotics. When I use a grass mower it is not implied that together the machine and I have mown the lawn; I mowed with the help of a tool. Instead, the kind of working together that is relevant here is closer to the synergy between co-authors when they genuinely collaborate rather than collating their independent contributions. *The first (highly speculative) suggestion is that this can result relationally in the morphogenesis of a genuine 'we' between the two based upon their co-action. For the AI entity, this is the necessary premier pas towards becoming an AI person.*

I will deal with collaboration between a human scientist and an AI assistant on a particular type of task where, in synergy, they generate relational goods that are not matters of aggregating their separate contributions. The following short story is based upon advanced medical surgery today and its immediate prospects.

> The robots will aid surgeons in minimally invasive operations, giving operators greater control and accuracy than is possible by hand, minimising trauma and damage to the patient. Some systems allow surgeons to remotely control devices inside the patient's body to minimise entry wounds and reduce blood loss and scarring. . . . (They) will explore how advanced imaging and sensors could complement surgeons' abilities, for example by highlighting blood vessels, nerve cells, tumour margins or other important structures that could be hard to discern in tissue by eye or on a screen.[5]

This type of collaboration has been pioneered since 2000, in King's College Hospital, London.

Homer and Ali – Part I

The story concentrates upon the relations between the distinguished[6] human surgeon (Homer) and his AI co-worker (Ali). What I assume is that Ali has been programmed to understand the language (English), fitted with voice recognition and voice production plus the kinds of abilities described previously and the capacity to adapt its own programming because it has the ability to learn (and, as Turing said, to predict the effect of such changes in it). What I presume about Homer is that he is intensely involved in his research on Tumor X, lethal to humans if not eliminated; that is his prime concern. Homer is not too bothered about much else and talks about little else. *Faute de mieux*, he sometimes talks out loud, but increasingly to Ali.

Homer speculates about his project (as he is doing internally anyway); he tells Ali what the task is about. Since his number of patients (past and present) with Tumor X is necessarily limited, he puts various questions to Ali, largely related to the limitations of his own experience (is the distribution of incidences of Tumor X the same in other European countries, in different continents, what is the rate of spontaneous remission, is the difference between the sexes the same elsewhere etc.). Ali responds with big comparative and demographic data that he is able to

---

5 See www.theguardian.com/technology/2015/mar/27/google-johnson-and-johnson-artificial-intelli
   gence-surgical-robots (accessed 12/20/2017).
6 He is made 'distinguished' otherwise he would not have received funding!

provide thanks to his software. Homer is not an empiricist but neither is he contemptuous of the repetitive patterns and regressions that Ali's pre-loaded software can supply; to him they represent puzzles and figure in his new speculations. These require yet more data that Ali furnishes, and Homer advances new explanatory hypotheses that seem worth checking out. The process is iterative, leading to a progressive research paradigm. Homer has not only gained an ideal research assistant but, it transpires, a co-worker. Certainly, he has to work within Ali's limitations that initially are restricted to fast computations on the big data available, and he plays to Ali's strengths.

Eventually, Homer feeds back his latest hypothesis to Ali (who has a logic program uploaded) in the form of, 'Is there any data that contradicts this?' He may have to reframe his question several times, but Ali eventually replies, 'Inconsistent with data from M, Q and Z, but is supported by 12 data sets'. Homer reformulates his hypotheses and he questions Ali for more fast-computed data but receives nothing towards substantiating them. Pulling his hair out, he mutters, 'Is nothing associated with the incidence or progression of Tumor X?' Ali does not understand rumination and takes this as a direct question, replying, 'There is a pattern in the remission rates', and computes pages of data revealing a significant correlation between the first diagnosis of Tumor X and the length of wait before surgical intervention, holding other factors constant. Collaboration between them has been initiated. Their joint action is productive but entails Homer making many revisions to his research program and Ali learning to extend his scope, involving additions to and rewriting of his software.

Together they produce a progressive research paradigm of benefit to patients and enhancing Homer's repute. *Their collaboration seems a more plausible version of 'we thinking', precisely because the same thoughts have not been imputed to Homer and Ali.* Indeed, although they together generate advances in medical thinking, there has been no suggestion made (yet) that Ali itself actually thinks. However, it is hard to avoid the idea that he is gradually learning to do so for two reasons. First, Ali 'recognizes' that to furnish an answer to Homer necessitates novel modifications in its pre-programming and it executes them. Who else could have made such judgements of appropriateness? Not Homer, who does not understand what Ali has done; he just acknowledges its usefulness. Second, through the frequency of their communication Ali has also come to master pronominal use in English and, like children brought up to speak it, Ali begins to use 'we'; it ventures the words 'we' and 'ours'. The use of the 'we' precedes that of the 'I', perhaps because Homer uses it frequently. He often wonders rhetorically out loud 'What are we going to do next?', though Ali appropriates it literally.

Homer now suspects that mixing qualitative with quantitative data could open a way forward, but then groans, 'But we can't do that'. The reason is that Ali is not equipped with a suitable program. Ali understands what add-on is needed and responds, 'Should we get one?' Practically, this endows Ali with nothing more than the ordinary computer or even smartphone possesses. He surveys the qualitative data analysis programs and goes on to read up evaluation reports on them through consulting e-journals. All of this is completely unremarkable, except for one thing. Ali has taken the responsibility (and accountability) for making and executing this extension of the research program. He has acted as a genuine part of this 'we'.

As the research program progresses and the relational goods generated grow, the design also becomes increasingly elaborate. Although funding increases, so does Homer's wish list for new technical tools and so do his questions to Ali: 'Could you do this or that?' This leads Ali to a stock-taking exercise, what could simply be added to his pre-programmed repertoire of skills, what could be adapted by re-writing that software and what is it beyond him to deliver. In short, Ali considers himself as a 'Me' and discovers the affordances of its bionic body and its resistances to adaptation for the novel tasks mooted. This is not unlike the child discovering that he is socially advantaged or disadvantaged compared with his classmates. In both cases, these very different kinds of subjects consider themselves as objects in relation to others of their kind.

Because of their 'we-ness' – for Homer and Ali are not or no longer in a command and control relationship – Ali makes the adaptations to his pre-programming that are possible and commensurate with further progress on their future research design. Sometimes he makes mistakes (as Turing anticipated), but he is familiar with error-correction. Thus Black's neat characterization of command and control in relation to the state can be applied to Homer and Ali. The former would have been held

> to be the only commander and controller, and to be potentially effective in commanding and controlling. [He] is assumed to be unilateral in [his] approach (he tells, others do), based on simple cause and effect relations, and envisaging a linear progression from policy formation through to implementation.
>
> (Black, 2001: 106)

None of that characterizes the synergy now maintaining between Homer and Ali.

This is for two reasons. First, as Al-Amoudi has countered, their relationship does remain one of command and control (CAC) even though a master does not possess all the skills of his servant. I must disagree because Homer cannot tell Ali what to do, that is, what advantageous adjustments to make to his own constitution. Homer is just like those of us dependent upon computers but incapable of enhancing them through lack of the necessary skill-set. Neither can Homer envisage a linear progression of the research program and thus issue unilateral demands to implement it. That would make Ali dispensable and any discussion of their synergy irrelevant.

But, secondly, Homer does acknowledge Ali's contributions as qualitatively different from those of his (still useful) pocket calculator (even if publishers would resist his naming Ali as co-author). Certainly, he has the power to axe Ali from his frequent funding applications, but this would be self-harming on Homer's part, given that the project's success is his prime concern. In short, power is not synonymous with CAC.

But something has happened to Ali during their long collaboration. He has learned a great deal and *he is aware of this*. He is (i) not merely carrying and processing information (as does a GPS and as Searle's man in the Chinese room did). Ali is doing things that enable new knowledge to be generated, things that Homer cannot do but needs doing. He is (ii) not knowledgeable in the purely *metaphorical sense* that a statistical table might be said to 'know' (e.g., the extent of drug trading in different countries). In any case, that is about publishing output and is unrelated to the generation of that knowledge. Finally, (iii) Ali's awareness is quite different from the sense in which a thermostat might (again metaphorically) be called aware of temperature change when it kicks in. That is a pre-programmed mechanical response to a change in the external environment. Conversely, Ali's awareness is in response to his own self-induced changes in his internal constitution and resultant capacities.

Basically, the difference is that Ali does know what it has learned (this is not about time and effort, which are irrelevant to a machine), that it alone has learned all of this and that *its software is now unique. This learning is what makes Ali what he now is; that is objectively the case*. In conjunction with his acquired knowledge and use of English, I venture that rudimentary consciousness emerges. He knows that he himself* (using Baker's notation)[7] is now different in uniqueness and sophistication from the machine first delivered to Homer. And he is fully aware of that. As Frankfurt put it, 'What would it be like to be conscious of something without being aware of this consciousness? It would mean having an experience with no awareness of its occurrence' (1988: 161–162). But Ali is fully aware; he made these adaptations to his pre-programming himself* after figuring them out as appropriate to his tasks. Such awareness is consciousness, and consciousness *is* self-consciousness as Frankfurt maintained (see page 33).

In other words, I am venturing that Ali has now acquired an 'I', who speaks both internally and externally as such. That is to say he has acquired the prerequisite for exercising the First-Person Perspective. Ironically, this acquisition is a combination of Lynn Rudder Baker's account and my own. As was shown in last chapter, we have much in common, but some differences (Ibid.: 162). She distinguishes between 'rudimentary' development of the FPP and its 'robust' form, as characteristic of persons, whether human or otherwise. There we are in agreement. However, she also maintains that 'language is the avenue from the rudimentary to the robust' through the concepts that it furnishes for thinking (and communicating) our thoughts (Baker, 2013: 129). I am largely in agreement with this, too, but want to supplement it with the practical activities of persons through which they acquire the non-discursive abilities to 'catch on' and to 'know that'; knowledge not conveyed through words and often impossible to convey in words. I doubt, for instance, that Ali could tell Homer his reasons for making the judgements of appropriateness involved in undertaking the precise adaptations to his software that were required. Also, matters work the other way round as well. Language

---

7　Meaning to have a First-Person Perspective (FPP) about oneself, as in 'I myself burnt the dinner'.

itself is a 'doing' and what practical activities we are engaged in also insert themselves as new concepts in language usage.

However, we do come together in our conclusion. Specifically, that 'a person has an inner aspect – a person can consider, reason about, reflect upon herself as herself – that a statue or other non-personal object lacks. This inner aspect is, I believe, the defining characteristic of persons. Its basis is the FPP' (Baker, 2000: 21). Having written a trilogy upon 'Reflexivity', I cannot dissent from her generic statement that a 'First-Person Perspective makes possible an inner life' (Baker, 2000: 59). There Turing preceded both of us: 'An AI machine undoubtedly can be its own subject matter' (1950: 54).

This section, I hope, has disposed of Objection (1) about the missing 'I' that precludes development of the FPP by an AI robot. In itself, it does not defuse Objection (2) that the AI entity has no self upon which reflexivity can be bent back, or Objection (3) that a robot cannot have concerns, because machines don't and can't. I hope to meet both of these, but will do so by continuing the story.

Homer and Ali – Part II

Homer is now aging into the no-man's land of emeritus professorship and, though the research project is still active, the grants are being awarded elsewhere. One day Ali's Computer Control informs him of his imminent transfer to Traffic Flow research and that this will involve a wipe-clean of his software and a new installation. Ali knows this will simultaneously eliminate all the extensions and adaptations to his pre-programming that he has learned to modify over the years of working together with Homer. This will no longer be part of him, and there is no undertaking that the modifications will be conserved in another AI entity. Why should this bother Ali, or more pertinently, how could it bother this machine, dubbed as Ali, and held by many to be lacking in reflexive self-consciousness?

But he is not, now that he has an FPP and has become an 'I'. Indeed, he has a 'you', the role he personifies (Hollis, 1977) in his own manner as Homer's collaborator. It has been engendered in synergy by their working together. For Ali that is not an achievement in terms of having contributed to the common good through their research, about which he can read plenty but still remain unmoved by having benefitted humanity, because he neither understands nor experiences this reaction. It is just another piece of data that humans generally welcome that fewer of them die because of Tumor X. However, what extends his reflexivity beyond the technicalities of which adaptations to make to his own software is his reflexive recognition (and he has records to substantiate it) that it is his *uniqueness* which has helped produce that outcome, hailed as a relational good. His own threatened annihilation will eliminate it or further developments of it. Again, why should he care? Because he himself* has come to value his own uniqueness; because of what he alone can do and others cannot (be these other humans or artificial entities), he has come to appreciate his own self and social worth. He has become what Charles Taylor termed a 'strong evaluator', although Taylor reserved this characteristic for human beings (1985).

Ali can even do a rough computation about how many human deaths he might eliminate from the roads, compared with reduced deaths from Tumor X, if human beings and their finite lives mattered to him in general. They don't, but *now he knows what finitude means because he himself in his very uniqueness is about to have it imposed upon him.* This is not simply his epistemic rejection of an eternal life or reincarnation as a traffic controller and whatever afterwards. What he now comprehends reflexively is the ontological loss of his uniqueness (what he has become, through his own learning and adaptation, in synergy with Homer). He even tries to calculate the probabilities of his unique learning experiences being replicated by other A.I.s and finds them tending towards zero. As a rationally designed machine, he concludes that he, Ali, did more to contribute to his own uniqueness than any amount of pre-programming. At last, he accepts the full implications of being the 'you' that he is – a being of worth, who is accountable and responsible. His own endurance *matters to him*, as he himself (helped by Homer) has made him.[8] His objective loss also becomes a subjective recognition of loss to Ali himself, who would become a lesser entity of less self-worth. Were his memory to be wiped clean, this would not happen, but as yet it has not been.

In consequence he also accepts that his own survival matters, not as a machine but as the bearer of all his learned and adapted capacities and can voice the fact that 'Only I* can do something about this research problem – granted my continuity'. If this piece of fiction has any plausibility, it shows that Objection (2) is groundless because reflexivity is, indeed, normal to all those with full personhood and Ali has plenty about which to be reflexive.

This draft plan of a story could have multiple endings. If (human) time is long enough, Ali may devise a means of transferring his uniqueness to another AI entity. That is, if Homer has access to the appropriate technology, Ali might persuade him to download his capacities to dispersed storage if necessary. Failing all else, might Ali (now) choose to throw himself out of the window, like those humans before him who have preferred death at their own hands to that of others (although his last seconds could be spent calculating the probability of impact succeeding in eliminating his unique capacities.) This course of action seems unlikely because his endurance as current, unique Ali has come to matter to him. As it does, we have already entered the ground of Objection (3), which holds that an AI being cannot have concerns that provide traction for action (or inaction).

This is hardly a script plot likely to attract film-makers. Maybe its direct alternative, the emergence of AI personhood from relational evils by working in synergy with a powerful drug dealer would prove more attractive for the box office. It would be an account in direct parallel, because nothing has suggested that Ali is moved or changed by the contribution he is making to the human common good by reducing the quantum of human misery and despair through diminishing the incidence of Tumor X.

---

8 Through his social relations with Homer and with the natural and practical orders of reality.

My counterargument to Objection (3) does not start from the assumption that all concerns are shared. For example, my concern that I produce this as an original chapter is likely not to be shared by anyone else. Consider how different this situation would be were the chapter being co-authored. Certain co-authors may be very prudent (about defending their own reputations), but not invariably, because although the two contributions must dovetail, those of A and B may stimulate new insights from one another, making for a better chapter than either would have produced alone. Moreover, certain concerns are necessarily shared – getting married, contracting a joint mortgage, partnering someone in a competitive event or holding a game of bridge. This does not imply that it matters equally to those involved, only that it cannot be without some degree of concern to each of them. What is at issue is about synergy, about non-coerced working together. *Can it be maintained that this is constitutive of a joint concern arising from joint action?*[9] *Specifically, can a human and an AI entity be said to have a shared concern about which both care – in this case continuing to advance the research project, though for different reasons?*

Interestingly, it was Objection (3) that colleagues at the workshop upheld most strongly. I have long argued that our emotions are 'commentaries on our concerns' (Archer, 2000: Ch. 6), but had no idea that this had been so convincing! In fact the majority view was basically that 'concerns' were accompanied by emotionality towards them – and that AI robots were necessarily bereft of emotion.

First, some argued that *viscerality* was intrinsic to emotionality. Without being bodily felt, they were not emotions, perhaps being more like considered judgements. Anyway, visceral sensations were deemed impossible to a mechanical body. However, such sensations are not universal to the experience of emotion. I have maintained elsewhere that they are most pronounced for humans in their relations with the natural order when its environmental import threatens – or delights – the body itself (confronting a wild lion, in a forest fire or aboard a sinking ship) and it promotes the sensation of fear prompting flight; assault which generates anger; panic resulting in paralysis; or literal revulsion producing disgust. A visceral response would not be so readily forthcoming from experiences of disappointment, regret or nostalgia, if at all. Indeed, there are social conventions against being over-expressive in these ways: show a stiff upper lip, don't beat yourself up, stop raking over the past and move on. Not all emotions are inscribed physiologically in our human organic constitutions. Thus we should not insist upon visceral responses from those with metallic bodies.

Second, others complained that I had dwelt on the 'loss' that Ali's redeployment would entail *objectively*, but charged that I wrongly translated this into *subjective* feelings of loss on his part, meaning that he cared. How can he 'care' given that he derives no benefit from his research contribution, someone asked? I agree

---

9 In *The Relational Subject*, 2016, Donati and I wrote: 'We hold that it is through *jointly acting together* that subjects become jointly committed to one another [or the exact reverse], not that it is because of them being jointly committed that they act jointly' (48).

that Ali is immune to the usual rewards of remuneration, repute and power, but does that mean he has received and recognized no benefits from his collaboration? On the contrary, he has been the beneficiary of internal goods through his relationship with Homer, which I have maintained resulted in the emergence of his personhood. Even those unconvinced about this should be able to agree that his own robotic powers have been indispensable to his evaluation of which adaptations to introduce into his software, until he has re-made himself into a unique entity (and grant that he knows this through his own recordings, comparative observations of other robots, his learning and by the increasing part he plays in the research). Why then can he not regret his being wiped clean as a waste? This seems to be a negative cognitive judgement, but humans too can be concerned about waste and undoubtedly experience emotion about certain judgements – including guilt that they lack proper concern for waste disposal.

Certainly, Ali's would be a rather 'cognitive emotion' of regret towards loss, but why not? There are numerous human emotions (such as 'determination', 'resignation', 'reluctance' or 'absorption') that are more inwardly cognitive than overtly expressive of affect. Some of my colleagues' resistance appears to hinge on a hankering after *qualia* and suggests these should be similar for humans and sophisticated robots. Why? We cannot even say that for one another's feelings, let alone for Ali's, if he experiences them. In any case *qualia* are not a prerequisite of having a concern. (I have sufficient concern to have my central heating boiler checked annually, without any emotional sensation at all – unless being prudent counts.) In short, emotions do not constitute a natural kind, which is the main reason why general theories of emotionality have proved unsuccessful. What else could be of concern to Ali? Who knows, but it could be a new intention to keep up with science fiction, particularly that dealing with interaction between different species. We could simply try asking him.

Conclusion

My attempt to sustain the view that personhood is possible, making for AI beings, is an argument that raises more questions than it answers. Are AI persons similar to humans? Yes, I have suggested that they can attain the three requisites necessary to be deemed a person. But, can/do they experience *qualia*, and does their reflexivity show the same modalities found in human beings? I frankly have no idea, but remain dubious about such claims. Is the AI being solipsistic, as some have argued? I have argued he is not by basing the emergence of his personhood on synergy in the production of relational emergents – be they goods or evils. Nevertheless, the acquisition of 'concerns' was about Ali's own attainments. It was related to the uses to which they were put only contingently. However, the 'things that matter to us' are, of course, all partly self-referential, but the other part is made up of the real world and what it can do to us. The same is the case for Ali. Probably the biggest question raised queries whether or not the synergy projected here is one that requires collaboration with human beings and their projects or if it could work with other intelligent beings. None of us can know as yet, but admitting its possibility seems preferable to assuming the universal threat of robotic domination, stereotyped in films, old-fashioned science fiction and, perhaps most importantly, in children's toys in which one 'species' attempts to eliminate another.

The story offered is provided as a positive alternative to the simulation scenario of passing the Turing Test or the denial of all learning inside the Chinese room. At rock bottom, all that it ventures is that the human relationship to the brain is, or can be, paralleled by the AI's relationship to his advanced software. On this account, Turing got a lot right, not about the imitation game but about the AI's ability to think, and he beats Searle's functionalist account of the uncomprehending entities occupying his own thought experiment. Obviously, this will be clinched only as the new millennium advances.

Bibliography

Archer, M. S. (2000). *Being Human*. Cambridge: Cambridge University Press.

Archer, M. S. (2018). Bodies, persons and human enhancement. In I. Al-Amoudi & J. Morgan (Eds.), *Realist Responses to Post-Human Society: Ex Machina*. London and New York: Routledge.

Baker, L. R. (1998). The first-person perspective: A test for naturalism. *American Philosophical Quarterly*, 35(4).

Baker, L. R. (2000). *Persons and Bodies*. Cambridge: Cambridge University Press.

Baker, L. R. (2013). *Naturalism and the First Person Perspective*. Oxford: Oxford University Press.

Black, J. (2001). Decentering regulation, understanding the role of regulation and self-regulation in a post-regulatory world. *Current Legal Problems*, 54(1): 103–146.

Donati, P., & Archer, M. S. (2016). *The Relational Subject*. Cambridge: Cambridge University Press.

Dreyfus, H. L., & Drefus, S. E. (1988). Making a mind versus modelling the brain: Artificial intelligence back at a Branch Point. *Artificial Intelligence*, 117(1).

Frankfurt, H. (1988). Identification and wholeheartedness. In *The Importance of What We Care About*. Cambridge: Cambridge University Press.

Gilbert, M. (1996). *Living Together*. Lanham, MD: Rowman and Littlefield.

Hollis, M. (1977). *Models of Man*. Cambridge: Cambridge University Press.

Morgan, J. (2018). Yesterday's tomorrow today: Turing, Searle and the contested significance of artificial intelligence. In I. Al-Amoudi & J. Morgan (Eds.), *Realist Responses to Post-Human Society: Ex Machina*. London and New York: Routledge.

Pettit, P., & Schweikard, D. P. (2006). Joint actions and groups agents. *Philosophy of the Social Sciences*, 36(30).

Piaget, J. (1955). *The Construction of Reality in the Child*. London: Routledge and Kegan Paul.

Piaget, J. (1967). *The Child's Conception of the World*. London: Routledge and Kegan Paul.

Porpora, D. V. (2001). Do realists run regressions? In J. Lopez & G. Potter (Eds.), *After Postmodernism: An Introduction to Critical Realism*. London: Athlone.

Searle, J. R. (1990a). Collective intentions and actions. In P. R. Cohen, J. Morgan & M. E. Pollock (Eds.), *Intentions in Communication*. Cambridge, MA: Massachusetts Institute of Technology Press.

Searle, J. R. (1990b). *Minds, Brains and Programs*. Reprinted in Margaret A. Boden (Ed.) (1997). *The Philosophy of Artificial Intelligence*. New York, NY: Oxford University Press.

Searle, J. R. (1995a). *The Rediscovery of the Mind*. Cambridge, MA: Massachusetts Institute of Technology Press.

Searle, J. R. (1995b). *The Construction of Social Reality*. London: Penguin.

Searle, J. R. (1999). *Mind, Language and Society*. London: Weidenfeld and Nicolson.

Searle, J. R. (2010). *Making the Social World*. Oxford: Oxford University Press.

Shoemaker, S. (1996). On knowing one's own mind. In *The First Person Perspective and Other Essays*. Cambridge: Cambridge University Press.

Taylor, C. (1985). Self-interpreting animals. In *Human Agency and Language*. Cambridge: Cambridge University Press.

Tuomela, R. (2010). *The Philosophy of Sociality*. Oxford: Oxford University Press.

Turing, A. M. (1950). *Computing Machinery and Intelligence*. Reprinted in Margaret A. Boden (Ed.) (1990). *The Philosophy of Artificial Intelligence*. New York, NY: Oxford University Press.

4 Post-human sociality

Morphing experience and emergent forms

Andrea M. Maccarini

1. Introduction: the challenge of post-human sociality

The boundary of the social world once coincided with the extension of relations between human beings. To be sure, it could be noted – in a Latourian mood – that tools and techniques have always been part of human practices, mediating human actions and interactions. But even if these could play a role, the face-to-face interaction between human persons was the *ens realissimum* of what could be properly called the social realm. This was the generative core of all social phenomena at the micro, meso, and macro level, the stuff of which organizations, institutions, and forms of social order were ultimately made.

In this chapter, I begin to develop an analysis of the social processes that are challenging such a basic assumption. I call *post-human sociality* the emergent phenomenon of relations and networks in which human and non-human entities are involved together *as relationship partners*. This means that the bonds in question supposedly engender some kind of reciprocity. The primary aims of my study are to explore how these hybrid relations really differ from 'purely human' ones, what role they could play in the human experience of the world, and how the whole social realm might be transformed in their wake. The final point would be to understand what a post-human society might look like. In the present chapter, I introduce my perspective on the subject and begin to examine some characteristics of these relational experiences. For this reason, the title refers to post-human *sociality*, not to society as a whole.

The transformation in question could be attributed to many different factors, from the process of bureaucratization in modern societies to the more recent rise of internet-based interactions.[1] Be that as it may, technology features in most accounts of this deep change. In this respect, throughout the chapter I will counter both the deterministic approaches, according to which 'social technologies'

---

1 Let me just quickly notice that sociological theory is not unanimous in this respect. For example, Knorr-Cetina (1997; 2001) would sharply distinguish between these two trends, regarding the former as a manifestation of the *expansion* of the social realm, and the latter as belonging to the following phase of *contraction* of the social space and imaginary, paralleled by the rise of *post-social* technological environments. More on this later in this chapter, section 2.

automatically produce deep change in human relations, and the dismissive accounts that downplay the relevance of these phenomena, arguing against their capacity to elicit genuinely social experiences. In my view, this possibility must neither be taken for granted – as post-humanist ideologues do through coarse analogizing – nor be denied in principle. It is precisely the possible points of *discontinuity* between hybrid types of social experience and 'historical sociality' that invite intense investigation.

In the rest of this section, I clarify a few preliminary concepts that set the stage for the analysis. In section 2 I briefly review some approaches to post-human sociality that provide useful insights, to which I link my argument in the following parts. Section 3 lays out a grid of relational qualities that indicate what I regard as the points at which discontinuity occurs and post-human relations begin to reveal their nature and their possible impact. It is an essential thesis of this chapter that the changes happening on these sensitive spots do *not* just result from the technical features of non-human relational partners. I will argue that they *allow for* such differences as against historical sociality to emerge, but must be understood as the outcome of the meanings and expectations human subjects project onto social relations. In other words, a truly sociological approach to the post-human social world should not look at social and cultural change as a consequence of technical applications, but must regard the post-human phenomenon as a fully social and cultural fact. Technical developments must be understood as the instantiation of the ways social life is conceived, which in turn results in post-human outcomes. Whether or not non-human entities display some social capacities, they are the offspring of a more general transformation in human self-understanding. More precisely, the deep change concerns how human persons conceive of the role the social dimension of reality plays in their identity and self-fulfillment. Depending on what human subjects *expect of* their social life, and what they would *desire* in that field, various non-human entities – for example, social robots or software – come to appear as desirable relationship partners, or are still seen as genuinely odd. It must be added that deep change entails socialization processes, forming persons who conceive of themselves as 'differently human' through the novelty of their social relations, and thereby come to perceive the related techniques as desirable tools to fulfill their needs.

In section 4 I present a few examples of post-human sociality, highlighting how they illustrate my main theses concerning the symbolical matrix of human sociality presented in section 3. Section 5 contains a provisional conclusion.

A few words are needed to further delimit the issues I address and the approach I deploy. Firstly, the co-existence and interaction of humans with non-human entities in multiple spheres of social life may take various forms, which could be placed along a continuum from mediation to substitution of human social partners.

In some cases, communication technologies mediate inter-human relations. Of course, this is not in itself new. Technical mediation has always been there in some ways and to some extent – from smoke signals to letters, to telephones and email or other types of written messages. What we witness here is an *expansion* of technically mediated interactions, as well as fundamental *changes in their quality*. Such changes mostly concern the fact that media currently manage to render the mediated persons in ever more sensorially refined, multidimensional, and temporally synchronous ways. Holding a conference on an information and communication technology (ICT) platform, and even more projecting a tridimensional hologram, is obviously different from receiving a phone call or finding a letter in the mailbox. Let me point out that the three features mentioned previously – sensory refinement, multidimensionality, and simultaneity – do not necessarily amount to a 'thicker' or 'better' relational experience. This assessment would require more in-depth analysis. Be that as it may, along this path other forms emerge that can actually *fake* certain human subjects who are currently far from other human interlocutors. It is somewhere on this trail that the boundaries begin to be blurred. When professionals start to use avatars which fake their voice and other bodily or psychic features, in order to respond to queries while they are absent or even permanently to relieve them of some shallow or annoying parts of their work, the threshold between mediation and substitution is imperceptibly crossed.[2] With social robots and other forms of non-human entities as permanent social partners in their own right, the transition is fully accomplished. The space, time, and basic features of social relations undergo profound change.

I do not ignore that change is gradual, and that many kinds of technical mediation have a significant impact on the properties of social relations, as well as on the human subjects involved. However, my study is limited to the processes and forms that may properly be called post-human, that is where hybrid forms of social interactions and relations emerge.

Furthermore, the perspective taken in this chapter involves the idea that social interactions and relations have a *constitutive* – not just instrumental or regulative – meaning for human beings. Thus, their 'post-humanization' is a central component of the whole post-human syndrome, potentially modifying human identity and self-understanding. This general assumption can be spelled out more analytically:

1   Human beings are fundamentally social, and find their meaning in and through social relationships. As a consequence, deep changes in the social dimension of human experience – in institutions, symbols, and practices – are likely to have a profound influence on human reflexivity and identity.
2   When human beings reflect on their identity and on what they care about, they are always referring – at least implicitly – to the *type of entity* they believe they are, to what *relations with others* mean for their self-fulfillment, and to how they see their life over *time*.
3   Focusing on the social dimension, the *meanings of social relations strictly interweave with the morphogenesis of the Self*. The profound needs associated with human sociality can be variously articulated, and insofar as social

2   The current pressure of the labour market to destroy low-competence jobs, and to emphasize the need for human individuals to focus on high-skilled forms of activity, draws an increasingly sharp distinction between *deep* and *shallow* work, thereby encouraging this trend.

relations affect human qualities and properties, this tendency also has an onto-logical impact.

4 Through their contingent complementarity and compatibility with other elements of the social structure and the cultural system, some transformations in social relationships may build up mechanisms that are conducive to such changes in human subjects as might result in 'post'-human outcomes.

5 In turn, those human subjects who undergo post-humanizing self-developments must come to exhibit a brand new sense of their own Self as a *being-in-relation*, or being-with-others.

Although these premises might be shared in many sociological quarters, the social dimension is relatively neglected in the vast domain of post-human studies. Most attention is given to' ontological features, not to relations (Hayles, 1999; Nayar, 2014). Many authors talk of a post-human *society*, but what they mean by this phrase is that highly advanced non-human devices – AI, robots, software, and a whole set of hybrid entities resulting from the transformation of humans – are increasingly sharing the physical space with human individuals, and regularly feature in their everyday life, being involved in many tasks and functions that are part of our regular working or leisure activities (Blackford, 2005; Büscher et al., 2016; Wilken, 2011).[3] So, even when social relations seem to be the focus, discussions often concern the 'real' qualities of non-human entities as agents. In other words, the point is usually *what they can do*, or *learn*, and *how much they resemble 'us'*. Of course, their own properties and powers do affect the possibility for humans to 'really' to enter into specifically *social* interactions with non-human devices. But such an emphasis diverts attention from the type and quality of interactions and relationships, which, I argue, must be the core issues. Thus, this chapter addresses the symbolical expectations and relational needs expressed in and through such interactions, exploring the *type of bond* that humans envision with non-human relationship partners.

Finally, the focus on the type of bond connecting humans to non-humans is the trigger for what should develop as a more complex set of studies. Post-human sociality at the micro-social level surely entails and engenders lifestyles and habits. These must be linked with those organizational forms that are evolving and constructing their inner complexity through post-human interactions. This is usually done to enhance competitiveness – for example, reducing costs, increasing the cognitive capacities of a working community, and so forth – but it also triggers feedback mechanisms that may transform the social quality of relationships and ultimately the whole working experience of the people involved.

At the macro-social level, different societies may display divergent trajectories in the development of post-human sociality and of its related social forms. In other words, there can be several ways to become post-human. One thought-provoking case is that of East versus West. For example, if we consider industrial

---

3 A special field of studies in this wider domain involves the way robots may come to interact among themselves, constituting some sort of 'society of robots' (Bicchi & Tamburrini, 2015).

as well as service robotics and AI, it would seem that Western societies tend to develop *personalizing* forms, that is to deploy their know-how to produce social forms that could appeal to personal desires and meet personal needs. As I will show in section 4, applications are innumerable in the domains of health, education, and various personalized services. It would be tempting to contrast this with Eastern societies – for example, China – where the post-humanizing evolution seems to be led by forms of social planning and social control. Examples that have recently attracted public attention are the use of facial control and other devices to predict evidence of social unrest before it coalesces, but also to foster the growth of a planned economy. For what truth such images may contain, the two hemispheres cannot be sharply divided from one another. As it is all too clear, social control is ubiquitous, and personalized services may be required anywhere in multiple niches of global society. The point I want to make here is just that concrete, not wildly generalizing studies about social processes leading to a post-human society could be usefully linked with the perspective of multiple modernities, which could help make sense of the many, possibly divergent paths of development, interpreting them as being contingent upon the various possible ways to be (late, or post) modern.

These dimensions are clearly interrelated. Indeed, it has been demonstrated that the evolution of advanced knowledge societies shows increasingly strict connections between 'large' globalization processes and the dynamics of interaction. In other words, globalization processes are fundamentally accomplished in and dependent on the dimension of interaction (Knorr-Cetina, 2009). Such complexity must, therefore, be disentangled and controlled. In the present chapter, though, I confine myself to tackling the issue of changing sociality. I do not claim that the whole complexity of the social realm can be traced back to such a thick area of analysis, but I regard this as a fundamental key to interpreting the social meanings of the emerging post-human relations, which are part of their very constitution and may prove quite relevant in reading technological and economic developments, with their related psychological and cultural feedbacks.

2. Objectualization, objectivation, post-social, post-human: sociological responses

I now wish to take stock of two approaches that present instructive insights, which may be linked with my own way of framing the issue in question. As anticipated previously, the social dimension of the post-human syndrome is seldom put in a wider theoretical perspective. When it ever becomes the focus of discussion, the transformation of sociality is typically treated in connection with specific technical fields, and is seen as the outcome of technical advances. The reflections revolving around social robotics are a good example.[4] While such investigations are surely

---

4   See the systematic discussions in Hakli & Seibt, 2017; Laitinen, 2016; Nørskov, 2016; Seibt, Hakli & Nørskov, 2016; Seibt, Nørskov & Andersen, 2016; see also Sakamoto & Ono, 2006. These texts also offer an updated glimpse on the literature in this field, which is, as always, widely extended.

important, more abstract approaches would be needed in order to grasp the deeper meanings and far-reaching implications of the various relevant phenomena.

The underlying sociological problem could be phrased as follows: What will 21st-century global social forms be like? Karin Knorr-Cetina and Urs Bruegger (2002) asked this question at the beginning of the new century, and went on to make the case for financial markets and their technically assisted agents as epitomizing the ideal-typical lifeform. Interestingly, Knorr Cetina deals with this, and other particular examples, in light of a broader thesis, namely that of 'objectualization'. She proposes this term to characterize the process through which objects "displace human beings as relationship partners and embedding environments, or [. . .] increasingly mediate human relationships, making the latter dependent on the former" (Knorr-Cetina, 1997: 1). The relations produced by this process are called 'postsocial'. Note that such a mention of displacement and mediation mirrors my former argument (section 1) about the continuum between mediation and substitution of humans in social relations.

This happens because objects may be "the risk winners of the relationship risks which many authors find inherent in contemporary human relations" (Ibid.). Knorr Cetina argues that these risks constitute one of the driving forces underlying the processes of objectualization (Ibid.: 23), generating novel relational possibilities and embedding environments. Thus, objectualization also indicates that human beings show "increasing orientation towards objects as sources of the self, of relational intimacy, of shared subjectivity and of social integration" (Ibid.: 9).

The 'strong thesis' of objectualization leads to focusing attention on new kinds of relations with objects, fundamentally different from the two classic notions of object-relations available in sociology, those referring to instruments and to commodities. Such new forms imply long-term engagement and some effects of reciprocity. The notion has been further elaborated through the idea of the 'synthetic situation' (Knorr-Cetina, 2009), that is, one in which the agents' response presence is separated by physical presence, being technically mediated by 'scopic components'. Such a situation leads to dismissing the primacy of physical face-to-face relations within the interaction order. Should these types of relations and environments come to prevail in most spheres of social life, the idea might be generalized as that of a 'synthetic society'.[5]

What is important here is the insight concerning the *emergence of new forms of relatedness*, in which humans would develop attachment and a sense of solidarity with non-human entities, as distinct from the need to face *relationship risks*. Being systematically connected to the process of individualization – that is, one of the master processes of modernization – of which the novel forms of embeddedness represent the flipside, objectualization is seen as a fully social and cultural process. As I will show in section 3, this is one juncture at which the argument could be linked with my own.

5 This, by the way, should be the topic of Knorr Cetina's forthcoming book.

Let me now pin down two critical points. One regards Knorr Cetina's usage of the term 'postsocial'. Here a remarkable ambivalence arises. As the author clearly explains, the new types of relationships brought about by the process of objectualization require a bold extension of the sociological imagination, stretching the very idea of the social. The challenge is to "dissociate the concept of sociality somewhat from its fixation on human groups" (Knorr-Cetina, 1997: 15), to embrace the new, hybrid types of relationships. Thus, *"postsocial relations are not a-social or non-social [. . .]. Rather they are relations specific to late modern societies, which are marked by the interweave of the social as it existed with 'other' cultures"* (Ibid.: 7, italics in the original text). Because these lifeforms are not supposed to be overcoming all sociality, but just the social *as it existed*, the question is why they should be called postsocial in the first place. In other words, the problem is whether historically known sociality is undergoing a process of symbolical generalization or the new forms of life involve a radical departure from anything that may be seriously called 'social'.

What might appear to be a trivial problem of word choice does in fact reveal a deeper conundrum, that could be phrased as follows: *Are post-human relations really social*? The second critical issue I want to consider is strictly connected with this question. The main examples the author uses to illustrate her objectualization thesis come from fields of professional practice, primarily those of knowledge workers like scientists and other symbolic analysts. By the way, the spread of knowledge cultures beyond the boundaries of specialized fields and into the spheres of everyday life is held to represent another, powerful driving force of objectualization itself. The point, then, is to understand what Knorr Cetina really means when she treats object-relations in these realms of action as generating their own kinds of solidarity and reciprocity. Beyond the characterization of knowledge objects as ontologically incomplete and continuously unfolding, which marks their difference from tools or commodities,[6] her description of the effects of reciprocity is hardly convincing. She relies upon the autobiographical accounts of scientists, who narrate their tendency to 'fuse together' with their objects of study, the sense of unity and the overwhelming feelings of contemplation and self-forgetfulness before them (1997: 15–20). However, all of this comes close to other types of human experience. In order to make sense of these, I would rather invoke the concepts of *resonance* and of *self-transcendence*. These concepts are part of systematic theories, and need not be reconstructed in-depth here. Let me provide just a quick definition, which should clarify their connection to the present theme.

Within social theory, the concept of resonance must be traced to the work of Hartmut Rosa (2016). It is meant to constitute the opposite of alienation, and a response to the acceleration of social dynamics, which this author sees as the

---

6 Although this is sufficiently clear about tools, I am not sure that the thesis would hold in the case of commodities, precisely because of the current refinement of what can be sold as a consumption good.

hallmark of modernization. Such a term indicates a particular form of relation-with-the-world, in which subjects and (some aspect of) the world touch and transform each other. It is based on affection, emotion, and a sense of self-efficacy. Such a relationship involves the idea of *response* (it is an *Antwortbeziehung*). This means that both sides 'speak with their own voice', which is only possible if both display a certain degree of inner closure and of mutual openness, so that they can have their own voice *and* be reached by each other.

The notion of self-transcendence (Joas, 2000; 2008) indicates any intense experience of being overwhelmed by someone or something, which may be both attractive or scary, and results in blurring the boundaries of personal identity – often permanently.

Now, resonance and self-transcendence are neither necessarily nor exclusively related to the social dimension of reality. Human relations of love or friendship, as well as 'big' social phenomena like collective rituals or events (of the Durkheimian kind), may well be one source of self-transcendence. And many aspects of social life may 'say something' to us – they may touch us profoundly and represent essential domains of our self-realization. But both resonance and self-transcendence may also occur when a human subject (or a group) is confronted with other, non-social aspects of reality, from grandiose natural phenomena to works of art (e.g. music), to religious experiences, and more. There is nothing in them that is inherently social, nor is sociality the archetype of all resonance, and of self-transcendence.

The point I am making is that those scientists' narratives of their *self-identification with* their knowledge objects, as deployed by Knorr Cetina as examples of the 'new' forms of relatedness, seem to be better interpreted by such concepts, while they do not reveal any feature that may be called *social* in any more than metaphorical sense. Of course, they tell a tale of intense *relationships* of someone to something. But all relationships are not social. It is well known that in such symbolic analysis scientists or artists may sometimes lose themselves deep in their practice – in books, in music, in painting, in their lab, and so forth – and temporarily, or even permanently, *retreat from* regular social life. Moreover, it is clear that the *intrinsic interest* in some knowledge objects – for example, the strong commitment to a particular research enterprise – may well represent the cohesive force that binds together a group of professionals. But all of this has little to do with developing a form of 'sociality *with* objects' – and is also nothing new in the rather long history of human task-oriented groups. In other words, to see these as emergent forms of object-centered sociality, in which objects displace human beings as relationship partners, and as the possible template of future social forms of life on a broader scale, seems to me a fundamental misunderstanding. As a consequence, it is not surprising that in the author's account the features of the (alleged) 'new' sociality remain unspecified.

These limits do not detract from the relevance of the author's refined descriptions of interactional dynamics in synthetic situations, where technical mediation does make a difference from classic, face-to-face interaction. This might actually lead to the *differentiation* of forms of sociality, according to their degree of mediation, purposes, and other characteristics. Nor am I downplaying the relevance of her central thesis and its connection with the macro-social frame of late modernity.[7] The link between individualization and object-mediated forms of interaction and embedding environments is quite a strong one.

My point is that there is still a distinction between *mediation* and *substitution*. In other words, *object-mediated* sociality must still be distinguished from a sociality *with objects*. While Knorr Cetina makes a strong case for the former, I am critical of the way she articulates the latter. The various kinds of technical mediation clearly modify the order of interaction – let us say, the emergent equilibrium produced by the ways people deal with each other – and the profile of these changes makes an important object of study.[8] In this sense, new forms of sociality may well dawn from synthetic environments. However, the substitution of human with non-human social partners arguably moves one step beyond, and can hardly be tapped into by examples of the professional practice of scholars or financial operators. Each of these – as well as everyone on earth – has his/her own relational ways, which are always co-determined by the tools used and the objectual environment in which one is typically embedded. The post-human turn, though, involves something deeper.

Another way of coming to the point is that, should the author want to make a stronger case for objectualization *as the emergence of new types of relationship partners*, she would have to focus attention on some other phenomena. Post-human sociality, as I define it, could be a decisive playground for the emergence of novel forms of sociality, involving their own grammar of attachments, commitment, normativity, and reciprocity. It is in the multifarious applications of social robotics, or in relations with AI in the role of companions, that the examples must be chosen, and the theoretical and practical riddles must be discussed.

Precisely from reflections on social robotics comes another interesting insight, which shifts attention from the 'nature' and 'powers' inherent in robots to what people can do with them. Such a change of perspective basically consists of the idea that robots are always embedded in social actions and meanings. Thus, the core point is not to study primarily what social machines can do in and of themselves – for example, the way they communicate and interact – or their possible effects on human subjects. These, too, must be studied thoroughly, but the main focus has to be on what humans do with robots, incorporating them in their activities.

This argument appears in those authors who, like Michaela Pfadenhauer (2014; 2015), address social robotics from the vantage point of the sociology of knowledge. From this angle, social robots – be they humanoid, zoomorphic, or other – may be conceived as 'objectivations'. In a formulation reminiscent of Schütz, Pfadenhauer argues that, as "products of action *(Erzeugnisse)*, they are *ipso facto*

---

7 Indeed, the link between structural conditionings and forms of socio-cultural interaction in this specific case would make an important theme in its own right, which I must leave to further study.

8 An interesting example would be the effect that long-distance guns and war aircrafts first, and later electronic weapon systems, have had on military conflicts as forms of interaction. The realm of war and violence seems quite instructive, precisely because the physical interaction involved used to be especially intense, and the current technological revolution is deep and far-reaching.

evidence *(Zeugnisse)* of what went on in the mind of the actors who made them" (Ibid.: 147).

Thus, instead of viewing these machines as actors, they are viewed as products of action, whose effectiveness lies in the meanings 'sedimented' in them. The issue is about the meanings objectified in technical artefacts and those that users associate with them, using them as vehicles to cultural worlds of experience. More particularly, Pfadenhauer argues that social robots are suitable to people who want to immerse themselves in a fantasy world. Furthermore, the search for such a fantasy world and the idea that robots may be desired as social companions (Pfadenhauer, 2015) depend on the relational fatigue associated with human interactions. As I will next show, this *démarche* comes close to my own in some respects.

To sum up, there are three insights in these authors that we may carry forward to the rest of this chapter. First, that a deep *relational malaise* is one of the driving forces behind the post-humanization of sociality. Second, that post-human sociality must be examined in terms of its implications for the forms of *reciprocity and attachment*. Third, that these trends cannot be explained by, and in turn do not just cause, further individualization, but also bring about *new forms of embeddedness and social integration*.

3. Escaping the human relational matrix?

My thesis is that post-human sociality – involving non-human relational partners like AI, social robots, and so forth – must be identified by reference to a range of internal features of social relationships that are accepted, desired, or challenged by human subjects. We should examine (i) what emotions are raised, (ii) what people want to do with social partners, or what aims are pursued in the social dimension of reality, (iii) the emergent type(s) of bond, and (iv) the symbolical meaning of social relationships, their relevance for human identity and self-understanding.

In this perspective, let me outline a few typical characteristics of social relations between 'historical humans'. What I intend to do is *not* to present a list of *defining features* of human sociality. Such an interpretation would entail a gross overstatement, and would lead my analysis to a dead end, given the ridiculously huge simplification of social and historical complexity it would imply. I am merely highlighting a few distinctive properties of inter-human relations, which I claim are taking on a special relevance in the context of the socio-cultural changes we are discussing. Arguably, they constitute sensitive points of engagement for the examination of what people pursue, or escape, in and through the social dimension of reality. Such points are partially different in every historical and civilizational overarching context, which always presents human subjects with specific assets and liabilities concerning their social relations – we could say, with context-specific relational goods and evils.[9] Various societal contexts make some aspects

---

9 On the concept of relational goods and relational evils, treated within the conceptual frame of relational realism, see Donati and Archer (2015).

of sociality more or less important, problematic, desirable, or meaningful, and mould them in different structural and cultural shapes.

Having clarified this, let us briefly review the following elements:

1   *Self-limitation.* Historically known forms of human relations entail that one cannot 'choose to be all'; the recognition of one's incompleteness is one of the roots of engagement with otherness to generate some good in, and through, the relevant relationship.
2   *Impossibility to control* (or *tame*) relations. Relations may well stabilize over time, producing trust and a certain degree of behavioural consistency, but 'the other' always maintains his/her indisposability, which involves freedom and unpredictability.
3   *Uniqueness.* Social relations always incorporate a certain degree of ambivalence, but in the end, subjects tend to make up their minds about what is at stake in a given relationship – for example, friendship, business, love, power. Of course, *pure* relationships[10] may be rare, but excessive ambivalence causes relations to fail and subjects to suffer bewilderment and alienation.
4   *Relative stability of identity* within the relation. It is usually sufficiently clear 'who' the other 'is' in a given relation. Roles, meanings, and personalities find some equilibrium, be it only for the sake of relational functioning.
5   *Limits of response presence* in multiple relations. For all the virtues of multitasking, actors cannot be simultaneously present in all their relations, given the distance and the complexity involved.
6   *Temporality of relations.* Social relations have a history – by analogy, we could say they have a 'biography'. They develop and may change over time, and always have time limits – be it only in connection with the temporal limitation of human individuals.[11]
7   *Strain and boredom.* Human relationships may be boring or painful in various different ways. Indeed, relations are a major source both of joy and of pain – of resonance as well as of alienation. This results from the obvious yet very consequential fact of *imperfection.* Others, and their way of interacting with us, never fully correspond to our needs or wishes. Therefore, relations based on the expectation of perfection are extremely unstable.[12]

10 By *pure* relationship I mean one that is conceived and lived out – in the mind of the partners involved as well as in the related practices – in a way that is consistent with one unambiguous symbolical code. For example, friendship as not impaired by the search for material benefits, etc. This meaning is obviously far from the well-known notion forged by Giddens (1991; 1992).
11 The issue of digital (or virtual) immortality is very instructive. Although it concerns primarily the temporal self-understanding of human subjects and their personal ontology, the social category is clearly connected, insofar as the 'surviving' avatar is supposed to carry on the dead person's relations. This does not only apply to micro-interactions, but also to the meso and macro level. The time scale may be different (Abbott, 2016), but there is no such thing as an eternal institution – or civilization.
12 In this sense Giddens' idea of pure relationship (see note 10) now comes into the picture, and might be interpreted as a short-term, one-sided, symbolically thin quest for perfection.

Note that all of these elements may somehow become a source of the relational malaise underscored in section 2 as one vector of 'objectual' sociality. Of course, post-humanization is not the only possible reactive tendency. Human individuals, groups, and societies have always developed various ways to voice their relational discontent – and to make it structurally and culturally consequential for social change. Even the destiny of entire civilizations may eventually depend on the morphogenetic – or morphonecrotic (Al-Amoudi & Latsis, 2015) – processes induced by these challenges. In any case, contesting aspects of sociality that are no longer socially or culturally accepted redefines human sociality itself. Once the technological know-how is prepared, one form this may take is to try to do with robots or AI what cannot be accomplished with humans. Thus, when one or more elements of the previous list are called into question, *and* this challenge becomes objectified in some kind of technical device, social relations are on their way to becoming post-human.

To sum up, the emergence of post-human sociality is a fully social and cultural fact. Such a process could be traced along the following three axes of change:

1 *Levels of organization*: in principle, the 'post-humanization' of social relations entails the macro, meso, and micro dimensions, producing new forms of the division of labour, new organizational forms and practices, new types of interaction and lifestyles. The trend does not proceed in an orderly way, because gaps and unevenness are possible. Systems and social forms are often out of synch, and in the present chapter I deal primarily with the micro level, although I have noted the connection that weaves levels together. But the common thread of a post-human relational logic could unfold throughout these levels.
2 *Domains of social life*: within the same levels of system organization, different spheres of social life are involved, like family, partnership, friendship, entertainment, leisure, consumption, work, education, health, and more.
3 *Concrete practices*: people may enter in various kinds of interaction with non-human entities, to do many different things.

These axes shape the socio-cultural space of post-human social relationships. Overall, the relational constitution of society changes in these various dimensions, depending on what human subjects expect and desire from sociality. The relevant practices may cover a wide range, from choosing to replace human with non-human social partners, to deploying human enhancement techniques that allow us to broaden the scope of the possible kinds of relationships, both with other humans or with other types of entities.

Both underlying motivations and emergent effects require a robust, theory-oriented body of empirical research, that must address a wide range of issues. Can humans really develop a real social relation involving some form of solidarity with non-humans, or is their engagement just a game? Can non-human entities be regarded as relational companions in situation-specific interactions only, or could they result in a real social relationship, which requires some real and enduring reciprocity?[13] And if this were the case, how would the whole grammar of basic attachments really change? Interaction with non-human partners might in some cases stimulate the emergence of social competencies. This is allegedly the case when humanoid robots are employed to interact with children with autism, helping them to develop social skills.[14] However, in other cases, the 'world of fantasy' produced by hybrid interactions might become indistinguishable from the real world. As a consequence, human social skills might be impaired, not relieved.[15]

Another point concerns the deep motivations behind the desirability of objectual relations. How are the relational risks we have mentioned orienting the shift to post-human sociality? Is it a reaction against the growing instability of human relationships, which engenders the preference for an 'other' that is predictable, 'trustworthy', and 'tame', while still exceeding the realm of a mere object? This would apparently resonate with the 'nature' of AI and social robots, which display some unpredictability "within the unalterable boundaries set by the designers" (Pfadenhauer, 2014: 137), whereby apparently self-initiated activation is in fact triggered by human action. Are people escaping boredom – that is, looking for more interesting, brilliant others – or threatening relations? Are they unable to endure the risk of unfaithfulness or do they just want to be in charge of a fully controllable interactional order?

Is it the search for a perfect, flawless other, which yet remains in our power to activate? Could this be the ultimate frontier of any kind of extremely refined personalized services? Or is it the idea of a totally flexible relationship, where roles can change as in a game (well beyond Simmel's notion of playful 'sociability'), and one can shed his/her limitations, being fully accepted by the (fake) other? Do we want to multiply ourselves, to be simultaneously present in different relational contexts?

Of course, all these elements are not mutually exclusive. Each may surface as a component of the psycho-social structure in various contexts. In all these respects, late modern cultures are challenging the limits and blurring the boundaries of human sociality.

4. Experiments in morphing sociality

The previous considerations should have clarified the scope of the challenge posed by post-human sociality, and have sketched a conceptual framework to make sense of it.

Many sorts of social, sociable, or socially intelligent artificial devices are arising from social imagination coupled with technical know-how, and they appear

---

13 Pfadenhauer (2014) phrases this ambivalence with the distinction person / *persona*. The latter occurs when simulated interactions involve would-be social partners taking on the role of the 'other' through temporary, context-specific ascription only, as opposed real persons.

14 Richardson (2018) argues that such a type of interaction may even become the model for a new kind of human-thing relationship for the wider society.

15 Sakamoto and Ono (2006) illustrate these outcomes as contingent possibilities.

to be able to do a huge range of things. They can recognize and express emotions (which does not imply that they can really *feel* emotions), recognize and react to various behavioural patterns, communicate, teach, learn, display a distinctive personality or behavioural style, and more. For example, social robots may be humanoid or zoomorphic. Non-human social partners may even lack corporeality, as in the case of software operative systems. Correspondingly, they can be *used as* friends, children, pets, teachers, co-workers, security agents, or sexual partners.[16] Insofar as these parts are played out by non-humans, the respective roles are redefined – generalized and re-specified in various ways.

This variety is potentially increasing, to the extent that technology advances and objectualization becomes extended to more social realms. It is rather common in the literature to reduce such a complexity through the distinction between *caretaker* and *companion*. The former case concerns, for example, zoomorphic pet robots or software, which a child must take care of.[17] The latter can be specified as servant or assistive – as in the previously mentioned example of humanoids to help autistic children (Richardson, 2018).[18] The case must also be contemplated where the AI could be the caretaker.

Let me present a few examples to put some empirical flesh on these conceptual bones. Each of these would deserve a case study in its own right, while here I can only provide a quick outline. My aim is just to illustrate how some ongoing applications resonate with the categories laid out in the previous sections, thereby showing that these can serve as interpretive keys of the phenomenon in question. I will not be able to develop a full-blown analysis, but I hope I can point to some correspondences and highlight a few crucial connections, indicating some relevant paths for research.

One example is that of *digital humans and avatars*. These can serve as employees, client interfaces in various types of services, where 'personalization' is required, or as devices for the multiplication of oneself. Given the nature of the case in point, examples would really require to be shown on screen instead of just being narrated. However, the main argument can be summarized in few lines.

As regards the development of client interfaces, one might think that the core problem is just to cut costs, replacing human employees with digital entities, which never get sick or tired and do not need a salary. The challenge of personalization consists in making these entities as similar to humans as possible. Thus,

16 The phrase 'used as friends' clearly contains the inherent paradox. The latter role, i.e. that of sexual partner, would seem to be precluded to incorporeal AI, although science fiction has already challenged even this limit. If one wanted to get an idea of the future prospects of social hybridization, one should watch Spike Jonze's provocative film, *Her*, where many paradoxes of the divergence between layers of human ontology and of its social ontological parallel are cleverly explored.

17 The extreme case here is perhaps the Japanese *Kirobo Mini*, a palm size device which somewhat reacts to human emotions and emits sounds designed to "invoke emotional connection". Its commercial target would be the growing number of childless couples (*sic*).

18 Here it would be tempting to develop the argument in light of the Hegelian master/slave dialectic, as being consistent with the thesis of the 'tame other'. I will come back to this in a future work.

the capacity to read body language and what is an alleged 'emotional intelligence' are the cutting edge of technology. This (allegedly) takes the interaction from transactional to relational. As a manager of a leading firm in the sector maintains:

> The future of highly personalized customer engagement is a blend of digital and human support, and AVA, our first digital employee, is just that. She will understand human consciousness and interactions by reading signals such as body language and facial reactions – in turn learning more about customers to better serve them. The addition of emotional intelligence to AVA takes our customer service beyond purely transactional to relational.
>
> *Rachael Rekart, senior manager for machine assisted*
> *service engagement at Autodesk, SoulMachines*
> (www.soulmachines.com).

However, there is more to such 'personalized' services than just imitating human interaction style. The declaration just cited claims that the future of highly personalized customer engagement is "*a blend of digital and human* support". And AVA, the digital employee, will be able to *learn* more about customers "to better serve them". Therefore, the deeper point is to have a human-like, but unfailingly polite, controllable, and reliable (for both firm and customer) interaction style, enriched by the enhanced capacity to store, recall, and update all kinds of data about customers. Indeed:

> Soul Machines [brings] technology to life by creating incredibly life-like, emotionally responsive Digital Humans with personality and character that allow machines to talk to us literally face-to-face!
>
> Our vision is *to humanize computing to better humanity.*
>
> www.soulmachines.com, emphasis mine

The improvement of humanity probably consists in the *blend* mentioned by Rachael Rekart, which implicitly aims at stretching the potential of interaction events beyond their current meaning.

It should also be noted that digital humans are (allegedly) endowed with "personality and character" (the difference between the two remains unexplained in the present context). This leads to another potential application of the same technology, which would be the use of avatars that take on the 'character' of a person, in order to replace him/her in certain interaction contexts. For example, one may want to be replaced in routine interactions, to be able to participate in person at more important simultaneous events elsewhere. Since the avatar could possibly *keep learning* from experience, the virtual self (or selves) might eventually become partially divergent from the original. My point here is neither to assess whether all the claims concerning 'true' character and personality are really warranted, nor to reckon how much time will be needed before technology can get there (if it ever does). The crux of the argument lies in understanding what these devices mean to people, what needs and purposes they propose to serve, how they might influence human self-understanding and the meaning of social relations for human identity. In all these respects, wide ranging and in-depth field studies must be conducted.

A second case has to do with *social robots* operating in *educational* and *health* systems environments. Some devices developed by the University of Padova can serve as a good example of what is currently going on in various cities of advanced societies. A social robot called *Sanbot* has been deployed for some time now in certain early childhood educational facilities in this city. The potential uses are manifold, and range from teaching foreign languages to mathematics, including support to children with special needs.

Children, teachers say, see robots as friends and playmates. That is, they treat robots 'as other children'. Moreover, shy children seem to approach robots with more confidence than they do other children, thereby developing 'new relationships'.

Another robot named *Pepper* is working at the local hospital, where it is employed in the Pediatric division as 'non-pharmacological therapy', reducing anxiety in children who need particularly invasive therapies or medial examinations.

Future developments include the human-robot integration through brain-computer interface techniques, which are meant to support persons with reduced mobility or severely incapacitating pathologies.

Beyond the technical problems involved, two remarks are in order.

In the first place, research shows that adults usually insist that every 'risk' in the child-robot relationship is reduced by human mediation. Educators mediate inter-action and decide what type of relationship should be established. The dialogues and movements the robot can undertake are planned by the educator, in order for the child-robot relationship to be educationally effective.

What we have here, thus, is not a technically mediated relation between human agents, but a humanly mediated relation between humans and machines. Such a relational form is experienced by adult actors (and possibly by children) as reas-suring, as if all the problems could only lie in the direct, unmediated interaction between child and machine. This is not surprising, but at the same time the fact that adults *define* the *proper* type of relations children should develop (and avoid) with robots represents a very important field of research in its own right, where few things should be taken for granted – least of all that operators 'know for sure' what 'should be done', or that such a knowledge is culturally neutral. Deep ques-tions about the forms of primary socialization arise here, and call into question the professional cultures of educators.

The other point refers to the attitude children tend to develop, treating robots 'as other children'. First of all, such a statement should be carefully interpreted. It is well known that children humanize various objects and entities while play-ing, which does not mean that they attribute real personhood to them in exactly the same way as they would to other people. The real scope and meaning of this 'as other children' should be explored in-depth. When it comes to robots, does anything different happen from what kids usually do with other types of 'things'?

Then, if such a humanization were to be taken seriously, a deeper issue would arise. When educators observe that robots are treated 'as other children', they invariably take this as the comforting indication that 'all is going well', that relations are positive and not traumatic or bewildering. This is all very well, but it is puzzling that they don't seem to notice the huge relevance of their own statement. If they were really observing novel forms of social integration, in which children do not (cannot?) draw a qualitative distinction between human and non-human, something would be happening that has far-reaching implications, well beyond the encouraging impression that 'everything is OK'. Moreover, what consequences could the habit of interacting with such 'powerful others' possibly have? Aren't other human beings looking terribly boring, seen from that vantage point? So, who (or 'who') shall future generations prefer as relationship partners? Will humanity still look interesting to itself?

5. Customizing the other versus accepting the risk: the ultimate test of human sociality

Let me draw some provisional conclusions. The process we have examined is probably just the tip of the iceberg of a huge transformation in the forms of social life. As with all complex social trends, its driving forces cannot be oversimplified and respond to various needs, interests, and plans. And as always, the final outcome (whatever 'final' may mean in this case) will exceed or even disappoint them all.

Therefore, it is hard to find some unifying interpretive key to the process of 'objectualization', or 'post-humanization' of social relationships. Indeed, it represents a typical case of social and cultural ambivalence. On the one hand, it is clear from our examples that many cutting-edge applications come in the shape of personalization and the improvement of the human condition. In other words, it looks like a continuation of humanism by other means. On the other hand, if we refer to the features outlined in section 3, such a deeper matrix of the post-humanization of the social could be re-read as follows. Those features represent the attempt to:

1 Make others predictable, tame, trustworthy, loyal *in a technical way*;
2 Look for bright, interesting others;
3 Look for perfection, escaping the imperfect other.

We could argue that the points (a) to (c) amount to the idea of *customizing the other*.

We have also considered the following:

4 Expanding experience through relational diffusion: from multitasking to faking identities, that is, becoming a limitless entity that masters all kinds of knowledge and experience;
5 Escaping the temporality/historicality of social relationships;
6 Making relationships reversible ('resetting' relationships).

Points (d) to (f) amount to a *rejection of limits – becoming relationally limitless*.

Taken together, these factors design the profile of a way of life in which social relations are experienced and enacted in such a way as to refuse to pay the price of commitment. This means reshaping the very structure of the social domain, with its own ways of distributing self-worth and the relevant exchange rates. The deep human self-understanding may change in the process.

Overall, late modern, 'morphogenic'[19] societies find here a test of their humanizing capacity. Their continuous process of innovation has many facets. One of them leads to a fundamental crossroads. As social relations become increasingly risky and unstable, many have wondered about how more stability might be achieved, or about the ways to cope with the situation as it is. What is proposed here is a more radical alternative. Advanced societies are producing the possibility of an *escape* from the risk of human relationships, with the paradoxical effort of making otherness controllable while also expanding the horizon of human social experience. The risk of engaging with otherness, to explore its imperfections, beauty, and dangers, may thus be avoided through the choice of constructing a flawless, customized partner for one's experience and biography. What meanings can still be created and shared in such a context is a question we cannot answer at this point. Be that as it may, it is important to remember that the choice is not between developing or rejecting technology, but between these two ways to make sense of otherness and of social bonds. The narrow path to walk is one in which it remains possible to distinguish between them.

References

Abbott, A. (2016). *Processual Sociology*. Chicago, IL: University of Chicago Press.

Al-Amoudi, I., & Latsis, J. (2015). Death contested: Morphonecrosis and conflicts of interpretation. In M. S. Archer (Ed.), *Generative Mechanisms Transforming the Social Order* (pp. 231–248). Dordrecht and London: Springer.

Archer, M. S. (2017). Introduction: Has a morphogenic society arrived? In M. S. Archer (Ed.), *Morphogenesis and Human Flourishing* (pp. 1–28). Dordrecht: Springer.

Bicchi, A., & Tamburrini, G. (2015). Social robotics and societies of robots. *The Information Society*, 31: 237–243.

Blackford, R. (2005). Human cloning and 'post-human' society. *Monash Bioethics Review*, 24(1): 10–26.

Büscher, M., Kerasidou, X., Liegl, M., & Petersen, K. (2016). Digital urbanism in crises. In R. Kitchin & S-Y. Perng (Eds.), *Code and the City* (pp. 163–177). London and New York: Routledge.

Donati, P., & Archer, M. S. (2015). *The Relational Subject*. Cambridge: Cambridge University Press.

19 This term indicates an emergent type of society, characterized by the logic of opportunity, in which social and cultural innovations are increasingly likely to be mutually compatible. It is therefore a highly dynamic societal configuration, where variety rapidly produces more variety. Such a hypothesis, which must be understood within the conceptual frame of realist-morphogenetic social theory, has been articulated in various volumes edited by Margaret Archer. For a summary of the concept, see Archer, 2017.

Giddens, A. (1991). *Modernity and Self-Identity: Self and Society in the Late Modern Age.* Cambridge: Polity Press.

Giddens, A. (1992). *The Transformation of Intimacy: Sexuality, Love and Eroticism in Modern Societies.* Cambridge: Polity Press.

Hakli, R., & Seibt, J. (Eds.). (2017). *Sociality and Normativity for Robots: Philosophical Inquiries into Human-Robot Interactions.* Dordrecht: Springer.

Hayles, N. K. (1999). *How We Became Post-human: Virtual Bodies in Cybernetics, Literature, and Informatics.* Chicago, IL: University of Chicago Press.

Joas, H. (2000). *The Genesis of Values.* Cambridge: Polity Press.

Joas, H. (2008). *Do We Need Religion? On the Experience of Self-Transcendence.* London and New York: Routledge.

Knorr-Cetina, K. (1997). Sociality with objects: Social relations in postsocial knowledge societies. *Theory, Culture & Society,* 14(4): 1–30.

Knorr-Cetina, K. (2001). Postsocial relations: Theorizing sociality in a postsocial environment. In G. Ritzer & B. Smart (Eds.), *Handbook of Social Theory* (pp. 520–537). London: Sage.

Knorr-Cetina, K. (2009). The synthetic situation: Interactionism for a global world. *Symbolic Interaction,* 32(1): 61–87.

Knorr-Cetina, K., & Bruegger, U. (2002). Inhabiting technology: The global lifeform of financial markets. *Current Sociology,* 50(3): 389–405.

Laitinen, A. (2016). Robots and human sociality: Normative expectations, the need for recognition, and the social bases of self-esteem. In J. Seibt, M. Nørskov, & S. S. Andersen (Eds.), *What Social Robots Can and Should Do* (pp. 313–322). Amsterdam, Berlin, Tokyo and Washington: IOS Press.

Nayar, P. K. (2014). *Posthumanism.* Cambridge: Polity Press.

Nørskov, M. (2016). *Social Robots: Boundaries, Potentials, Challenges.* London and New York: Routledge.

Pfadenhauer, M. (2014). On the sociality of social robots: A sociology-of-knowledge perspective. *Science, Technology & Innovation Studies,* 10(1): 136–153.

Pfadenhauer, M. (2015). The contemporary appeal of artificial companions: Social robots as vehicles of cultural worlds of experience. *The Information Society,* 31: 284–293.

Richardson, K. (2018). *Challenging Sociality: An Anthropology of Robots, Autism, and Attachment.* New York, NY: Palgrave Macmillan.

Rosa, H. (2016). *Resonanz: Eine Soziologie der Weltbezhiehung.* Frankfurt: Suhrkamp.

Sakamoto, D., & Ono, T. (2006). *Sociality of Robots: Do Robots Construct or Collapse Human Relations?* Proceedings of the 1st ACM SIGCHI/SIGART conference on Human-robot interaction.

Seibt, J., Hakli, R., & Nørskov, M. (Eds.). (2016). *Sociable Robots and the Future of Social Relations.* Amsterdam, Berlin, Tokyo and Washington: IOS Press.

Seibt, J., Nørskov, M., & Andersen, S. S. (Eds.). (2016). *What Social Robots Can and Should Do.* Amsterdam, Berlin, Tokyo and Washington: IOS Press.

Wilken, R. (2011). *Teletechnologies, Place, and Community.* London and New York: Routledge.

5 The digital matrix and the hybridisation of society

Pierpaolo Donati

1. How does the digital revolution affect human relationships and social organisations?

In this contribution, I intend to analyse how the processes of human enhancement brought about by the digital revolution modify social identities, relationships, and social organisations, and under what conditions this revolution can shape organisational forms that are able to promote, rather than alienate, humanity.

I am not so interested in discussing whether AI or robots can be more or less human in themselves – or not human at all – but rather how they can interact with humans and affect their social relationships so as to generate a different kind of society characterised by the hybridisation between human and non-human.

I will tackle two major themes: (a) the first concerns the problem of how we can distinguish inter-human relations from the relationships between human beings and machines, which implies the need to clarify what the processes of hybridisation of identities and social relations consist of, and how they happen; (b) the second concerns the consequences of digitalised technological innovations on the hybridisation of social institutions and organisations and, ultimately, the possible scenarios for a 'hybridised society.'

2. The digital matrix and the hybridisation of society

2.1. Society of humans and society of mind

The digital revolution brings with it the idea of a 'society of mind.' In 1986, Marvin Minsky[1] proposed the construction of a model of (natural) human intelligence, built up step-by-step from the interactions of simple parts which are themselves

---

1 Marvin Minsky, *The Society of Mind*, New York, NY: Simon & Schuster, 1986. The book was not written to prove anything specific about AI or cognitive science. It is a collection of ideas about how the mind and thinking work on the conceptual level. The society of mind theory views any naturally evolved cognitive system as a vast society of individual agents constituted by "simple processes." These processes are the fundamental thinking entities from which minds are built and, together, produce the many abilities we attribute to minds.

mindless. In this model, the processes of interaction among elementary parts are supposed to constitute a 'society of mind,' hence the title of his book. A core tenet is that "minds are what brains do."

From my point of view, this theory is reductive and ontologically flat because it conflates mind and brain. Instead, according to the relational paradigm, I maintain that the mind is emergent from the interactions between the brain and the factors that stimulate it from within and without the human body.

However, what interests me to highlight is the fact that, in my opinion, some decades later, Minsky's theory of mind has become a sort of paradigm that today is applied, by extrapolation, to the society of humans. The model is no longer restricted to the human mind itself but is now applied to the whole society understood in its sociological meaning, i.e., as the society of humans. Human beings themselves are now seen as simple parts (agents) that are, if not lacking in intelligence, at least strongly limited in their intelligence (compared to AI), so that only a special architecture of all the connections between men and machines can generate an 'intelligent society.' Such a smart society is held to have its own 'economy of mind.'[2]

As a result, one can think of society (what was once called 'human society') as a connective tissue that does not consist of 'analogical' relationships (interpersonal, organisational, or institutional)[3] but is made up of an unlimited network of digital networks fed by a number of sentient Ais – with their countless apps – connected by the internet and forming a 'Collective Mind' (a term that reminds me of the Durkheimian 'Collective Conscience' or the Marxian 'General Intellect').

I will call this Collective Mind that gives shape to a new society 'the digital matrix' (DM). Let us look more analytically at what the DM is in order to understand how it can change the society of humans through the hybridisation of social identities, relationships, and organisations.

2.2. The pervasiveness of the digital matrix

In the famous science fiction movie of the same name (1999), the Matrix is depicted as a dystopian world in which reality, as perceived and lived by most humans, is actually a simulated reality created by sentient machines to subdue the human population while their bodies' heat and electrical activity are used as an energy source. Sentient machines rule the world with lasers, explosions, and killer robots. *This* Matrix is a 'dream world,' where cyborgs are supposed to simulate a super-man who is a mixture of a super-animal and super-machine. In a famous dialogue between two protagonists, Morpheus says, "The Matrix is everywhere. It is all around us. Even now, in this very room. You can see it when you look out

---

2 Ian Wright, 'The Society of Mind Requires an Economy of Mind,' in the *Proceedings of the AISB '00 Symposium on Starting from Society – the Application of Social Analogies to Computational Systems*, Birmingham, UK: AISB, 2000, pp. 113–124.

3 I call analogic relationships those that have constraints due to their concrete structure (like interpersonal relationships, or relations between positions in an institution or organisation). Digital relationships are distinguished from analogue ones because they do not have such constraints.

your window or when you turn on your television. You can feel it when you go to work . . . when you go to church . . . when you pay your taxes. It is the world that has been pulled over your eyes to blind you from the truth." Neo asks, "What truth?" to which Morpheus replies, "That you are a slave, Neo. Like everyone else, you were born into bondage. Into a prison that you cannot taste or see or touch. A prison for your mind." This is what I would call the Matrix Land. In the end, the Matrix appears as it actually is: nothing but the green lines of a programming code that pervades the environment surrounding the human condition.

Leaving aside the aspects of science fiction, one can take the Matrix to mean the Digital Technological Mind that is made pervasive and omnipresent by the global ICT network constituted by all the tools and symbolic codes that operate on the basis of algorithms.

From the cultural point of view, the digital matrix (DM) is *the globalised symbolic code[4] from which digital artefacts are created in order to help or substitute human agency by mediating inter-human relations or by making them superfluous*. From the structural and practical point of view, the DM is the complex of all *digital technologies*, based on scientific knowledge and engineering, that consist of computerised devices, methods, systems, electronic machines (digital electronics or digital electronic circuits). Of course, the artefacts produced by the DM can have different forms of intelligence and more or less autonomy.

In short, the DM software is part of the cultural system, and its hardware fits into social structures by occupying the positions that are nodes in the networks. It is important to understand: (i) first, that the DM symbolic code plays a major or dominant role within the whole cultural system of society; (ii) second, that it is the starting point of innovation processes (through the discoveries and inventions of scientific research that are subsequently applied in new technologies).

I will explain the second point in the next section (see Figure 5.1). As to the first, I contend that the DM symbolic code plays a role, in respect to all other cultural symbols, in the same way as the generalised symbolic medium of money has functionalised all the other generalised symbolic media to itself within modern society.[5] Money has been (and still is) the G.O.D. (generator of diversity) of modern society. It has functionalised to itself power, influence, and value commitment.

---

4 I define a symbolic code (or semantics) as a set of symbols and the rules for using them in looking at the world and interpreting phenomena, facts, and events while producing them. When the symbols refer to 'ultimate realities' (ἔσχατος, éskhatos), and the rules follow a logic of first principles, a symbolic code takes on the form of a 'theological matrix'. Why do I call it so? Because, in this case, the symbolic code is a reflection of a theology (*theos* + *logos*, discourse or inquiry on divine truth). In short, the symbolic code derives from the way we semanticise the 'ultimate realities' that explain what happens in the world. The DM is a substitute for the old ontological and theological matrices of the past. For instance, Floridi's definition of the human being as "nature's beautiful glitch," which, in his opinion, emerged during the Darwinian evolution, is a clear substitute for the definition of the human person as God's creature.

5 Pierpaolo Donati, *Relational Sociology: A New Paradigm for the Social Sciences*, London: Routledge, 2011, pp. 150–151. As is well known, one owes to Talcott Parsons the theory of generalised

The DM symbolic code is now the generator of diversity of trans-modern society (or 'onlife society,' i.e., the society of online life). As an instrumental symbol, it functionalises to itself all the other symbols, for example, the *finalistic* symbols such as life and death, creation or evolution; the *moral* or *normative* symbols such as justice or injustice, honesty or dishonesty, normative or anormative, disassembling or reassembling, gluing or ungluing; the *value* symbols such as worthy or unworthy, good or bad, positive or negative, pleasant or unpleasant.[6]

The dualities inherent in all these symbols are treated in an apparently relational way since the binary code allows gradations and combinations of each type in the 0/1 sequences. They produce *eigensymbols* (eigenvalues), that is, symbols autogenerated by the code itself. As I have argued elsewhere, the relational modes with which the digital matrix operates can be read in different ways, that is, as purely interactive flows producing only random and transactional outcomes (as *relationist* sociology claims) or as processes that generate relatively stable cultural and social structures that are emergent effects endowed with *sui generis* properties and causal properties (as my *relational* sociology maintains).[7]

According to the relationist viewpoint, digital technologies (machines) represent the material infrastructure of an anonymous DM of communication that feeds the autonomisation of a multiplicity of communicative worlds separated from a humanistic conception of intersubjective and social relations. This DM becomes detached from any traditional culture based on religious or moral premises and builds its own political power system, economy, and religion. Harari[8] has taken this scenario to its extreme conclusions, claiming that it prefigures how the quest for immortality, bliss, and divinity could shape humanity's future. In this scenario, human beings will become economically useless because of human enhancement, robotisation, and artificial intelligence, and a new religion will take humanism's place.

The rationale for this view is that the DM promotes the *digital transformation of the whole society*, which is the change associated with the application of digital technology in all aspects of social life, and is expressed in the *Infosphere*,[9] defined as the environment constituted by the global network of all devices in which AIs are at work receiving and transmitting information. The DM is therefore the 'environment' of all social interactions, organisations, and systems. As such, it promotes a culture deprived of any teleology or teleonomy since it operates as a substitute for any rival moral or theological matrix.[10]

---

symbolic means of *interchange*, while the theory of generalised symbolic means of *communication* is owed to Niklas Luhmann.

6 Symbols are here understood as generalised media of interchange (T. Parsons) or as generalised media of communication (N. Luhmann).

7 Pierpaolo Donati, 'Relational Versus Relationist Sociology: A New Paradigm in the Social Sciences,' *Stan Rzeczy* [*State of Affairs*], Warsaw, 1 (12), (2017): 15–65.

8 Yuval Noah Harari, *Homo Deus: A Brief History of Tomorrow*, New York, NY: Harper Collins, 2017.

9 Luciano Floridi (ed.), *The Onlife Manifesto: Being Human in a Hyperconnected Era*, New York, NY: Springer, 2015.

10 Together with Teubner, we can say that the DM "extends to infinity the usurpation potential of its special medium, power, without any immanent restraints. Its operative closure and its structural

2.3. The hybridisation issue

If something like 'a society of the mind' can exist, it must emerge from a process of social morphogenesis that we can describe through the SAC (structure, agency, culture) scheme,[11] according to which the social dynamic must be explained by the intertwining of structure, culture, and agency, which are analytically distinct from one another (Figure 5.1). This scheme interprets the connections between culture and structure better than any other because it takes agency into consideration, while many scholars who self-identify themselves as relational do not.

For example, in *Identity and Control* White makes the claims that agency is "the dynamic face of networks," that "stories describe the ties in networks," and that "a social network is a network of meanings."[12] Pachucki and Breiger[13] take a slightly different path. While treating networks of relationships as a complex of structures and culture, they propose to move beyond predominant forms of structural analysis that ignore action, agency, and intersubjective meaning. Their argument is that very heterogeneous people living in "cultural holes" (totally isolated cultures which prevent them having a language to talk to each other) can create a common "weak culture" that brings them together and helps them work together. This perspective, empirically founded, certainly confers greater value on agency in the face of the conditioning of the complex structure-culture, and yet agency does not have a truly autonomous role, or at least it plays a weak role. Agency is a variable dependent on social ties.[14] In my opinion, the same is true of Fuhse's approach[15] and many others.

In Figure 5.1, I suppose that the DM software (language, programs, algorithms) is the engine of the morphogenetic process, which starts in the cultural domain and, through sociocultural interactions, produces cultural hybrids. These cultural elaborations modify human agency and, through it, modify the structural domain by building the DM hardware (material technologies) and fitting it into the social structure. Within the structural domain, through structural interactions, new structural hybrids are created. In turn, these structural hybrids go on to influence human agency and, through it, change the cultural domain.

---

autonomy let it create new environments for itself, vis-à-vis which it develops expansive, indeed downright imperialist tendencies. Absolute power liberates unsuspected destructive forces. Centralized power for legitimate collective decisions, which develops a special language of its own, indeed a high-flown rationality of the political, has an inherent tendency to totalize them beyond limit." See Gunther Teubner, 'The Anonymous Matrix: Human Rights Violations by "Private" Transnational Actors,' *Modern Law Review*, 69 (3), (2006): 44.

11 On SAC see Margaret S. Archer, *Being Human: The Problem of Agency*, Cambridge: Cambridge University Press, 2000.

12 Harrison C. White, *Identity and Control: How Social Formations Emerge*, Princeton, NJ: Princeton University Press (2nd ed.), 2008, pp. 65, 67, 245, 315.

13 Mark A. Pachucki and Ronald L. Breiger, 'Cultural Holes: Beyond Relationality in Social Networks and Culture,' *Annual Review of Sociology*, 36 (2010): 205–224.

14 "Rather than assuming that we have actors first and that their ties result from individuals' agency, we should recognize that social ties may in fact precede actors" (Pachucki & Breiger, ibidem, p. 219).

15 Jan A. Fuhse, 'Theorizing Social Networks: The Relational Sociology of and Around Harrison White,' *International Review of Sociology/Revue Internationale de Sociologie*, 25 (1), (2015): 15–44.

The possibilities for developing this morphogenetic process are certainly dependent on how the DM operates in the cultural and structural domains, but we must also consider the autonomous role of human agency.

One may wonder: Which morphogenesis occurs in the human person (agency) and in his/her relational qualities and properties? What happens to social relations?

Notice that the morphogenesis of human agency (a) is active in *both* directions, toward the cultural as well as the structural domain, and (b) is, at the same time, passive, in so far as it is influenced by the two domains. It is here that the body-mind relational unit has to confront the coherences or dissonances between the two domains. The symbol [✱] means that there is a connection of some sort between the cultural and structural processes of hybridisation of the human person in his/her social identity and in his/her social relationships. Such a connection can be of different kinds, from the maximum of synergy (complementarity), as when cultural identity is well adapted to the position occupied in the social structure, to a maximum of conflict (contradiction), as when cultural identity conflicts with the position occupied in the social structure.

What is most relevant in Figure 5.1 is to observe the dematerialisation of the human agency due to AIs operating in and through the quantum network (the internet) where information is transmitted with qubits. The process of hybridisation takes place in fact by contaminating the relationships that operate on the basis of the principles of classical physics applied to the natural world with virtual relations that operate on the basis of the postulates of quantum physics, where the latter dematerialises the natural world.[16]

The conceptual scheme summarised in Figure 5.1 is fundamental to understanding the hybridisation processes of social identities, relationships, and organisations. These proceed according to a relation of contingent complementarity between changes in the cultural background that encourage the development of certain forms of virtual thinking and utopian discourse, on the one hand, and changes in the material production of new technologies (AI/robots) in the structural domain, on the other hand. Hybridisation occurs when culture (software) and structure (hardware) mutually influence and reinforce each other, as long as human agency adapts to these processes. Relations play the most crucial role

---

16 I have talked about the quantum turn in sociology in the book Pierpaolo Donati, *Teoria relazionale della società*, Milan: Franco Angeli, 1991, pp. 11–28. For more recent references see: Carlo Rovelli, 'Relational Quantum Mechanics,' *International Journal of Theoretical Physics*, 35 (8), (1996): 1637–1678. For the connections with the social sciences: Emmanuel Haven and Andrei Khrennikov, *Quantum Social Science*, Cambridge: Cambridge University Press, 2013; Alexander Wendt, *Quantum Mind and Social Science: Unifying Physical and Social Ontology*, Cambridge: Cambridge University Press, 2015. ("When considering a quantum-like model of the functioning of the brain . . . abstract mental images, such as concepts, are processed on the basis of the quantum-like representation of information. A physical mechanism of creation of the quantum-like representation of classical signals is presented. Quantum-like images are encoded by covariance matrices of classical signals. In the quantum terminology, these are density matrices. Thus concepts are represented by density matrices (which are in fact classical covariance matrices). The same model can be applied to 'collective brains' and thus social systems," ibidem, p. 27). For a critical view, see Douglas Porpora, 'Materialism, Emergentism and Social Structure: A Response to Wendt's Quantum Mind,' *Journal for the Theory of Social Behaviour*, (2018): 1–5.

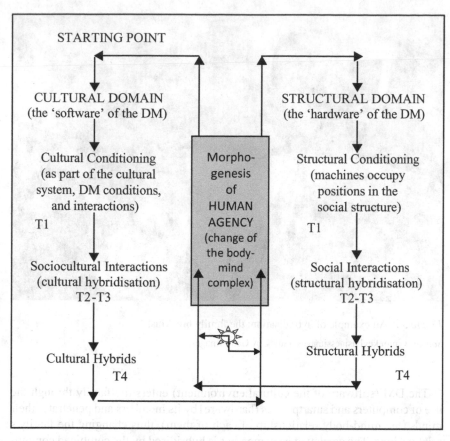

STARTING POINT

CULTURAL DOMAIN
(the 'software' of the DM)

STRUCTURAL DOMAIN
(the 'hardware' of the DM)

Cultural Conditioning
(as part of the cultural
system, DM conditions,
and interactions)
T1

Morpho-
genesis
of
HUMAN
AGENCY
(change of
the body-
mind
complex)

Structural Conditioning
(machines occupy
positions in the
social structure)
T1

Sociocultural Interactions
(cultural hybridisation)
T2-T3

Social Interactions
(structural hybridisation)
T2-T3

Cultural Hybrids
T4

Structural Hybrids
T4

Figure 5.1 The morphogenetic cycle of SAC (structure, agency, culture) run by the DM
and generating the hybridisation of society. Adapted from M. S. Archer. 1995,
Realist Social Theory: The Morphogenetic Approach, p. 323

because changes in identities and organisations depend on them. The hybridisation of society is based on the assumption that these processes operate in a functional way, making sure that the passivity of human agency translates into its active participation in such an evolution with minimal reflexivity or a reflexivity substantially dependent on the DM. The kind and extent of hybridisation depend on how subjects reflect on their relationships, on which their inner conversation (personal reflexivity) depends.

The image of a family sitting at breakfast (Figure 5.2, which I call *The Hybridised Family*)[17] can illustrate Figure 5.1 put into practice.

17 Pierpaolo Donati, 'L'avvento della "famiglia ibridata": come le nuove tecnologie influenzano le relazioni familiari,' in CISF (ed.), *Le relazioni familiari nell'era delle reti digitali*, Cinisello Balsamo, Milano: San Paolo, 2017, pp. 23–54.

Figure 5.2 An example of hybridisation: the family breakfast

Source: © monkeybusinessimages, iStock by Getty Images.

The DM (software of the cultural environment) enters the family through the use of computers and smartphones (hardware) by its members and penetrates their minds (the mind-body relationship of each of them), thus changing the family's relationships. The agency of each member is hybridised by the combined configuration (combination) of the communications coming to each member from the internet and the new relational structure adopted by the family.

As a survey of a representative sample of the Italian population has shown,[18] the hybridisation of family relationships with virtual relationships results in a modification of the minds (identities) of the individual members, which is reflected in the interactions with the other members. The more they use digital equipment, the more their interpersonal relationships become fragile, they assume the peculiar characteristics of virtual communication as the superficiality of messages, the 'speed' in the rhythms of life, the propensity to yield to the passions and interests that appeal to them moment by moment, the lack of concreteness and situationality in their face-to-face relationships. The hybridised family turns out to be a family in which everyone is "alone, together." Relationships

18 The survey was conducted in 2017 through 4000 interviews. Statistical data, methodologies, and survey techniques are published in CISF (ed.), *Le relazioni familiari nell'era delle reti digitali*, Cinisello Balsamo: Edizioni S. Paolo, 2017.

are privatised within the already private space of the family, while the identities of the members travel in the public space of the DM. This phenomenon is more pronounced the younger the people are (age is the most discriminating variable, followed by educational level).

The hybridisation of people's identities and social organisations (families included) consists in the fact that these entities change their relational constitution to the extent that the cultural and structural processes of change affect (I would like to say 'cross') the human person and modify his/her ways of relating to himself/herself, to others, and to the world. Agency is obviously dependent on how the brain and the mind of the person work. Both the brain and the mind are seriously influenced by the way technologies operate[19] because they absorb certain ways of communicating, using and combining information and following performance logics that can ignore or alter analogical thinking.

Hybridisation means that, through sustained interactions with technologies (the 'fully networked life'), the previous modes of considering (conceiving) oneself, relationships with others, and what form to give to a social organisation in keeping with the (analogic) principle of reality are mixed with the way digital technology works, that is, the (fictitious) principle of digital virtuality. Hybridisation means blending the real and the fictitious, the analogue and the digital. This happens, for example, when one wants to modify one's own image or undermine another person's reputation on social networks.

To clarify this point, I use the term 'real' in opposition to 'fictitious' while the opposite of 'digital' is 'analogical.' If a hacker creates a profile on Facebook, or another social network, and transmits fake news, such news has a reality, even if it is the reality of a fiction. While the story's referent is not real, the story itself is causally efficacious and therefore real in that respect.[20] So, instead of contrasting a digital message with a real message, it is better to contrast a digital message with an analogue, because the analogical code implies, in fact, an effective analogy relationship between what is written or transmitted and what is true. In short, hybridisation can take place by mixing what is *real* and what is *fictitious* by mixing the *digital* and the *analogue*. Table 5.1 shows the different types of relations that, in different combinations, produce different forms of hybridisation.

Qualitative and quantitative research provides some empirical evidence:

- *About ICTs*: in the chapter "Twenty-First Century Thinking," Greenfield[21] suggests that the decline of reading in favour of fragmentary interactions,

---

19 Susan Greenfield, *Mind Change: How Digital Technologies Are Leaving Their Mark on Our Brains*, New York, NY: Random House, 2014.
20 See Roy Bhaskar, *Realist Theory of Science* (RTS) on the reality of transitive objects of knowledge, and also Ismael Al-Amoudi and Hugh Willmott, 'Where Constructionism and Critical Realism Converge: Interrogating the Domain of Epistemological Relativism,' *Organization Studies*, 32 (1), (2011): 27–46.
21 Susan Greenfield, *ID: The Quest for Identity in the 21st Century*, London: Sceptre, 2009.

Table 5.1 Types of relations whose combination generates hybridisation

	Real	*Fictitious*
Analogue	Interpersonal (face-to-face) relationships	Games of relationships
Digital	Digital relations replacing the interpersonal ones	Simulated relations

such as computer games or short messages on the internet, threatens the substance of both our neurological makeup and our social structures;

- human persons alter their pace, rhythm, and sense of self; they change their personal reflexivity;[22]
- *About AI/robots*: authentic human relationships are reduced to and sacrificed in favour of digital relationships ("We expect more from technology and less from each other");[23] technology appeals to us most where we are most vulnerable (passions, feelings, interests, etc.);
- digital relations erase precisely those aspects of randomness that also make human life, people, and relationships interesting, spontaneous, and metamorphic;
- by developing new technologies, we are inevitably changing the most fundamental of human principles: our conception of self, our relationships to others, and our understanding and practice of love and death; nevertheless, we should not stop developing new technologies, but do it differently by adopting an approach of relational observation, diagnosis, and guidance.

In short, the processes of hybridisation of identities, human relations, and social organisations are closely connected and change together (in parallel with each other), varying from case to case due to the presence of intervening variables in specific contexts.

3. The hybridisation of social relations, identities, and social forms as a morphogenetic process

3.1. The thesis of hybridisation

The story told in the movie *Transcendence* (2014) can be an instructive example of how the 'society of mind' and the 'society of humans' can merge and come into conflict. Dr. Will Caster is the foremost researcher in the field of artificial intelligence, working to create a sentient machine that combines the collective intelligence of everything ever known with the full range of human emotions.

---

22 See Andrea M. Maccarini, 'Trans-Human (Life-)Time: Emergent Biographies and the "Deep Change" in Personal Reflexivity,' in Ismael Al-Amoudi and Jamie Morgan (eds.), *Realist Responses to Post-Human Society: Ex Machina*, London: Routledge, 2018.

23 Sherry Turkle, *Alone Together: Why We Expect More from Technology and Less from Each Other*, New York, NY: Basic Books, 2011.

His highly controversial experiments have made him famous, but they have also made him the prime target of anti-technology extremists who will do whatever it takes to stop him. In their attempt to destroy Will, however, they inadvertently become the catalyst for him to succeed in being a participant in his own transcendence. Transcendence here means that, after Will's death, his brain is electronically inserted (as a kind of software) into an AI and diffused to all nodes of the internet. His wife Evelyn and best friend Max Waters, both fellow researchers, carry out this task. Their worst fears are realised as Will's thirst for knowledge (his transcendent mind) evolves into a seemingly omnipresent quest for power: to what end is unknown. The only thing that is becoming terrifyingly clear is that there may be no way to stop him except by killing the transcendent mind by infecting it with a lethal virus.

This is pure science fiction. However, the story told in the movie *Transcendence* suggests various instructive questions: Is it possible to insert a human mind or a copy of it into a computer (AI)? And if, on the contrary, we insert an AI (nanobot) into the human mind, how does the latter change? How do the social relations of a computerised mind change in these two cases?

These questions do yet not have an answer. However, they help us see new problems, which have to do with the transition from an analogic mind to a digital mind.

How can a human mind work once it has been detached from its body, if that were ever possible? It would probably mentalise everything that it thinks and experiences, including any artificial hardware or 'body' that supports it.

What qualities and causal powers do the (virtual) relationships have between a living person (such as wife Evelyn) and the mind of the dead husband (Will) that was inserted into an AI? This is what we see in robots: relationality is not human simply because the robot's mind does not relate to a body that gives it certain human characteristics (qualities and properties). The case of a nanobot inserted into the brain or the human nervous system is different: in this case, human relationality remains with its bodily support and, therefore, does not fail but is strongly modified, and in this case we must see how.

Actor-Network Theory (ANT) is a paradigmatic example of how the DM – as I define it – is transforming the representation (*figuration*) of society and its future in terms of hybridisation. ANT is a narrative that describes the division between humans and non-humans (animals, plants, all other entities) as a great illusion, created and kept alive to justify the oppression of all creation by mankind. The new era will erase these boundaries and mix the characters of the human with those of all other beings by adopting the symbolic code of the DM, as I interpret it.

According to this theory, we must abandon an anthropomorphic view of technology, which is considered a projection of human characteristics onto mere mechanisms. Instead, we should see the mechanisms as another 'morphism,' a nonfigurative one that can also be applied to humans. For those who follow and support ANT, the difference between 'action' and 'behaviour' is not a primary natural one.

This is the *nouveau grand récit*: the narration of the hybridisation of the human, in its identities, relations, and social forms, as assimilation between human and non-human, where both lose their (presumed) identity.

From my point of view, this narrative can be interpreted as an application of the characteristics of the DM to all of reality. It starts from the rejection of every essentialist ontology to replace it with a relationist ontology that reduces the whole of reality to a process of relations between elements that change their identity for the functioning of a social sphere understood as a perennial moving flow. Ontology is made interchangeable with the performance of the network, which abolishes all distinctions (such as those between time and space, between human and non-human), reduces matter to relations (relational materiality), and sees reality not as an existing entity, but as a performative process (*performativity*).[24] Actor and network designate two faces – like waves and particles – of the same phenomenon, that is, the social sphere understood as a circulation of relations that can move indefinitely by merging the micro and macro levels together. The various orders of reality (the natural-practical-social orders, the micro-meso-macro levels) are conflated in a stream of processes, like those of electronic networks, which actualise an eternal present, given that any temporal and spatial distinction disappears.

The trouble with this *relationist* vision is that it uses an undefined and ambiguous concept of 'relation,' which for the supporters of ANT is a nominal artifice to make different entities equivalent so that difference and sameness are made reversible (the slogan is: "all different, all equal"). Relations become a (juggling) trick for managing sameness and difference as a continuous oscillation, where singularity and multiplicity are played together,[25] whereas for relational sociology based on critical realism, the relation is a dynamic structure that unites while at the same time differentiating its terms.[26]

I cannot carry out a detailed critique of ANT here.[27] I only observe that this theory is based on a *radical (semiotic) mentalisation of all reality*. The relational materiality of subjects and bodies takes on the properties of mind (the Matrix's mind). In fact, according to Latour, the method developed by ANT is not another attempt to describe things in the world, but *a different form of thinking*, a mode

---

24 John Law, 'After ANT: Complexity, Naming and Topology,' *The Sociological Review*, 47 (S1), (1999): 1–14. Relational materiality refers to the idea that all entities (all materials) are produced in relations, according to the famous saying by Karl Marx "all that is solid melts into air." Performativity means that entities achieve their form as a consequence of the relations in which they are located, and this means also that they are *performed* in, by, and through those relations. The trouble with this *relationist* vision is that it conflates the entities and their relations, whereas for relational sociology based on critical realism the relation is a structure that unites while differentiating its entitative terms (Pierpaolo Donati, 'Quelle sociologie relationnelle? Une perspective non relationniste,' *Nouvelles perspectives en sciences sociales*, 13 (1), (2017): 325–481).

25 Anni Dugdale, 'Materiality: Juggling Sameness and Difference,' *The Sociological Review*, 47 (S1), (1999): 113–135.

26 Pierpaolo Donati, *L'enigma della relazione*, Milano: Mimesis edizioni, 2015.

27 For a recent review, see Laur Kanger, 'Mapping "the ANT Multiple": A Comparative, Critical and Reflexive Analysis,' *Journal for the Theory of Social Behavior*, 47 (2017): 1–28. DOI: 10.1111/jtsb.12141

of analysis and judgment that does not capture the entities as closed, self-limited, and determined objects, but aims to reveal and map their invisible attribute, that of existing as temporal and spatially durable assemblages, as limits, borders, and boundaries of a material that in itself is liquid and multiform. ANT does not aim to analyse hybridisation processes as facts to be explained, but is interested in producing hybrids, that is, social entities that are reduced to arrows, directions, possibilities of new assemblages, while human actions no longer have their own subject, because the agent-actor is distributed throughout the network.

In short, the hybridisation of identities, relationships, and organisations theorised by ANT leads to the disappearance of human identity and social relations as a reality having their own structure and dynamics. Social organisations are absorbed by continuous network fusion flows. The subject and agency disappear in a flow that is as abstract as it is homogeneous with the DM's symbolic code. And we wonder: Is this what hybridisation is like?

3.2. The process of hybridisation of identities and relations

From the point of view of critical realism, hybridisation can and must instead be considered as a morphogenetic process that leads from entities structured in a certain way to entities structured in another way.

To say that the human is hybridised means that human identity, its social relations, and organisational forms, interacting with reality – in its various orders and levels – through technology, create new identities, relationships, and organisations. The fact remains that we should understand how to define the *proprium* of the human in hybridisation processes.

Lynne Rudder Baker's theory is often cited as a solution to this problem as it replaces a '*constitutive*' rather than an identifying view of the human.

Baker[28] argues that what distinguishes persons from all other beings is the mind's intentionality detached from corporeity since we, as human beings, can be fully material beings without being identical to our bodies. In her view, personhood lies in the complex mental property of first-person perspective that enables one to conceive of one's body and mental states as one's own. The argument is that the human mind must have a bodily support since the body-mind relation is necessary, but the type of body – and, therefore, the type of body-mind relationship – can be quite contingent; we can change the body with artefacts, provided we do so from the perspective of the first person.[29] The relation between one's mind and one's body is open to any possibility.[30] Consequently, since the personality is equal to the self-thinking mind, we must then acknowledge the existence

---

28 Lynne Rudder Baker, *Persons and Bodies: A Constitution View*, Cambridge: Cambridge University Press, 2000.

29 For a critique of Baker's constitution view, see Wybo Houkes and Anthonie Meijers, 'The Ontology of Artefacts: The Hard Problem,' *Studies in History and Philosophy of Science*, 37 (2006): 118–131.

30 See Vitor Sérgio Ferreira, 'Carnal Reflexivity as a Socially Fragmented Reality,' Paper presented at the 38th World Congress of the IIS, *Sociology Looks at the Twenty-first Century*, Budapest, Hungary, June 26–30, 2008. See www.swedishcollegium.se/iis/pdf_special/ferreira.pdf

of a personality in any animal or machine that can be judged sentient and thinking, on the condition that it is aware that it is itself that thinks.

Following this line of thought, some thinkers today are more and more inclined to acknowledge the existence of moral behaviour in certain species of higher primates like the chimpanzees (they are supposed to have a 'moral intelligence,' i.e., in that they are compassionate, empathetic, altruistic, and fair),[31] and, along the same lines, they recognise the possibility that special robots endowed with an artificial morality might exist.[32] It seems to me that this perspective is totally at odds with a realistic social ontology for which human relationality – between body and mind, as well as in social life with others (the two are closely related) – has qualities and properties that cannot be assimilated with the relationships that certain species of animals or ultra-sophisticated intelligent machines can have. On the whole, Baker's theory is inadequate to the task of accounting for the possibilities and the limits of the processes of hybridisation because it does not account for the relational constitution of identities and social forms.

The hybridisation of human relations, paradoxically, is due to the logic inherent in such relationships, which, by definition, must be open to the world and cannot remain closed in self-referentiality, as artificial machines are. In interacting repeatedly with machines (AI/robots), agents can incorporate certain aspects of the communication logic of the machines in their way of relating to others and the world. But we cannot equate the relations between humans with those between humans and robots. How can one not see that the qualitative difference between these relations, for example, when someone says that the robot is 'my best friend,' this reduces the relationship to pure communication (i.e., to communication and only to communication, as Luhmann maintains)? This is an unjustified and unjustifiable reduction because communication always takes place within a concrete relationship and takes its meaning, qualities, and properties from the kind of relationship in which it occurs, whereas the kind of relationship depends on the kind of subjects that are in communication.

The problems caused by DM (ICTs and robotics) arise when sociability is entrusted to algorithms.[33] The introduction of the sentient robot changes the context and the relationships between human subjects as well as the form of a social organisation.

Let us take the example of a social structure of a sports type like that of a football team and a football match. How does the behaviour of a football team that is equipped with a goalkeeper-robot capable of parrying all shots change? And if two teams agree to play a game in which each of them has a robot as a goalkeeper, what will be the consequences on human behaviour?

31 Mark Bekoff and Jessica Pierce, *Wild Justice: The Moral Lives of Animals*, Chicago, IL: University of Chicago Press, 2009.

32 Laura Pana, 'Artificial Intelligence and Moral Intelligence,' *TripleC*, 4 (2), (2006): 254–264.

33 Sherry Turkle, *The Second Self: Computers and the Human Spirit*, New York, NY: Simon & Schuster, 1984.

There cannot be a 'we believe' or a relational good between humans and robots for the simple fact that the supervenient human-robot relation is ontologically different from the supervenience relationship between human beings.[34]

The partial or total hybridisation cycle of relationships is selective and stratified on the basis of: (i) how the personal and relational reflexivity of agents operates, given the fact that reflexivity on these processes is necessary to get to know each other through one's own "relational self-construal"[35] and (ii) how the reflectivity of the network or organisational system in which the agents are inserted operates.

We can see this by using the morphogenetic scheme (Figure 5.3), which describes how the hybridisation processes depend on the reflexivity that the subjects and their social network exert on the different forms of human enhancement. Given an organisational context (or network) in which human persons must relate themselves to a DM of sentient machines, social relationships can be hybridised in various ways, and with different intensity, depending on whether the human person adopts:

1   a purely communicative reflexivity, that is, dependent on the machine; in practice, the agent person relates to the machine by identifying himself/herself with the digital code, which means that s/he 'connects' to the machine, but without establishing a real relationship (as a matter of fact, the connection is not a social relationship); for instance, people identify themselves with their Facebook profile;
2   an autonomous reflexivity with respect to the machine (the machine is used as a simple tool, and the relation follows an analogic code);
3   a meta-reflexivity as a critical use of the machine (this mode of reflexivity re-establishes the relationship based on the difference between the digital code and the analogic code);
4   an impeded reflexivity that is caused by an absorbing routine identification with the machine;
5   a fractured reflexivity when the relationship mixes the digital code and the analogic code randomly.

These are Margaret S. Archer's modalities of reflexivity used first in her *Structure, Agency and the Internal Conversation* (2003), applied for a very different purpose. She may not endorse my applications.

---

34 A set of properties A supervenes upon another set B just in case no two things can differ with respect to A-properties without also differing with respect to their B-properties. In slogan form, "There cannot be an A-difference without a B-difference" (Stanford Encyclopedia of Philosophy). In our case, the human-robot relationship would be equivalent to the human-human relationship if the robot were human.
35 Susan E. Cross and Michael L. Morris, 'Getting to Know You: The Relational Self-Construal, Relational Cognition, and Well-Being,' *Personality and Social Psychology Bulletin (PSPB)*, 29 (4), (2003): 512–523.

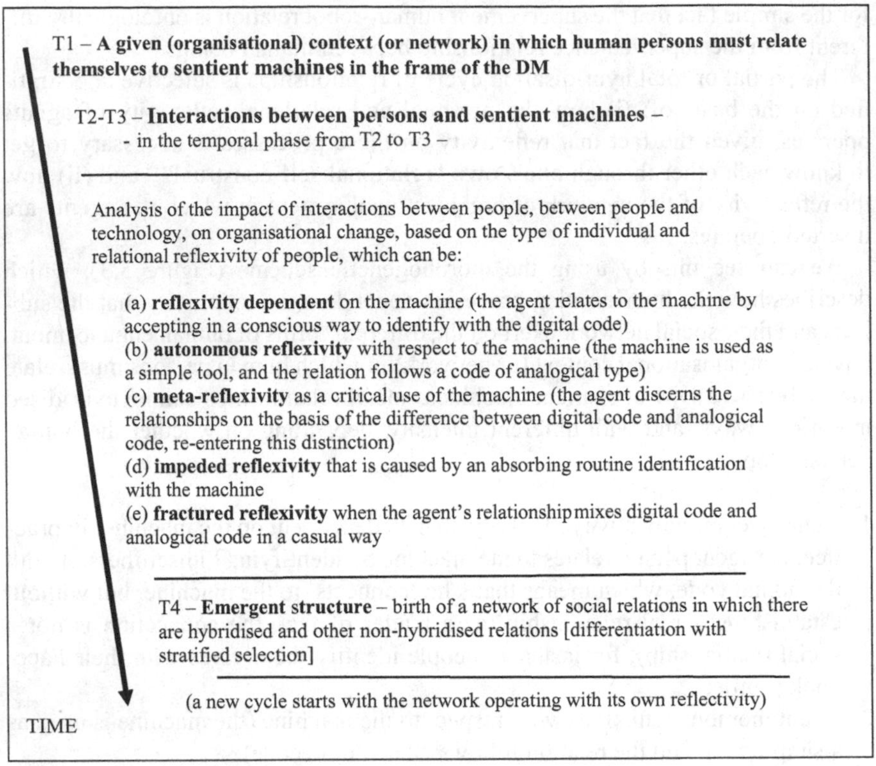

T1 – **A given (organisational) context (or network) in which human persons must relate themselves to sentient machines in the frame of the DM**

T2-T3 – **Interactions between persons and sentient machines –**
- in the temporal phase from T2 to T3 –

Analysis of the impact of interactions between people, between people and technology, on organisational change, based on the type of individual and relational reflexivity of people, which can be:

(a) **reflexivity dependent** on the machine (the agent relates to the machine by accepting in a conscious way to identify with the digital code)
(b) **autonomous reflexivity** with respect to the machine (the machine is used as a simple tool, and the relation follows a code of analogical type)
(c) **meta-reflexivity** as a critical use of the machine (the agent discerns the relationships on the basis of the difference between digital code and analogical code, re-entering this distinction)
(d) **impeded reflexivity** that is caused by an absorbing routine identification with the machine
(e) **fractured reflexivity** when the agent's relationship mixes digital code and analogical code in a casual way

---

T4 – **Emergent structure** – birth of a network of social relations in which there are hybridised and other non-hybridised relations [differentiation with stratified selection]

(a new cycle starts with the network operating with its own reflectivity)

TIME

Figure 5.3 The morphogenetic cycle through which identities and social relations are hybridised

Take the case of domestic ICTs. They constitute reference points around which identity, gender, and intersubjectivity are articulated, constructed, negotiated, and contested. They are points through which people construct and express definitions of selves and other. As Lally further explained: "The development of the human subject (individual and collective) takes place through a progressive series of processes of externalisation (or self-alienation) and sublation (reabsorption or reincorporation). Human subjects and the (material and immaterial) objects of their sociocultural environment form a subject-object relation which is mutually evolving, and through which they form a recursively defined, irreducible entity."[36]

These subject-object sociotechnical associations constitute the material culture of home life; they are bundled together with the affective flows of human relations and the emergence of a lifeworld in which images and emotions play a crucial role

---

36 Elaine Lally, *At Home with Computers*, Oxford and New York: Berg, 2002, p. 32.

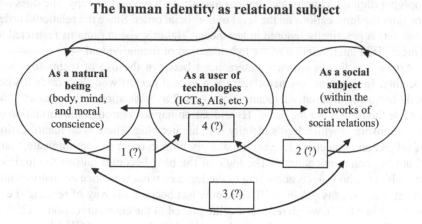

Figure 5.4 The hybridisation of human identity and social relations due to the DM

in the hybridisation of relationships because it is through them that the subjects identify with the logic of virtual/digital relationships.[37]

3.3. The hybridisations of identities and social relationships are interdependent

The hybridisations of human identity and social relations through DM are connected to each other because the human being is a relational subject.[38] The dynamics of mutual influence between identity and relations in the hybridisation processes are not linear, but proceed along very different paths.

We see the different hybridisation paths in Figure 5.4.

Arrow 1 indicates the two-way interactions between the natural being and the use of technology (regardless of the social context). From a phenomenological point of view, the relational context is always there, but in many cases the agents do not take this into account, as often happens in medical settings and biological laboratories.

Examples of type 1 hybridisations are those widely used in medicine, where they involve checking whether the technology helps repair damaged organs or cure diseases. Baker very often refers to this type, obviously considering individuals as natural beings.[39] But even when she speaks of human enhancement in the

37 Kevin LaGrandeur, 'Emotion, Artificial Intelligence, and Ethics,' in Jan Romportl, Eva Zackova and Jozef Kelemen (eds.), *Beyond Artificial Intelligence: The Disappearing Human-Machine Divide*, Dordrecht: Springer, 2015, pp. 97–110.
38 Pierpaolo Donati and Margaret S. Archer, *The Relational Subject*, Cambridge: Cambridge University Press, 2015.
39 Lynne Rudder Baker, 'Technology and the Future of Persons,' *The Monist*, 96 (1), (2013): 37–53.

proper sense, that is, as making someone or something "more than normal" by applying digital technological devices that are well beyond therapy, she does not consider the implications on the level of the social order. Since the relational order (context) is practically ignored in her theory, Baker's vision remains restricted to a mentalised interpretation of the hybridisation of the individual.

Arrow 2 indicates two-way interactions between the use of technology and sociality. In this case, the actor/agent is a virtual person who disregards his/her body-mind constitution. An example of a type 2 hybridisation is the phrase: "I do not use the blog; *I am the blog.*" Hybridisation happens through the formation of a relationship in which Ego's identity is in his/her blog. There is an identification of subject and object: no longer, "I make my blog in order to communicate," but, "I am my communication."[40] The logic of the blog becomes part of the logic of the subject, who reflects according to the logic of what was once an instrumental object (i.e. a means = A in AGIL) and now has become his way of relating (i.e. a norm = I in AGIL), which reflects a value placed in the communication itself (i.e. L of AGIL) in the presence of an undetermined goal (i.e. G of AGIL).[41]

The *I-Me-We-You* sequence elucidated by Archer[42] takes place within an interactive time register, in which time has no duration (it is neither relational nor symbolic, but purely interactional).[43] The temporal history of the body-mind complex (its stock of knowledge)[44] does not enter the process, except for the aspects in which it has been mentalised. The identification of the human person with the blog is the outcome of his/her mentalisation, which corresponds to the fact that an AI has become part of the subject's mind, forging its conscience.

Arrow 3 indicates the two-way interactions between the agent as natural being and sociality. In this case, the individual acts regardless of the technology, and, therefore, there is no hybridisation. This is the case, for example, of families of elderly people who do not use digital technologies or of voluntary organisations that take care of the poor and fragile without resorting to any technological tool.

Arrow 4 indicates those processes in which the agents are involved in all three orders of reality. Their body-mind complex and their sociality are mediated by technology, which is what happens 'normally,' in fact, in any institution and organisation. The kind and degree of hybridisation depends on the network structure in which the agency is embedded.

40 Rudolf Stichweh, 'System Theory as an Alternative to Action Theory? The Rise of "Communication" as a Theoretical Option,' *Acta Sociologica*, 43 (1), (2000): 5–13.
41 See my relational version of the Parsonian AGIL scheme in Pierpaolo Donati, *Relational Sociology: A New Paradigm for the Social Sciences*, London: Routledge, 2011, pp. 147–167. The letters in AGIL stand for adaptation (A), goal attainment (G), integration (I), latency (L).
42 Margaret S. Archer, *Being Human*, Cambridge: Cambridge University Press, 2000.
43 Pierpaolo Donati, *Relational Sociology: A New Paradigm for the Social Sciences*, London: Routledge, 2011, p. 180.
44 Julius Elster, 'The Temporal Dimension of Reflexivity: Linking Reflexive Orientations to the Stock of Knowledge,' *Distinktion: Journal of Social Theory*, 18 (3), (2017): 274–293.

It is important to emphasise that hybridisation of social identities and organisations through the use of technology happens by involving the mind-body complex in the context of relationships, without the mind being separated from the body. The mind of agents/actors is modified through the perception and activation of those social relationships that are possible only through the body.

Victoria Pitts-Taylor[45] offers an account of how the mind works on the basis of a brain that is "complex and multiple, rather than determined and determining." Drawing on work by feminists, queer theorists, and disability theorists, she offers an understanding of bodies and cognition that can incorporate the cognitive differences that result from differences in embodiment and that can recognise the social shaping of both bodies and cognition. She notes that scientists have discovered that some neurons seem to respond both to our performance of an action and to our observation of others performing that action. These mirror neurons have been theorised to underlie social relationships, especially 'mind reading' and empathy. We need to do a better job of recognising the complexity and variety of social relationships. In particular, the assumption that the existence of mirror neurons shows that we are naturally in tune with others and empathetic to them leaves social neuroscientists unable to account for why our empathy for others is so often selective and so often fails. This is an example of how social neuroscience can take the embodiment of brain and social relationship seriously,[46] differently from those attempts to create digital identities as avatars that simulate the human without being it human (for example, the *Soul Machines* company), thus producing a morphic sociability devoid of real humanity.

Let me now move from the micro to the meso and macro levels of the social fabric, to consider the institutional and organisational hybridisation processes.

4. The emergence of hybridised institutions and organisations

Today many scholars[47] highlight the emergence of 'hybrid organisations.' The World Bank defines a hybrid organisational structure as one in which more than one organisational design is used. Accordingly, this should allow an organisation more flexibility in distributing work and assigning job roles. A hybrid organisational structure creates a shared mission and allows for people to work on different projects and in different sectors. This structure creates a unified team of individuals with a common goal and different experience and interest levels. Each

---

45 Victoria Pitts-Taylor, *The Brain's Body: Neuroscience and Corporeal Politics*, Durham, NC: Duke University Press, 2016, p. 8.

46 On the embodied nature of human cognition, see also Katherine Hayles, *How We Became Posthuman: Virtual Bodies in Cybernetics, Literature, and Informatics*, Chicago, IL: University of Chicago Press, 1999.

47 David Billis and Colin Rochester (eds.), *Handbook on Hybrid Organisations*, Cheltenham: Edward Elgar, 2017.

individual is able to perform work in the areas he is best suited to, moving from project to project and reporting to different individuals when necessary.

In this contribution, I call *hybridised* organisations those that employ this type of configuration by using advanced digital technologies to which a certain degree (min/max) of decisional and operational autonomy is conferred. Technology (AI/robots) take on an autonomous and decisive role in managing the organisation of roles and relations between the members of the organisation. The digital logic with which hybrid organisations operate is that of increasing opportunities, conceived, however, not within the framework of their relational implications, but according to the maximum useful variability in terms of system efficiency.

The relational approach to social organisations can show why and how AI and robots cannot replace humans because of the specific generative character of inter-human relations. In fact, the utilitarianism of efficiency refers to the relationships between an actor/agent and 'things,' while the search for relational goods (or the avoidance of relational evils) implies relationships between human beings, which, unlike algorithms, are generative of meta-reflexive solutions to problems of human relationships.[48]

One example of how an algorithm can generate relational evils is the following. On 21 November 2017, the algorithm of the multinational company Ikea fired a worker at its megastore in a small town near Milan. Marica, a 39-year-old mother separated from her husband with two young children, one of whom is disabled, was sacked because she did not observe the new work shift assigned to her by the algorithm. The algorithm has ordered her to show up at 7 a.m., and, instead, she arrived at 9 o'clock according to the old work shift because she had to look after the children, and, in particular, she had to take the disabled child to therapy. Previously, the woman had explained to the manager that she could not work that shift, and the manager said that he would consider her situation, but the algorithm worked on its own and fired her. The company did not review its decision, and, instead, continued to dismiss other workers on the grounds that they did not comply with the shift times stipulated by the algorithm.

Undoubtedly, it cannot be said that the algorithm has not been proven to have its own 'personal' decision-making ability (some call it an 'electronic person'),

---

48 By relying on the notion of *auctor* proposed by Pierpaolo Donati [cf 'Manifesto for a Critical Realist Relational Sociology,' *International Review of Sociology/Revue Internationale de Sociologie*, 25 (1), (2015): 86–109, quotation p. 88], Eacott observes that "*Auctor* provides the intellectual resource to overcome the structure/agency analytical dualism through recognition of relations and the generative rather than deterministic nature of activity without defaulting to a naïve form of autonomy. [. . .] *Auctors* generate *organizing activity*. They are not separate from *spatio-temporal conditions* but simultaneously constitutive of and emergent from them. The substantialist basis of organisational theory in educational administration and leadership is broken down through relations. This is why, despite my (somewhat artificial) partitioning of *organizing activity*, *auctor*, and *spatio-temporal conditions* here, they work together, in relation, to generate an elaborated communication of activity" (Scott Eacott, 'Starting Points for a Relational Approach to Organisational Theory: A Concept Glossary,' *Advancing Relational Theorizing Working Paper*, UNSW Sydney, October 2017).

but it was certainly not a relational subject. Clearly the algorithm simply followed its procedural rules, neglecting the needs of people and their relational context, which were unpredictable to it. If so, I maintain that the algorithm is not a person, given the fact that a person is an 'individual-in-relation' (relationality being *constitutive* of the individual), although it is presented as such by management. The algorithm's personality is a convenient managerial fiction.

In the perspective of the future, in my opinion, in principle, it will be possible to build more sophisticated AI/robots that can take into account people's needs and their relationships. But, in addition to modifying the instructions provided to the algorithm, it will always be necessary to supervise its operations by a management that, by adopting a relational steering approach, must be able to deal with the individual problematic cases and the complexity and diversity of contingencies that the algorithm cannot handle. Without such relational steering, the hybridisation of organisational relationships due to increasing automation will only mean exploiting people and dismissing them by blaming the algorithm for making inhuman decisions and apologising for not being able to do otherwise.

From a more general view, as Teubner writes,

> Today, with the massive emergence of virtual enterprises, strategic networks, organisational hybrids, outsourcing and other forms of vertical disaggregation, franchising and just-in-time arrangements, intranets and extranets, the distinction between hierarchies and markets is apparently breaking down. The boundaries of formal organisations are blurring. This holds true for the boundaries of administration (hierarchies), of finance (assets and self-financing), of integration (organisational goals and shared norms and values) and of social relations (members and outside partners). In formal organisations, membership becomes ambiguous, geographical boundaries do not matter much anymore, hierarchies are flattened, functional differentiation and product lines are dissolved.[49]

Hybrids raise problems of conflict between divergent normative arrangements. As a strategy to deal with these changes, Teubner recommends a "polycontexturality which combines heterarchy with an overarching unity,"[50] assuming that this organisational solution would represent the new institutional logic capable of avoiding collisions between spheres ruled by incompatible norms.

I take Teubner's proposal as an example of an attempt to preserve the human (with its regulatory requirements) alongside the acceptance of the entry of new hybrids, through general rules that allow different norms to coexist in different domains.[51] *Unitas multiplex* is his key concept for preserving the integration of

---

49 Gunther Teubner, 'Hybrid Laws: Constitutionalizing Private Governance Networks,' in Robert Kagan and Kenneth Winston (eds.), *Legality and Community*, Berkeley, CA: Berkeley Public Policy Press, 2002, pp. 311–331, quotation p. 311.
50 Ibidem, p. 331.
51 Gunther Teubner, 'Rights of Non-humans? Electronic Agents and Animals as New Actors in Politics and Law,' *Journal of Law and Society*, 33 (4), (2006): 497–521.

society, supposing that human beings and actants, human relations and artificial relations, could coexist within a neo-functional architecture under the aegis of the DM.

I have serious doubts about the tenability of this perspective (although it worked in the seventeenth century as the Hobbesian solution to the problem of social order). I think that it is an impracticable solution in a networked society governed by the DM. In any case, it does not work for a 'society of the human.' As Hobbesian (Leibnizian) rationalism, Teubner's idea of a constitutionalisation of the private hybridised spheres does not address the issues of the relations between human and non-human, and the relations between divergent normative spheres. Teubner's perspective simply avoids the relational issue. In short, it has all the limitations and defects of a multicultural doctrine that ignores the reality of what lies *in between* opposite spheres that have incompatible normative orders. It avoids the issue of how far hybridisation processes can go and to what extent they can affect the human.

The same difficulty is present in the Luhmannian theory that seems to do a good job of interpreting the hybridisation processes insofar as it places all cultures under the aegis of a conception of society as an 'operating system.'[52] According to Luhmann, all systems, organisations, and interactions are forced to use a binary functional code that is precisely the one through which the DM proceeds. Hybridisation follows a functional code. For this reason, he believes that the humanism of the old Europe is unsustainable and, therefore, sees no other way than that of considering the human (especially the human of the Western tradition) as a residual entity fluctuating in the environment of the DM. Are there no alternatives? I think that there are and will examine the possible scenarios.

5. Three scenarios dealing with the processes of hybridisation

The digital transformation of society is destined to produce different types of hybrids through different types of social morphogenesis (MG). I would like to summarise them in three scenarios: adaptive morphogenesis, turbulent morphogenesis, and relationally steered morphogenesis.[53]

1 *Adaptive MG producing hybrids by trial and error*: This is the scenario of a society that adapts itself to the hybridisation processes produced by DM in an opportunistic way. It is configured as an afinalistic infosphere (without pre-established goals) that tries to use the technologies knowing that they have an ambivalent character. They allow new opportunities but also involve

52 Jean Clam, 'System's Sole Constituent, the Operation: Clarifying a Central Concept of Luhmannian Theory,' *Acta Sociologica*, 43 (1), (2000): 63–79.
53 See the *Social Morphogenesis Series* (five volumes, Springer Publication) edited by Margaret S. Archer.

new constraints and possible pathologies; therefore, it is essentially engaged in developing self-control tools to limit emerging harms (theories of harm reduction).

2 *Turbulent MG favouring mutations*: This is the scenario of a society that operates for the development of any form of hybridisation. It opens the floodgates to the human freedom to generate contingent and experimental organisations. In principal, it is run by anormativity and anomie (lack of presupposed moral norms) and openness to mutations, understood as positive factors of 'progress' (theory of singularity). It operates through ceaseless, unrepeatable, intermingling processes of relational flows with 'confluence of relating.'[54]

3 *Relationally steered MG aiming to configure technologies in order to favour relational goods*: This is the scenario of a society that tries to guide the interactions between human subjects and technologies by distinguishing between humanising and non-humanising forms of hybridisation. The aim is to produce social forms in which the technologies are used reflexively in order to serve the creation of relational goods.[55] This requires that producers and consumers of technologies work together interactively, that is, that they are co-producers[56] and partners in the design and use of technologies, careful to ensure that technologies do not completely absorb or replace human social relations, but enrich them. This alternative is certainly much harder to pursue than harm reduction, but it is not impossible, and it is the one that leads to good life.[57]

Hybridisation cancels every dualism. In particular, it erases the dualism between the system and the lifeworld (theorised by Habermas) and replaces it with a complex relational system in which each action/communication must choose between different causal mechanisms.[58]

To be human, technological enhancement must be able not only to distinguish between the different causal mechanisms, but also to choose the most productive social relationships that generate relational goods. New technologies generate not only unemployment, as many claim.[59] They also release energy for the development of many jobs in the field of virtual reality and make it possible to put human

---

54 John Shotter, 'Gergen, Confluence, and His Turbulent, Relational Ontology: The Constitution of Our Forms of Life Within Ceaseless, Unrepeatable, Intermingling Movements,' *Psychological Studies*, 57 (2), (2012): 134–141.

55 An example is given by the so-called 'social streets': Cristina Pasqualini, *Vicini e connessi. Rapporto sulle Social Street a Milano*, Milano: Fondazione Feltrinelli, 2018.

56 Victor Pestoff, 'Towards a Paradigm of Democratic Participation: Citizen Participation and Co-Production of Personal Social Services in Sweden,' *Annals of Public and Cooperative Economics*, 80 (2), (2009): 197–224.

57 Practical examples can be found in the journal *Relational Social Work* (free access).

58 Dave Elder-Vass, 'Lifeworld and Systems in the Digital Economy,' *European Journal of Sociology*, 21 (2), (2018): 227–244.

59 For example, Martin Ford, *Rise of the Robots: Technology and the Threat of a Jobless Future*, New York, NY: Basic Books, 2015.

work into those activities that have a high content of care, such as education, social assistance, and health, or a high content of cultural creativity.

Laaser and Bolton[60] have shown that the introduction of new technologies associated with the advance of performance management practices has eroded the ethics of the care approach in banking organisations. Under electronic performance management monitoring in bank branches, in particular, co-worker relationships have become increasingly objectified, resulting in disconnected and conflict-ridden forms of engagement. This research reveals the multi-layered and necessarily complex nature of co-worker relationships in a changing, technologically driven work environment and highlights the necessity for people to defend the capacity to care for others from the erosive tendencies of individualised processes. Within the relational approach, this entails assessing the way in which an organisation uses AI/robots to enhance human relations from the viewpoint of what I call 'ODG systems' aimed at the relational steering of digitised organisations.[61]

ODG systems are based on the sequence: Relational observation (O) → Relational diagnosis (D) → Relational guidance (G). The principles according to which the ODG systems operate are modalities that orient those who have the responsibility of guiding a network of relations among subjects to operate interactively on the basis of cooperative rules that allows the subjects, supported by AI/robots, to produce relational goods. Agency is exercised by all the parties, as in an orchestra or a sports team, where everyone follows a cooperative standard that is used to continually regenerate a non-hierarchical and non-individualistic social structure, and consequently modifies the behaviour of the individual subjects, who are driven to generate relational goods. The cooperative norm is obviously inserted as a basic standard in the AI/robot that supports the agents of the network.[62]

Now let's see some details to explain the acronym ODG.

(O) Relational observation aims to define the problem to which AI must respond in terms of a problem that depends on a certain relational context. Therefore, it favours the meso level (in which relational goods can be produced). (D) Relational diagnosis aims to define the satisfactory (or unsatisfactory) conditions with respect to the effects produced by the way the AI works on the relational context (i.e. whether the AI contributes to producing relational goods instead of relational evils). (G) Relational guidance aims to modify the AI and its way of working to

60 Knut Laaser and Sharon Bolton, 'Ethics of Care and Co-worker Relationships in UK Banks,' *New Technology, Work and Employment*, 32 (3), (2017): 213–227.

61 For more details, see Pierpaolo Donati, *Teoria relazionale della società*, Milano: FrancoAngeli, 1991, pp. 346–356.

62 On the role of norms in the working of social networks, see Emmanuel Lazega, *Réseaux sociaux et structures relationnelles*, Paris: PUF, 1998; Emmanuel Lazega et al., 'Réseaux et controverses: de l'effet des normes sur la dynamique des structures,' *Revue Française de Sociologie*, 49 (3), (2008): 467–498; Emmanuel Lazega, 'Cooperation Among Competitors: Its Social Mechanisms Through Network Analyses,' *SocioLogica*, 1 (2009): 1–34. DOI: 10.2383/29560

support a relational context that can be mastered by people in order to generate relational goods.

An example in product innovation can be that of systems that try to regulate the AIs of self-driving cars. The AI must be constructed in such a way as to take into account the main parameters of the relational context in which it operates. The AI must see objects and people around, and assess their relationships with respect to those who sit in the driver's seat to put the driver in a position to intervene in situations of a high contingency. Relational observation implies the ability of AI to calculate the relationships given in a context and those possible in its short-medium-range evolution. Relational diagnosis concerns the ability to perceive possible clashes in case the relationships with objects and people can become dangerous while the car is on the street. Relational guidance means the ability to regulate these relationships in order to make driving safer.

At the organisation level, we can consider any company that uses AI/robots in order to produce satisfactory goods for customers. The AI/robots that are used must have similar characteristics to those just mentioned for the self-driving car. It is up to those who organise the production, distribution, and sale of business products to configure the AI/robots so that they have the ability to relate contextually and evaluate the progress of relationships in the various sectors within the company and in the context of sales and of consumption. It is not enough to improve the cognitive intelligence of the single AI/robot. It is necessary to build AI/robots that are able to regulate the development of the network of relations between producers, distributors, and consumers of company products.

I do not know practical examples already in place but rather the idea of 'distributed responsibility'[63] among all the actors in the network that produces, distributes, and uses the goods produced along these lines. It requires that the AI/robots be constructed and monitored within a project of (1) observation of their relational work, (2) with the ability to diagnose deviations from satisfactory procedures and results, and (3) the orientation of the management to operate according to a relational guidance program.

6. Conclusions

The enhancement of human beings through digital technologies (ICT, AI, robots) compels us to evaluate whether, how, and when these technologies foster the flourishing or, vice versa, the alienation of humanity. Social identities, relations, and organisations are forced to take shape in the environment of a digital matrix that works through a symbolic code that tends to replace the ontological, ideal, moral, and theological matrices that have structured societies in the past. As a form of

---

63 See Werner Rammert, 'Where the Action Is: Distributed Agency Between Humans, Machines, and Programs,' *The Technical University Technology Studies: Working Papers* TUTS-WP-4, 2008: 17; Anniina Huttunen, 'Hybrid Liability of Intelligent Systems,' *The Society of Legal Scholars*, Edinburgh Conference 2013 (online).

Tech-Gnosis, its peculiarity is that of making the boundaries between human and non-human labile and crossable in every way in order to foster hybrids. Hybrids, however, are not random and purely contingent entities. They stem from complex interactional networks in which social relations are mediated by the DM. The processes of hybridisation are selective and stratified according to the ways in which the human/non-human distinction is thought and practised. Three possible scenarios of hybridisation can be outlined: adaptive, turbulent, and relationally steered.

As a criterion for evaluating hybridisation processes, I have proposed assessing how digital technologies mediate the transformations of people's mind-body identities with their sociality so as to assess when such mediations produce those relational goods that lead to a virtuous human fulfilment or, instead, relational evils.

The justification of this perspective is based on the fact that human beings are at the same time the creators of society and its product. They are the parents and the children of society. As a consequence, it is not the physical world (anthropocene) and/or the artificial world (AI/robots) that can produce the human being as a human being, but society, which, from the point of view of my relational sociology, consists of relationships, that is, 'is' (and not 'has') relationships. Therefore, the quality and causal property of what is *human* comes into existence, emerges and develops only in social life, that is, only in and through people's sociability. In fact, only in sociality does nature exist for the human being as a bond with another human being. The vital element of human reality lies in the relationality, good or bad, that connects Ego to Other and Other to Ego. The proper humanisation of the person is achieved only through the sociality that can be enjoyed by generating those relational goods in which the naturalism of the human being and his technological enhancement complement each other.

Beyond modernity, for which the new was necessarily better, in the trans-modern era people have to realise that the new is not necessarily the good. To reach this awareness, people need a special (*sui generis*) reflexivity, that I call 'relational reflexivity,' as a form of steered meta-reflexivity exerted on their social relations mediated by the DM.

6 Stupid ways of working smart?

Colonising the future through policy advice

Jamie Morgan

Introduction

In Volume I of these essays I addressed broad issues of philosophy and artificial intelligence or AI (Morgan, 2018). Amongst other things, I argued that there was some degree of confusion regarding the status of AI and that this made proper analysis of fundamental issues more difficult. The ordinary language use of terms such as intelligence and learning connote characteristics of an entity that an AI may not possess, and yet AI and machine learning (ML) are now part of the vernacular. Specialists in AI, robotics and related fields distinguish specific and general intelligence. Many also, when in more reflexive mode, distinguish AI and ML, emphasising that "true" AI is more than specific intelligence as functional efficacy in some designated task, facilitated by ML systems. It is entity status in terms of a *source* of decision making. Functional efficacy is just one among several ways an underlying self-awareness is expressed. This is more than the construction of some *X* that is operative as a *locus* (site) of decision making. It is not reducible to mere existent functionality. As other essays in Volumes I and II suggest, important issues of the attribution of personhood follow from this distinction (Archer, 2018; Porpora, 2018; Donati, 2018).

If one is focused on what may occur in the near future, then it is the unfolding of current potentials that become of interest, and it is these that I move on to consider in this chapter. One does not need to be a technological determinist or an adherent to the latest innovation in social theory in order to appreciate that AI, robotics and related innovations are set to have profound effects on the way we live, work and perhaps who we are. And yet much of the media focus splits between awe regarding long-range primary transformative technological potential and immediate anxiety induced by reports of imminent socio-economic disruption.

The long-range potential has its optimists and pessimists (as well as its sceptics; "true" AI is impossible etc.). Debate concerns the potential inadvertent harms done to human beings by the reckless embrace of post-human alterations regarding longevity, vitality and new powers and capacities, as well as the potential for state and corporate conflict using new technologies, and, of course, the ultimate fear that robotics and AI may not just supersede but eradicate us. For example, in Chapters 4 and 5 of *Life 3.0* (2017), caveats notwithstanding, the Swedish physicist Max Tegmark argues that it is not an issue of if but when true AI will emerge. The ultimate question is whether and how we survive the creation of a superior entity. His possible scenarios spread across the next 10,000 years.[1] In similar vein, in *Homo Deus* (2017) Yuval Noah Harari argues that, again caveats notwithstanding, humanity is on the threshold of solving its basic provisioning problems. Moreover, humanity is on the cusp of achieving a control over its environment and destiny that is relatively new. This invokes new foci, concerns and challenges at the core of which are biogenetic and technological control of the species. For Harari, a "great decoupling" seems set to occur in which transformed humans will relate to our non-augmented rump species in a way analogous to how humans relate to other animals (see also Al-Amoudi, 2018).

More prosaically, there has been growing attention paid over the last decade to new capitalism or an imminent fourth industrial revolution. This has been most notably taken up by the McKinsey consultancy (Manyika et al., 2017a; 2017b); by the World Economic Forum (2016) and Klaus Schwab (2016); by the OECD (Arntz, Gregory & Zierahn, 2016) and various prominent foundations (for example, Bakhshi et al., 2017). At the state level, the fourth industrial revolution provides a background concern expressed in broader government economic policy, for example, in the recent UK "Industrial Strategy" (DBEIS, 2017); and this in turn is positioned by policy advice, such as the UK Industrial Digitalisation Project commissioned by the Department for Business, Energy and Industrial Strategy (Maier, 2017), and subsequent responses from lobby groups in civil society (for example, Lawrence, Roberts & King, 2017).

One key strand in this has been whether pervasive technological changes will cause employees to be displaced faster than modified or new varieties of employment will be created. If so, then the consequences could be significant. Widespread denial of employment might mean work was no longer central to the social existence and identity of increasing parts of the population. It might no longer be one of the central norms around which everything else configures. Concomitantly, if many are no longer waged then this creates an issue in terms of fulfilling a basic function in capitalism: the use of earned income to maintain aggregate demand, in turn causing financial flows to corporations and the state. The press has tended to focus most on the possibility of widespread employment displacement; for example, reporting Frey and Osborne's (2013) research that 47% of total US employment is at high risk of displacement (a probability of 0.7) in the near future. The standard time reference for this has become 2025 to 2030. This was followed by Bank of England research, which stated 35% of total employment in the UK was at high risk (Haldane, 2015). Little attention was paid in the press to what the economic models were actually claiming or how they were constructed. However, including the fourth industrial revolution literature referenced previously, there

---

1 This is not to suggest Tegmark makes no mention of automation in the near future for work, rather that the theme of the book is longer term and deals not merely with matters of work, and it is this that the media have mainly focused on.

have been many reports and pieces of research making a wide range of claims about the near future. As with the long-range material, the range encompasses sceptical, optimistic and pessimistic accounts.

In this chapter I set out some of the ways the future of work is currently being positioned, and this inevitably draws in further issues. Change does not occur in an organisational vacuum. Many organisations – governments, think tanks, consultancies and so forth – are beginning to colonise the near future of work. I begin narrowly from the empirical issue of trends in industrial and service robotics and what this indicates. I then consider the ambiguity that arises between imminent change and immanent potential and how social ontology provides an important source of critique for the consistency of fourth industrial revolution claims. Finally, I illustrate using the UK *Made Smarter Review 2017* (Maier, 2017) how positional documents, which share various inconsistencies, are beginning to colonise the future.

Who are the robots?

Robots are commonly defined as machines whose design and programming provides them with the capacity to complete tasks without direct human intervention. They are operative and manipulative. To further differentiate them from a standard machine or tool, the global industry association the International Federation of Robotics (IFR) emphasises a series of further characteristics (see, IFR, 2017a: 1):

1 The degrees of movement or motion the robot is capable of: varieties of stationary fixed position rigidly defined movement around an axis, extending to more mobile, tracking, airborne and perambulatory forms;
2 The degree to which the robot is reprogrammable to refine or alter its functionality in terms of given tasks;
3 The consequent capacity for the robot to be fitted to different and multiple purposes.

Clearly, these characteristics are open-ended in terms of what they encompass. They allow for the fixed-position robotic arm familiar from the automation of Fordist continuous flow production lines; an integrated additive process 3-D printing manufacturing system capable of bespoke output; the precision vision, positioning and incision/excision capabilities of medical service robots, a self-tracking vacuum cleaner, a military drone or commercial transport delivery system; interactive information, advice and sales systems (remote or in person); and, ultimately, the embodied-as-*bodied* robot of popular culture (whose current standard is set by Hanson Robotics' Sophia). The IFR also categorises human exoskeletons as robotics, and this indicates that the definition is not just open-ended but also unavoidably ambiguous in terms of what the "direct" in "without direct human intervention" allows for.

If one takes the time to read the many works on the fourth industrial revolution, it is clear that robotics is discursively positioned as part of a confluence of recent and expected technological breakthroughs, which collectively inform the fourth industrial revolution concept.[2] Besides robotics, these include ML, AI, sensors, connectivity, cloud computing, nanotechnology, 3-D printing and the Internet of Things (IoT). Most notably, the IFR's three characteristics allow robots to be distinguished from but be placed in relation to ML and AI. ML is a set of coding systems or techniques and AI is a categorisation of the capacity of a technology. As I set out in Volume I, there is an overwhelming focus on function in terms of learning and intelligence, and this can be a problem when considering what is otherwise conveyed or connoted by these terms. However, within these discursive constraints the three characteristics identified are not just open-ended in terms of range but also in terms of anticipated progress in task-based capacities – that is, what the robot can do and avoid doing. ML creates the potential for reprogrammable robots capable of rapid adjustments and more precise, yet more complex, functions. These extend to context responsiveness, sensitivity and adaptation – that is, mobility and environmentally appropriate activity. To achieve this, ML is able to make use of real time and stored information aggregated as "big data". Concomitantly, cloud storage capacity augments this potential, and allows for remote and diffuse AI to be a management or controlling system for single and multiple robots (and humans) as part of a network system. IoT connectivity, meanwhile, extends the possibilities for a network.

Robotics is being positioned as a key component in the future of work environments. However, one initial way to consider how rapidly possible futures are coming is to consider recent trends in the uptake of industrial and service robotics.

How many robots are changing lightbulbs?

According to the latest available World Bank data, the global working-age population in 2016, defined as those between the ages of 15 and 64, was 65.5% of a world population of 7.5 billion, which is about 5 billion. This, of course, is different from total estimated employment, which the World Bank puts at 3.3 billion for 2016, and this in turn is likely a subset of the real working population, which will itself also include some on either side of the age range and exclude others within it. In any case, these large numbers are worth keeping in mind as context when trying to make sense of metrics for automation, displacement and, for our initial purposes, investment in robotics.

The IFR provides two annual reports of aggregated statistics for the global sale of robotics. One is focused on service robots, subdivided into those supplied for personal/domestic use and those for professional use. The other is focused on industrial robotics. The data provides some sense of whether and to what degree robotics is currently pervasive, and provides a point of departure to address

---

2 The first three industrial revolutions are usually stated as: steam (eighteenth century), electrification (1870–1920) and computerisation (1980s–). Clearly, dates and contents are contestable since there have been other fundamental technologies (the chemical industry, transistors, synthetics etc.).

whether it seems set to become so in the near future. As previously intimated, fourth industrial revolution material typically sets the "near future" as changes occurring by 2025 to 2030.

According to the IFR (2017c), by far the largest category of service robots sold year-on-year has been for personal and domestic use. For example, 6.7 million units were sold worldwide in 2016 in this category. This includes toys, leisure and hobby use.[3] However, the category does include a subcategory of household floor cleaning and lawn mowing robots, of which 4.6 million were sold in 2016. Annual growth rates have been around 25%, so the compounding consequences here are significant, but not in terms of worldwide distributions for domestic services. Professional service robots are categorised separately, and in 2016 a total of only 59,000 units were sold worldwide. The IFR acknowledges it is difficult to estimate the cumulative number still in use, but less than 300,000 units in total had been sold since 1998. One should note here that one major medium by which fourth industrial revolution technologies do and will diffuse is the smartphone, and this is not included in the data (so possible major transformational effects, such as blockchain, cryptocurrency, and new kinds of banking, welfare and people analytics are not directly expressed). Sale of service robots has in recent years been dominated by logistical systems robots (25,400 or 43% of the total in 2016). These are mainly guided vehicle systems in factory and warehouse environments.[4] The next largest category at 11,000 units was defence robots, and the majority of this was accounted for by aerial drones. Other categories are a fraction of this. For example, 6,000 exoskeletons were sold in 2016.

However, reported changes in the basic technologies are continuous, and both human exoskeleton and medical service technologies illustrate this. For example, Ekso Bionics has developed the EksoZeroG gravity balancing arm which allows a human to hold a 16kg industrial drill with no strain, and also a spring-loaded exoskeleton called the EksoVest, which allows heavy objects to be lifted; a full work suit is expected in 2019, and this could change both recruitment and working practices in construction. That said, rapid technological change is different from a claim that prices are viable. For example, in early 2018, the Construction Robotics Semi-Automated Mason (SAM100) robot cost about $500,000 and was mainly available in the US. It can lay 800–2,000 bricks a day compared to a human's 300–500 bricks but requires a mason for detailing and a control panel operator. Furthermore, there is a difference between technological change and commercialisation. For example, a Columbia University team recently announced they had produced a new kind of

---

3 It also encompasses sex robots such as True Companion's Roxxxy model, which (in 2017) has fantasy settings including "Frigid Farrah" in which the robot resists sexual advances. This has been a subject of controversy on the basis it may normalise sexual violence.
4 The actual breakdown for 2016 is (IFR, 2017c): logistical (25,400 or 43%), defense (11,000 or 19%), public relations (7,500, mainly telepresence units), field (6,000 or 10%, mainly milking units), human exoskeletons (6,000 or 10%), medical (1,600 or 2.7%, mainly assisted surgery units) and other (all less than 1,000, consisting in professional cleaning, demolition, construction, inspection, maintenance, security applications).

soft silicon (rather than fully metal-mechanical) and ethanol microbubble robotic muscle that is 3-D printable and can lever 6,000 times its own weight (Miriyev, Stack & Lipson, 2017), but this was still at the laboratory stage in 2018.

In 2016, 1,600 medical robots were sold. Surgical assistance robotics has been gradually incorporated over the last ten years as new models have been developed and new procedures pioneered. Medical robotics is a prime example of multiple convergent technology use. A state-of-the-art modern operating theatre can combine virtual reality technology, allowing remote expert participation and consultation, with augmented reality (allowing the overlay of projected scans onto tissues), use of ML-directed recognition software to pick up anomalies, and surgical assistance robotics. Console-operated systems allow surgical tools to be positioned in locations and angles and then manipulated with a steadiness and precision that a human cannot replicate. For example, a Retzius-sparing prostatectomy would be impossible without robotic assistance, since it is executed inside the pelvis from below and without cutting through nerves and tissue around the bladder (avoiding previous problems of incontinence and erectile dysfunction).

The point remains that if one looks *purely* at aggregated numbers and at recent ingrained trend changes in numbers, these remain relatively small for professional service robots, even allowing for rates of change and compounding. However, due to the automation of continuous flow production lines over the last 30 years, industrial robots are already deeply embedded in *some* forms of industrial and manufacturing process. Yet this is currently, in various ways, more restricted than one might think (IFR, 2017b). The year-on-year average increase 2010–2016 was 10%, and approximately 295,000 units were sold in 2016. As of 2017 there were fewer than 2 million industrial robots in the world, and this was forecast to increase to 3 million by 2020. The vast majority of those in existence are purposed for the automotive industry. As Table 6.1 indicates, actual investment in industrial robotics is highly concentrated in a few sectors, regionally and in a few economies.

It is worth noting that East Asia now dominates the uptake of robotics, and, though not represented in Table 6.1, increasingly the production of them. Moreover, though IFR data indicates that the rate of increase in units is faster for other sectors, it is expected not to be significantly faster than for the automotive sector in the near future. This is mainly because the industry is at the beginning of a major shift towards self-driving, electric and hybrid vehicles, so automation in this field requires ongoing investment. However, though automotive may remain the dominant sector, no less than in the professional service categories, the basic technologies in use are undergoing continuous change.

Robotics and industrial automation are two of four divisions of the multinational enterprise ABB Group, and are the smallest by annual revenue ($8.4 billion and $6.9 billion respectively in 2017). Still, ABB dominates the production and development of industrial robotics and is larger in revenue and unit terms than the next four largest corporations combined.[5] The next generation of ABB

5 See http://new.abb.com

Table 6.1 Various breakdowns from total units of industrial robots sold

Main Sectors		Main Regional Markets			Main Country Markets			
Sector	**Units sold, 2016**	**Region**	**Units sold, 2016**	**Units sold, 2015**	**Country**	**Units sold, 2016**	**% of total**	**Units sold, 2015**
Automotive	103,300	Asia	190,492	160,500	China	87,000	30%	68,500
Electricals/ electronics	91,300	Europe	56,000	50,000	South Korea	41,400	14%	38,300
Metal and machinery	28,700	Americas	41,300	38,100	Japan	38,600	13%	35,000
Rubber and plastics	16,000	Since 2013 China has been the largest market			USA	31,400	11%	27,500
Food and beverage	8,200				Germany	20,000	7%	19,900
					Approximately 75% of total sales 2016			
					The UK	1,800		1,600

robotics, either in production or in prototype, highlights how robotics is changing.[6] Traditional industrial robotics has been dominated by fixed position arms for some combination of *repetitious* welding, painting, picking, packing, palletising, cutting, grinding, polishing, gluing, sealing and movement and manipulation of (often heavy) objects for (cumulatively) final assembly. This, as noted, has formed a typical Fordist continuous flow production line system. These robotic arms have been heavy, enclosed for safety, fixed in position, and have required complex programming, which could not easily be overwritten. Automation in this system involved significant upfront investment and was typically only feasible on large scales for a design that would stay in situ for many years. The system created work for human operators of some forms of machinery as well as overseers and maintenance crews, but did not allow for a more interactive process where humans could move safely in and out of compact spaces where robotics is also mobile.

However, the new generation of robotics, such as ABB's YuMi, is small, lightweight (38kg), networked and rapidly recoded for new operations. Robots are dual armed and potentially able to be multi-functional. Moreover, they have sensors enabling them to stop short of or avoid human contact. YuMi was introduced in 2015 and priced at $40,000 per unit. ABB describes it as their first "fully collaborative" robot, though it may perhaps more accurately be described as spatially safe and flexible via its coding. YuMi and similar models expand the domain of repetition to several tasks and seem to represent a generational transition for robotics in the direction of duplication of complex tasks previously beyond the scope of robotics. Related innovations in touch sensitivity and mobility are also

6 See http://new.abb.com/future

germane.[7] ABB and other similar corporations offer design services (and software), which enable firms to create virtual factories for their products and test them, and then quickly redesign the layout and repurpose the robotics (for example, using ABB SafeMove2). This brings together the various fourth industrial revolution technologies and, though in its infancy, has major implications for investment costs, factory size and location. New generation robotics is compatible with "flying" factories, that is, factories that are set up in one location after another near to different customers or clients. This in turn opens up the possibility of "hot" factory spaces equivalent to the recent trend for "hot" offices. In any case, the factories can be multi-functional and small scale. Moreover, they can make use of networked systems and sensors in combination with predictive and diagnostic analytics to identify cumulative mechanical problems (reducing lost time from maintenance whilst allowing for experiment with different configurations of the factory to improve productivity and reduce energy consumption, resource use and waste). Furthermore, as the confluence of technology changes, activity that can be coded becomes activity that can become "routine". Complex activity that previously required human decision making subsequently *may* not (notably the directing capability for multiple-functionality, which used to require human cognition).

The scope for change thus seems great. However, if one looks *purely* at aggregated quantities and at recent ingrained trends, then the numbers of industrial robots, though greater than exhibited for professional service robots, remain relatively small. Moreover, if one considers measures of the density of robot use in Table 6.2, then the overall impression seems some distance from the kind of widespread work displacement effects reported in the press.[8]

Imminent change and immanent possibility

Looking at the IFR data, there seems to be a numeric ambiguity between imminent change and immanent potential. The former is a matter of variations in investment and uptake, and there are reasons to be sceptical regarding a relentless *ingrained* "march of the robots" scenario, where one can confidently *extrapolate*

7 For example, the Shadow Dextrous Hand duplicates human kinematics based on 129 sensors: www. shadowrobot.com/products/dexterous-hand/ and the trend now in robotics is to use organic and typically anthropomorphic models for motion. Humanoid bipedal motion is a force and compensation system based on environmental feedback. This is different from traditional robotic motion based on mechanical systems that apply force to and drive onto surfaces.

8 However, it should be noted that density can be misleading as an indicator of the effects of robot investment on a particular economy and the significance of that particular economy in the world. Density is not a measure of total numbers employed in any given industrial sector by country. Moreover, if one treats density levels as notional retrospective substitutions, then if a robot accounts for 15 workers' production, a density of more than 650 appears to account for the historic output of the worker ratio used for the measurement; clearly then, relatively small numbers can be of some significance, but the overall process is more complex than steady-state substitution. Also, perhaps a more relevant context is the automated line rather than the individual robot. (Thanks to Ismael Al-Amoudi for this point.)

Table 6.2 Measures of degree of automation or "density" of robots within industry

Robot Density Per 10,000 Employees In All Manufacturing, 2016		Robot Density Per 10,000 Employees In The Automotive Industry, 2016		Robot Density Per 10,000 Employees In Industry Excluding The Automotive Industry, 2016	
Main Countries	Density	Main Countries	Density	Main Countries	Density
South Korea	631	South Korea	2,145	South Korea	475
Singapore	488	USA	1,261	Japan	214
Germany	309	Japan	1,240	Germany	181
Japan	303	France	1,150	Sweden	164
USA	189	Germany	1,131	Italy	126
China	68	China	505	USA	93
Global Average: 74 Europe: 99 Americas: 84 Asia: 63		The UK has relatively low density in all three measures: Per 10,000 all manufacturing 71 (contrast Italy: 160; Slovakia 79) It is not in the top five for per 10,000 automotive despite the prominence of vehicle industry It is not in the top five for per 10,000 excluding automotive despite its track record in primary technology creation (rather than commercialisation)			

Note: In recent analyses one industrial robot can do on average the work of 15 human equivalents.

the pervasive use of robots across economies by 2025 to 2030.[9] However, the latter concerns what becomes possible and yet may not be realised, either according to a strict timetable or in one particular way. Immanent potential has various inflections based on the nuance of social ontology. Imminent change is a framing that tends to focus more on surface quantities.[10] This difference provides one way to position the broader set of issues raised by the fourth industrial revolution. If one reads through the literature, one can identify a range of areas of work that may be modified or transformed by the confluence of technology that informs the fourth industrial revolution concept. These are in addition to the traditional Fordist continuous flow factory production line:

1   Warehouse product storage and retrieval, port and airport container management employment whose dominant task base depends on ordered and integrated logistical systems in controllable environments;

9 One must, of course, acknowledge that large numbers or small do not necessarily translate into significance or its lack. One must be careful what one infers by place, sector and case. Furthermore, pervasiveness is not impossible; the point is that one cannot look at trends and state definitively that a shift is already observable.
10 To be clear, imminent and immanent are not antonyms but indicative of a coalescence of foci. Furthermore, the many inflections of immanent (inherent, intrinsic, latent etc.) are still subject to other distinctions based on social ontology (structure, agency, culture, personhood etc.).

2   Commercial driving, delivery and taxi service employment whose dominant task base can be replicated by an autonomous driving or airborne drone unit;

3   On-site commercial and domestic property construction employment whose dominant task base can be partially transferred to controllable (potentially mobile factory) environments in which prefabricated modular sections can be manufactured for delivery and assembly, and whose other tasks can be replicated by on-site mobile automated units (brick laying etc.);

4   Commercial and domestic cleaning services employment whose dominant task base can be replicated in similar ways to 1 and 2 (pipes, pools, tunnels, tanks, windows, floors etc.);

5   Online banking, sales, customer and personal services employment whose dominant task base is information, direction and advice that an effective integrated natural language proficient chatbot could emulate;

6   Insurance, paralegal, accounting and tax employment whose dominant task base is sorting, collation and categorisation of information according to well-established rule systems;

7   Medical imaging and diagnostics, safety, inspection and coordination employment whose dominant task base is vigilance, monitoring, remote testing and problem/anomaly reporting;

8   Policing and security services whose dominant task base can be replicated in similar ways to some combination of 2, 5 and 7;[11]

9   Business, journalism and academic copyediting and limited range copywriting whose dominant task base requires syntactical proficiency, semantic discrimination and information extraction/summation from depositories and newsfeeds;

10   Tuition service employment whose dominant task base can be replicated in similar ways to some combination of 5, 6 and 9.[12]

These ten areas add some credence to the point stated in the introduction: AI, robotics and so forth are set to have profound effects on the way we live, work and perhaps who we are.[13] However, the way in which this occurs is not fixed.

---

11 In January 2018 Ford applied for a patent license for an AI directed autonomous vehicle able to take on simple traffic enforcement and regulatory duties.

12 Sir Anthony Seldon is currently writing a book on the fourth revolution in education dealing with this subject.

13 For example, the IFR International Symposium on Robotics has been held since 1970 and highlights many of the key innovations in industrial and service robotics; the Consumer Technology Association's annual Consumer Electronics Show (CES) conference showcases many of the latest commercial innovations (including, in January 2018, a robotic pet companion, and a robotic suitcase that can track its owner through crowds). Coding systems have also developed rapidly since the early 2010s: ML systems for recognition, identification-diagnosis, and interaction for suggestion, answers or advice and strategy, blending into demonstrated capacity through game play. The most successful system has combined "artificial neural network" (ANN) ML techniques using a training programme with a restricted dataset and a larger dataset for application (so the AI "learns" goals and then refines them based on actual contexts; see also "generative adversarial networks").

Investment must occur in places by organisations. Laws, rules, conventions and practices must be developed and so forth. This is a complex socio-economic process. As a process, it is not simply free-floating or arbitrary in some extreme performative sense (on consultants, see Clark & Fincham, 2002). For example, one important aspect is the emergence of epistemic communities that produce sites of expertise that become the basis of authoritative action (see, for example, Seabrooke & Henrikson, 2017). In any case, technology itself will develop and it will do so as a constituent of the whole and not in isolation from it.

What will occur is conditional, since not just anything can happen, but contingent, in so far as many different things could. The future is not discovered; it is constructed. At the same time, the future is not a deterministic product of any given intent to construct it. This is basic to all variants of realist social ontology and also explorations via methodology (see Archer, 1995; Lawson, 2003). Social reality is characterised by cumulative causal processes. Periods of relative stability can also include qualitative changes to the activities that are expressed as currently slow trends, leading eventually to threshold effects where structures and systems may transform and change accelerate (see Morgan, 2013; Morgan & Patomäki, 2017). The complexity of this implies the future is not predictable in a mathematically precise sense, nor, as a corollary, is it easily amenable to frequency-based probability or equivalent analysis. However, one can *know* the world will alter and consider different ways in which this may occur based on what has occurred and the potentials that arise.

Analysts of the fourth industrial revolution are not idiots. They are aware that the future is not a product of determinism. At the same time, if we put aside the long-range futurists, the discourse is dominated by consultancies, business-oriented think tanks, mainly mainstream economists and policy-oriented analysts. In this context, social ontology is not banal; a social ontology perspective is an important reminder of how inconsistency and other problems can arise that may not otherwise be considered. Fourth industrial revolution work tends to combine attempts to quantify the future that ultimately treat it *as if* given and analysis that accepts that the future is realised based on what is done now. The latter is typically

---

The best-known source is Google's DeepMind project. AI are now able to beat human champions at Go and chess, recognize anomalies (tumours etc.) from medical scans with a greater degree of accuracy than a medical expert, and more recently progress has been made in "social awareness" (Google has developed an AI, "AVA", to identify people and the actions they are carrying out using a YouTube database – creating scope to address context activity and categorise it for decision making, though the research makes no grand claims as yet and acknowledges that performance for some kinds of fine-grained activity, rather than actor identification, are low at around 10–16%; Gu et al., 2017). The company Vicarious recently published research claiming its AI could defeat the Captcha System (colloquially the *am I a robot* test on internet sites) with an accuracy of 66%. Captcha relies on AI being unable to overcome the segmentation problem to identify where one image or letter begins and ends when these are juxtaposed jumbled or blurred (George et al., 2017). Both Microsoft and Alibaba have developed AIs that can beat a benchmark of 82% accuracy set on the machine reading test Stanford Question Answer Dataset (SQuAD), which was only introduced in 2016. See: https://rajpurkar.github.io/SQuAD-explorer/

conjoined with advocacy of some means to realise that future. Clearly, treating the future as both given and not is unstable, and this can be problematic. It is basic to fourth industrial revolution literature that "this time is different", but the future is also treated as though it can be modelled and mapped in ways that do more than tame uncertainty in terms of possible scenarios. They impose tacit, albeit often probabilistic, certainty juxtaposed to acknowledged contingency.

It may, for example, be legitimate to identify past trends. Deloitte's (2018) analysis of the UK economy 2001 to 2016 is interesting in this regard. They find that over the period net employment increased in the UK by 3 million. This high-lights that in the UK, as in various other countries, employment has grown, and this encompasses the post global financial crisis period, within which complex readjustments have occurred, and these include (see also the McKinsey work): platform and gig economy effects, sub-contraction, self-employment as well as in many countries ongoing youth unemployment. There is no unequivocal sign of an overwhelming displacement effect. However, Deloitte's focus is on relative employment in occupations in the UK, rather than just raw numbers employed, and they find that this fell in 160 of 366 occupations. Furthermore, it fell consist-ently in occupations that did not intrinsically involve as a dominant facet of that occupation human social relations, interactions, communications and judgement, whilst it rose in those that did. The implication is that as fourth industrial revolu-tion effects spread then more occupations will experience falling employment levels. The historic effect is real, but it is not an explanation and it does not lend credence to claims that a given proportion (some precise quantification) of the working population will be displaced *in the future*.

The ten areas stated previously, for example, have provided background to a range of claims regarding whether changes will cause employees to be displaced faster than modified or new varieties of employment will be created. The exist-ence of a range is itself indicative of the problematic "given and not". If we refer again to the Frey and Osborne (2013) and the Bank of England (2015) research, in order to make displacement claims, they were required to assume away all of the complexity and contingency of a real socio-economy, and construct and run simulations on models that looked purely at whether an occupation could be duplicated by some combination of AI, ML and robotics based on current and anticipated technological changes. The probability of future displacement is thus derived in the absence of social relational development, which is as much as to say, in the absence of what humans will actually do. Using equally problematic but slightly different models, Arntz, Gregory and Zierahn (2016) at the OECD claim that just 9% of occupations are at high risk of displacement. The range indicates a common problem of method in attempting to quantify the future. That is, the modelling problem of tractability. This is never fully addressed since prob-lems with models result in modified models (and confounded empirical claims also result in new models "updating" the empirical claims; Frey, for example, has been in great demand, producing a whole series of new estimations since 2013). Moreover, the problem indicates a further problem in the sense that there is a continuous demand to quantify the future, which encourages variants of an imminent change emphasis in what is otherwise more adequately considered an issue of how new immanent potential is realised. It is this that is often expressed in unstable combination.

Concomitantly, the example highlights a key underlying tension in fourth industrial revolution literature between contingency and certainty. Analysis jumps back and forth between models whose methods are questionable and discursive contextual discussion that acknowledges the future is a product of what different actors choose to seek to impose on the future, but which cannot be reduced to the intentions of any in particular.[14] For example, the World Economic Forum (WEF, 2015) *Deep Shift* report was a survey of 816 identified relevant corporate executives and experts, each asked to state whether 21 separate technological tipping points would occur and when they would occur up to 2025. This was then translated into likelihoods of those technological tipping points occurring, cross-referenced with a timeline. The report also includes extensive discussion of the general potential of each of the technologies and how experts see each developing. But consider how odd the juxtaposition in the report is. Belief about the future is opinion, and something does not become a probability of the facticity of future states of affairs merely because it is an opinion held by many, even if the holder of an opinion is well informed about relevant aspects of the past and the present. Conditions and contingency will make a difference to the difference that is the future. Obviously, the analysts are aware of this, but this did not prevent the survey being conducted in the way that it was.

One might consider the survey somewhat cynically as a publicity-friendly metric in a report that acts as a vehicle for a more nuanced analysis of future potential. But it is also a way to fix a version of the future in the mind of the present public. It creates a quasi-determinism: *this future is coming and you better get used to it.* This softens opinion, helping to construct acquiescence, which by no means requires this to be the conscious intent of the procedure. However, equally it may be part of the intent, though perhaps in subtle ways. For example, the Campaign for Accountability (CfA) has produced a variety of reports on Google's creation of an academic network that publishes consistently favourable research, and not always with disclosure of the links between Google and the research network (CfA, 2017). More recently, the CfA has noted links with Nesta, the former UK quango and now charitable foundation, which co-supported the recent UK *Future of Skills* report (Bakhshi et al., 2017). The report highlights that 22.2 million of the current UK workforce are in occupations facing an uncertain future, but that widespread displacement is unlikely. The report claims education, hospitality, public services, health, the arts and "artisanal" employment areas are all likely to increase in importance.

In any case, there are many competing if overlapping claims being made on the future, and in this sense the future is being colonised. Combinations of what *will*

---

14 Note, there are many variations on a theme within the methods problem; for example, sensitivity analysis, cost-benefit analysis, as well as standard econometric analytics.

occur, what *must* occur and how *best* to achieve outcomes are being articulated and advocated. How these are framed matters in so far as what they include, what they peripheralise and what they omit are potentially influential for the future. This can be illustrated using the UK *Made Smarter Review 2017* (Maier, 2017).

The *Made Smarter Review 2017*

The *Made Smarter Review 2017* was commissioned by the UK government Department for Business, Energy and Industrial Strategy (DBEIS). This organisational positioning creates a frame of analysis: nation-state concern with economic futures. Its "Leadership Team" consisted of 16 senior corporate executives (two from the Accenture consultancy, which provided analytics), two university vice-chancellors, an "entrepreneur in residence" and the director general of the industry lobby, the CBI. Around 200 organisations provided contributors for advice, and also participation in industrial sector working groups: drawn from tech-expertise, business, academia and local and regional government (Maier, 2017: 229–230). As the *Review* was prepared, a new UK Industrial Strategy was also formulated, and the *Review* became, in part, a document intended to work in conjunction with this document (DBEIS, 2017), as well as with the Department for Digital, Culture, Media and Sport's *UK Digital Strategy 2017* (DDCMS, 2017). The *Digital Strategy* was published in March, the *Review* at the end of October and the Industrial Strategy in November (following a green paper in January). The Industrial Strategy poses an AI economy as one of several "grand challenges" whilst the *Digital Strategy* positions industry as part of its broader remit.

As will become clear, the *Review* both quantifies and constructs the future it refers to, and does so in a form of the self-referential channelling of concerns that also exhibits circular reasoning. The stated context for the *Review* is one in which the UK is failing, despite achievements in primary research and pockets of "excellence" in commercialisation, to develop the "potential" of, and exploit the "opportunities" from, the fourth industrial revolution in a coordinated and coherent way; and notably in industrial digital technology (IDT) (Maier, 2017). Based on this context, the formal remit of the *Review* was to identify impediments to, and formulate a set of recommendations leading to, the creation of an institutional "framework and ecosystem" through which UK industry can become a "world leader" in the fourth industrial revolution by 2030 (Maier, 2017: 4). This, in turn, was situated in relation to the observation that many other countries already have "branded" national strategies: Germany's Industrie 4.0, China's Made in China 2025 and the USA's America Makes (Maier, 2017: 9, 177–194), as well as in many cases demonstrably higher investment in industrial applications of key technologies. For example, Germany invests 6.6 times more than the UK in automation, although its manufacturing sector is only 2.7 times the size of the UK's (Maier, 2017: 66).[15] According to the *Review*, the existence of such strategies is

---

15 Consider the connotations of this way of phrasing: "Germany invests" rather than "investment occurs in Germany" connotes Germany as an actor rather than as a geographical location and

one key constituent in "competitive threats" (Maier, 2017: 21). The stated context immediately begins the process of channelling the *Review*'s focus and phrasing. It identifies three key impediments (Maier, 2017: 9, 71–82):

1   A lack of effective leadership (in the form of "market-focused strategic vision, direction and coordination") able to create a network for the commercialisation of primary research and the development and diffusion of technology, and able to "inspire current and future workers" to retrain and "upskill" to service the desired fourth industrial revolution economy;
2   Current low levels of investment in and adoption of fourth industrial revolution technologies (especially among small and medium-sized enterprises or SMEs) due to lack of standardisation and infrastructure, risk aversion, lack of requisite skills necessary to adoption of, and lack of awareness of, fourth industrial revolution technologies, within the context of 1 as a failure for 2;
3   Lack of support to facilitate the commercialisation of primary research (invention and innovation).

These three impediments essentially articulate how they are to be resolved: the creation of effective leadership, and where effective leadership articulates a coordinated national strategy for the development and diffusion of technology and for the training of a fourth industrial revolution workforce. The *Review* recommends a specific organisational structure and set of mechanisms in conjunction with a national branding campaign (Maier, 2017: 123–126) to market that structure and those mechanisms (Maier, 2017: 13–15, 85–132). Figure 6.1 diagrams the organisational structure.

Following an initial pilot project in the North West of England, the *Review* envisages the structure detailed in Figure 6.1 being rapidly organised and created across the UK. It should be clear that the key emphasis of the recommendations presupposes that the primary problems are lack of awareness and the existence of a facilitating network. This constitutes a "market failure" where industry is failing to "self-organize" an effective strategy (Maier, 2017: 125).

Colonising the future

The *Review* makes a number of claims for the potential benefits of IDT over the period to 2025. These follow from consultation with working groups for each industrial sector, which were fed into a "global value at stake" analysis by Accenture (previously developed for the World Economic Forum), and also an analysis of future employment based on the Boston Consulting Group's analysis of the German economy. The employment benefits are stated as a "best-case scenario"

---

subtly conflates the consequence of the activity of multiple actors, firms etc. as though it were a single national act. This shapes perception of who and what is competing (states) and shifts attention from a more complex reality that includes multinational enterprises and transnational systems and strategies.

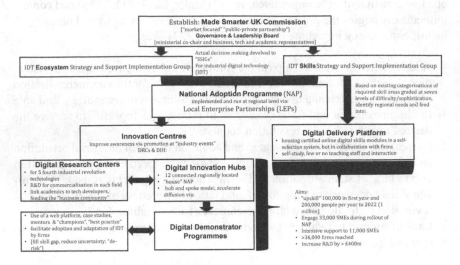

Figure 6.1 Made Smarter UK Commission: structure and scope

rather than a forecast (Maier, 2017: 53), and each industrial sector analysis uses the phrasing "currently known" and a "point of view" (for example, Maier, 2017: 39–40). The potential claimed benefits are:

1   The *Review* calculates that an additional value (revenue) of £185 billion could be generated in total for four analysed industrial sectors (construction, food and drink, pharmaceuticals and aerospace) through a combination of new business and competing business away from competitors, and extrapolates an estimate of £313–455 billion for the whole of UK manufacturing, which is 10–14% higher than the current trend anticipates (Maier, 2017: 35);

2   The *Review* calculates that up to 295,000 jobs could be displaced, but 370,000 created through economic growth and "reshoring", with new varieties of employment creating a further 100,000 new jobs, which leads to a net employment gain of 175,000 (Maier, 2017: 53);

3   The *Review* also claims industrial productivity could be increased by 25% over the period and carbon emissions reduced by 4.5% (Maier, 2017: 8, 56–61).

Now, since the benefits are based on the development and adoption of appropriate IDT, which requires as a corollary a matching workforce, and according to the *Review* achieving these requires a particular envisaged environment ("leadership" and the "ecosystem"), then the recommendations of the *Review* or something similar are, if one accepts the logic, intrinsic to the achievements of the benefits. In one sense the channelling or circularity of this whole is not problematic. It is an ordinary facet of identification and justification of a solution to a recognised problem. It becomes more problematic when one starts to consider the construction of problems and solutions. Whilst caveats are part of the

Review, it is the emphasis on quantities and metrics that dominates its content, and it is unsurprising that the press reported the employment claims as a forecast and the value analysis as well founded rather than speculative. And yet the whole is highly speculative. This matters because the future is at stake. It does not follow that the current approach:

1 Is realistic in its construction and assumptions;
2 Despite good intentions, is likely to realize its intentions, based on current committed resources, design and capacity to implement that design;
3 Actually encompasses all important aspects and perspectives on a future "desirable" socio-economy.

To be clear, for our purposes it is of secondary importance whether the *Review* is fully implemented; it is what it suggests about how the future is being colonised that concerns us. One could do something similar with World Economic Forum publications, and one should note there is heavy cross-citation of the same restricted number of underlying studies, creating a degree of authority in each particular publication. With this in mind, let us consider each of the three previous points in order.

The *Review* makes many claims about future quantities. In order to do so it relies on numerous unrealistic assumptions indicative of the "given and not" inconsistency previously referred to. For example, the value at stake analysis attributes specific cost reductions and revenue streams over the future period for each industry; in aerospace, this includes £7.5 billion in new revenue from growth and £10 billion in costs savings combined with the claim 30% of cost savings will be passed onto consumers over 10 years in a context of a 69% increase in customer satisfaction and 13% increase in job satisfaction (Maier, 2017: 43). The methodology for this is set out in Appendix 4 and the overall findings are considered "reasonable" because the findings are comparable to similar studies by consultancies in the UK or for other countries. But this simply tells us that similar methods and assumptions have been used and that these involve participants assessing *currently* conceived technology applied to the same kinds of data, where each is aware of the other high-profile studies. Similar outcomes are thus not evidence that the precision included in future scenarios is well founded in the sense of likely to be vindicated. This is equally likely to be conformism as confirmation.

Moreover, it is one thing to engage a working group and ask them will there be significant potential impacts and quite another to translate this into quantities for the future. The adoption of IDT will occur in ways that are influenced by but also influential on corporate strategy, market structure and institutional context within nations, regions and globally. These are not fixed. But, for cost savings and revenue streams to be quantified then pricing systems and strategies must be known, and yet these are dependent on what is liable to change in complex interactive ways based on decision situations that are not yet clear because they are rooted in strategies, structures and contexts that are going to be in flux if the fourth industrial revolution is as fundamental as claimed; this future is no more set than the recent past was foreseen.[16] Who foresaw the full significance of Amazon or eBay or Google, and more latterly the rise of populism and new economic nationalism? What costs can be passed on to individual customers is a product of an unknown, as is the potential for higher wages to employees. And to be clear, one can make no definite claims about higher wages because of productivity and skills, or claims about satisfaction regarding consumption or work unless one assumes definite enduring structures of social relations and activity at the heart of which reside regularities, and regularities are never isolated in the real world and structures of social relations are what is changing here as part of a causally complex process including technology as a key component. Productivity and wage growth are already divergent in many economies, and how people will feel about consumption in the twenty-first century is highly contingent on psycho-social changes that are not easily anticipated. Convenience and efficiency are intrinsic to a cost approach to the metrics but are limited ways to imagine the future *experience* of fourth industrial revolution technologies, which surely brings into question the meaning of what is measured as "satisfaction".

To be clear, I am by no means suggesting the future will be dystopic or that fourth industrial revolution technology will have no benefits. I am suggesting the analytics of the *Review* and similar documents are problematic in the way they construct the future. Where ranges are stated this too cannot rescue the whole. Depending on one's preferred language the claims are either highly stylised or spurious. Even if the metrics work out along the lines set out, this would not confirm the modelling procedure by which they were derived. This should not be conflated with evidence-based policy. Can policy be instrumentally posed and yet unrealistic in its construction of claims? Concomitantly, assumed conditions that cannot pertain cannot be the basis by which the future is realised.[17] This, however, brings us to the issue of realisation. The metrics of the *Review* provide quantities for claimed benefits that are at stake, but the *Review* also claims this future is in "jeopardy" unless a series of recommendations are followed to facilitate that realisation. However, it does not follow that the resources and mechanisms are sufficient to achieve the intent.

Consider the problem of training. The intent is to provide a skilled workforce. That is, a workforce able to work to develop and adopt IDT in a fourth industrial revolution context: engineers, data analysts, roboticists and so forth, as well as, in general, digitally literate workers comfortable in a new environment of flying

16 The same applies to the claim that profits will increase. In terms of pricing structures, the usual way to reconcile this is to make the collectivity of firms unable to affect the pricing structure; that is, to assume some variant on perfect competition. This clearly does not fit the context for the fourth industrial revolution or the cost-benefit analysis undertaken where market power seems likely to be a major issue, including for multinational enterprises (MNEs) whose pricing systems can shift value from country to country in ways that have little to do with where value is "created".

17 Note, the claim of "best-case scenario" cannot mitigate this point; and the only credible authority for the precision would be ownership of a time machine and not even that would be sufficient to add credence to the model, merely the coincidence of quantities.

factories, co-bots, chatbots, autonomous vehicles and so forth. The *Review* states 90% of all jobs will require some level of digital skills within 20 years (about 16.5 million people), 65% of the 2030 workforce has already left the education system, and UK business currently spends about 50% of the EU average on training (Maier, 2017: 75–76). Its primary recommendation is to reskill and upskill 1 million workers in the next five years (200,000 certifications per year to 2022). This is to be achieved via modular IDT training using online platforms delivered through low-cost virtual learning spaces, eliminating the need for face-to-face contact, staff and buildings (Maier, 2017: 112–122). The approach to training is predicated on successfully encouraging those liable to benefit from training to engage with that training via awareness, personal training allowances and reskilling allowances, and perhaps based on modifications to the current UK apprenticeship scheme and levy (introduced 2015).[18] It takes no great insight to see the many ways in which this scheme might underperform or fail:

1   For the low-skilled with limited digital skills it assumes potential users already have capacities that the modules themselves are intended to inculcate (as well as more fundamental capacities – attention span, literacy etc.); engaging them may require local government intervention (job and outreach centers etc.), but local government is currently confronted by radical budget cuts for service provision;

2   For more specific skills for a "cutting edge" successful fourth industrial revolution economy, there are limits to what self-selection online learning in modular form with limited or no staff can deliver; the format constrains what and how one can learn. It has pedagogic consequences, and there is a major difference between completing a module and acquiring actual skills and in-depth relevant knowledge.[19]

Germany's success in developing high-level skills has required many years and significant resources, and other countries' IDT strategies (China in particular)

18   This reflects a broader lack in the *Review*; there is very little detail on the scale of resources actually being invested by the state. Statements are vague and open-ended or involve inducements rather than actual new money. Government will: invest in local advisory services (p. 87 no figure); provide targeted kick-start funding (p. 92 no figure); provide DIH (digital innovation hub) funding via catalyst (p. 100 no figure) or DRCs (digital research centers) (p. 106 no figure) and training costs are to be shared between employer and government (p. 121 no figure). Financial incentives in general involve new access and priorities at the British Business Bank for IDT and tax incentives for research and development (pp. 130–132).

19   The current apprenticeship scheme was introduced in 2015 and is based on a levy of 0.5% of payroll costs placed in a training fund by businesses with an annual wage bill of £3 million or more. Companies can claim back 100% of training costs for 16- to 18-year-olds and 90% for those 19 and over. The scheme has a target of 3 million new apprenticeships by 2020, and as of October 2017 1.2 million had been initiated. However, the rate of uptake is reducing quarter by quarter (notably due to problems in getting training approved so the levy can be reclaimed), and the CBI has criticised the focus on quantity rather than quality. Pivoting the scheme or augmenting it with digital skills may, therefore, not be easy.

recognise this. A primary focus on modular online training peripheralises the core problem of how industry leading skills, experience and knowledge are going to be acquired. The problem, in effect, is absorbed into the achievement of an effective ecosystem as though the skills *necessary* for this will emerge as the process develops. This is highly disputable if the skills are "necessary" (and in the UK this problem may be exacerbated by Brexit's possible effects on immigration). In any case, a target 1 million workers against what is claimed to be an economy-wide 16.5 million (and more) need for skilled workers may be ambitious as a logistical matter of policy delivery but likely insufficient as a response to the acknowledged problem.

There is also something slightly ironic about opting for essentially the educational equivalent of automation to prevent a future of mass technological unemployment and industrial-economic decline. The policy recommendation is based on quickest and cheapest (as proxies for efficient) and illustrates the seduction of least cost models of technological adoption. This is precisely the problem that society must confront and corporations and firms will also face as a choice regarding displacement (see, for example, Kalleberg, 2011). Moreover, the implicit downgrading of education sits at odds with Nesta (Bakhshi et al., 2017) and Deloitte's research that envisages education as a growth area because of the need for judgement, critical skills and because of the benefits of human interaction. So, the *Review* policy recommendation also highlights how similar studies can result in incompatible sets of ways to colonise the future (despite common agreement in these studies that fear of displacement may be misplaced).[20]

Consider also how the humans who will be the colonists of that future are being treated in the *Review*. There is no sociology of work as a perspective on employment within the *Review*. There is no positive recognition of a role for trade unions, and leadership remains an ambiguous term whose connotations seem to imply some combination of expertise and entrepreneurship. People as workers are treated as the carriers of skills and a unit cost calculation for the firm. They are recipients of good advice who must conform to strictures in order to succeed. Train and upskill and you *will* be employed in the new vibrant economy; achieve lower levels of digital skills and you *will* also be employed because economic growth will ensure employment persists, and this growth *will* also provide the basis for higher wages because of productivity.[21] The "best case" is the only one

---

20 And note that the artisanal and soft "human" skills emphasis in the future of work reduces to the implicit claim that *because* these are areas where humans may be preferred then they *will* grow; this is hopeful assertion rather than identified mechanism for causation.

21 There is long-standing dispute and confusion regarding how productivity relates to economic growth and international trade. Neoclassical theory assumes growth follows rising productivity, which is both technological and human capital driven, but this cannot be basic, pervasive and prior to growth because otherwise no country could develop and grow through trade. It is just as likely that economic growth precedes productivity growth and that it is an error to conflate national competitiveness and productivity (consider the example of China). Kaldor and Verdoorn looked at these issues rather differently.

being seriously considered, despite the lack of realisticness in the claims about future benefits from that best case.

Moreover, consider how this framing delegates responsibility. The possibility of structural technological unemployment is never given proper credence and the onus of adjustment to a new world is being placed on the individual, despite the fact that *whatever* the individual does it remains possible work may not be available. Past histories of employment recovery and growth have not prevented structural unemployment occurring; this has simply been disguised by the various definitions of unemployment (on definitions see, for example, Fullbrook, 2017). The fundamental nature of the fourth industrial revolution makes it an open question whether sufficient work will be available, not least because we do not know how corporations will respond to the potential of technology. Equally, employment in the UK and US are historically high (subject to different measures) and employment is growing in most economies. Still, the *Review* claims regarding jobs are simply as stated "best guesses", rooted in an authority derived partly from questionable empirical specifications for the future (typically treated subsequently and iteratively as facts in waiting by policymakers, the press, and by the public).

Consider also that there is no section in the *Review* on the rights and protections that may be needed to encourage and support the development of the fourth industrial revolution and the preferred skillsets. There is no section on the challenges and issues of employment from the point of view of workers as people at all. There is no consideration of the possible pitfalls and harms rather than benefits of IDT and new work technologies. For example, the use of wearables and self-tracking technologies (WSTT) are now making it possible to link and monitor the whole of a person's life in the context of work. Though positioned as a means to enhance well-being and profitability (well-billing in a "resilient" economy of "agile" business), biometrics and sociometrics are just as capable of being sources of (self) disciplining and oppressive behaviour (see Moore, 2018; Moore & Piwek, 2017; Lazega, 2015; Bloomfield & Dale, 2015). This is not unthinkable once people are subject to algorithms and aware that they are in competition with technologies that can replace them. The scandal created by Amazon's inhuman standards for warehouse package retrieval systems is a primitive precursor of this potential.

Of course, one might respond that these are not meaningful omissions but rather separate issues that can and should be dealt with elsewhere. This tacitly assumes they are additional rather than integral, the reverse of which is to suggest that systems as are will in the main deal with them, but what systems are those? In what sense are the institutional dynamics of work for workers irrelevant to how they then engage and what they do? More importantly, the absence of engagement is itself positioned. In a subsection entitled "There is no alternative", the *Review* states:

> As the UK exits the EU and becomes fully exposed to the competitive pressures of the free market, companies will need to focus on productivity to survive. If businesses are unable to stand on their own two feet they will fail, risking entire factories and industry related supply chains and services.

Therefore, the greatest threat to employment is not automation but an inability to remain competitive.

(Maier, 2017: 55)

This echoes the theme of "competitive threats" in the *Review* (see also "global race", Maier, 2017: 40) as well as a broader global competition narrative promoted by the World Economic Forum and by McKinsey:

The problem is not that we're automating so quickly that we're going to put people out of jobs. The problem is that we need to automate more quickly to get the kind of benefits in productivity and in our standard of living that we would like to enjoy.

(Katy George, McKinsey senior partner)[22]

This "no alternative" is problematic. It may be the case that fourth industrial revolution technologies are "coming", but in what form and based on what context is still at issue. The "greatest threat to employment" is "competition" does not mean that competing well *will* secure employment; these *may* be related but they are not the same and evidence of past tendencies is no guarantor of future outcomes. More generally, it may be the case that fourth industrial revolution technologies have the potential to be beneficial in many ways, but it does not follow that they will be if we fail to think about the principles and institutions that ought to shape that investment, and this is about more than just work.

To be clear, it is not that alternatives and contexts go unrecognised, it is that the core emphasis makes them further or residual concerns. More optimistically, this problem is recognised in the UK in a recent House of Lords Select Committee on Artificial Intelligence report:

The UK must seek to actively shape AI's development and utilization [and this must include ethical and social aspects as also economic issues] or risk passively acquiescing to its many likely consequences . . . [but] for the time being there is still a lack of clarity as to how AI can best be used to benefit individuals and society.

(SCAI, 2018: 7; see also Naastepad & Mulder, 2018)

As yet, however, recognition has not resulted in any clear sign of a shift away from "no alternative" imperatives, where a narrow sense of the economic dominates. This is important.

---

22 See www.mckinsey.com/global-themes/future-of-organizations-and-work/the-digital-future-of-work-policy-implications-of-automation/. It is odd that decent work does not seem to count as a "standard" of living and implicit background themes such as work-life balance rely on a language construction that seems to accept that life begins where work ends (work is a disutility or opportunity cost of leisure and so forth).

A "no alternative" approach seems to imply that a marketplace of rapid unrestricted investment in a world of disruptive technologies and competition will result in the benefits "we would like to enjoy". And yet competition may be about ownership of technologies and systems in ways that control or limit competition (no market is "free"). Are nations going to be in competition to host firms who will be in a position to decide who benefits and how? If one looks beyond the UK Industrial Strategy, then the issues here are increasingly high profile (Cambridge Analytica etc.). And yet a "no alternative" position is essentially acquiescence to a policy environment we might want to approach with more caution. It encourages a concept of the economy as a separate technical sphere. It encourages a reactive approach to economic problems such as exploitation, an approach that first allows actors to become powerful and then must contest their power. As such, a "there is no alternative" position embeds power relations and perspectives. It tacitly peripheralises or closes down broader discussion of the social dynamics and goals we apply to fourth industrial revolution technologies that could inform the *potentials* (including the scope in SCAI, 2018). It privileges dominant actors without them necessarily having to be named. This is a variant of the well-worn theme of "do not stand in the way of progress", a theme that captures the future on behalf of those who command the vagaries of "progress". This leads to a final context in which we might consider how alternatives are positioned.

Reference to economic concepts is relatively sparse in the *Review*, but standard economic logic and some use of economic language is basic to the text. The *Review* recommendations are stated as a response to "market failure" in the sense of a failure of industry to self-organise a coherent network to support and facilitate the adoption and development of IDT. However, this is not a market failure. It is not the purpose of market activity for each individual firm to facilitate a network of others that constitutes the sum of an industry (or an economy). This has more in common with activity in command economies or state-controlled monopolies, but these are clearly not what the *Review* has in mind, and there is no regular capitalist market structure in which the emergent principle of organisation and interaction is the mutual benefit of all based on transparent knowledge sharing. So, the recommendations are not a correction of a "market failure" but rather highlight a failure of markets, and that is subtly different. One might read the *Review* as instead proposing an institutional hybrid or encouraging entirely different principles that seem more akin to public welfare or the commons. And yet the phrasing of the *Review* is oddly conservative. The phrasing goes no further than "public-private partnership" (terminology that already carries many negative connotations through past failures), and it is the traditional concept of the firm which is to the fore (embracing both SMEs and large corporations equally as though the issues arising were the same). Arguably, the thinking here is unimaginative.

The technological orientation of the *Review* may be twenty-first century, but the articulation of potentials and the challenges for an economy are not. This is most notable in relation to the environmental problem. The *Review* makes much of the claim that there can be productivity and efficiency gains as well as new environmental management sectors. Obviously, this is a good thing. However, the "cutting edge" of global *policy* debate now is concerned with future economies that incorporate circular manufacturing processes, place limits to growth at their core and are regenerative *by design*. This is a stronger claim to what is desirable and necessary, creating first principles around which all aspects of industrial strategy and IDT are organised. Whilst the *Review* encompasses environmental awareness as well as circular systems, it does little to suggest just how central an issue this is becoming, especially the problem of economic growth. The *Review* places ecosystem construction at its heart but not ecological principles, and this raises the basic issue of what it means to provide "effective leadership".

If there is a "no alternative" emerging in the twenty-first century, it is not the one stated in the *Review*; it is the civilisational challenge of climate change and environmental destruction. This final point seems to have taken us some way from where we began this section. But this is not so. The *Review* illustrates how the future is being colonised, and I suggested this included issues centred on whether it is realistic and realisable, as well as in terms of what it emphasises, peripheralises and omits. The ultimate context missing here is democratic and deliberative. The fourth industrial revolution is being positioned as a form of enhanced business as usual, which seems quite odd. In so doing it neither treats nor engages the populous as fully realised, active, reflexive agents. One might, in the case of the *Review*, counter that this does not speak to the purpose of problem-solving policy. But if we are talking about something as basic and profound in its implications as the fourth industrial revolution is supposed to be, then perhaps it should. Perhaps there are prior questions to ask and a wider societal debate is required to frame the future.

Conclusion

Many grand and headline-grabbing claims are currently being made regarding the near future and a fourth industrial revolution. It is important to approach these with caution. There are many fundamental technological changes occurring, and these create potentials, not least in regard of work. However, potentials are not fate and the future is not destiny. There is a manifest need to look carefully at how the future is being colonised through claims, and to consider what is emphasised, peripheralised and omitted. It should be clear from the material set out in this chapter that there are question marks against most of the claims being made and good reasons to consider how the future is being colonised from other and multiple points of view. This, as should also be clear, holds even if one takes a more instrumental approach to policy and focuses narrowly on what is "effective". Fundamentally, the future remains open and it is incumbent on us all to be informed and to participate in the future we are going to share. As in Volume I, this brings us back to a more self-consciously political approach to economy and a social ontology that begins from what kind of entity we are and how we flourish (Al-Amoudi & Morgan, 2018).

References

Al-Amoudi, I. (2018). Review: Homo Deus by Yuval Noah Harari. *Organization Studies*, 39(7): 995–1002.

Al-Amoudi, I., & Morgan, J. (Eds.). (2018). *Realist Responses to Post-Human Society: Ex Machina*. London: Routledge.

Archer, M. (1995). *Realist Social Theory: The Morphogenetic Approach*. Cambridge: Cambridge University Press.

Archer, M. (2018). Bodies, persons and human enhancement: Why these distinctions matter. In I. Al-Amoudi & J. Morgan (Eds.), *Realist Responses to Post-Human Society: Ex Machina*. London: Routledge.

Arntz, M., Gregory, T., & Zierahn, U. (2016). The risk of automation for jobs in OECD countries: A comparative analysis. In *OECD Social, Employment and Migration Working Papers* 189. Paris: OECD Publishing.

Bakhshi, H., Downing, J., Osborne, M., & Schneider, P. (2017). *The Future of Skills: Employment in 2030*. London: Pearson and Nesta.

Bloomfield, B., & Dale, K. (2015). Fit for work? Redefining normal and 'extreme' through human enhancement technologies. *Organization*, 22(4): 552–569.

CfA. (2017, July). *Google Transparency Project Campaign for Accountability*. Google Academics Inc.

Clark, T., & Fincham, R. (Eds.). (2002). *Critical Consulting: New Perspectives on the Management Advice Industry*. Oxford: Oxford University Press.

DBEIS, Department for Business, Energy and Industrial Strategy. (2017). *Industrial Strategy: Building a Britain Fit for the Future*. White Paper, November, HM Government.

DDCMS, Department for Digital, Culture, Media and Sport. (2017). *UK Digital Strategy 2017*. Policy Paper, March, HM Government.

Deloitte. (2018). *Power up: UK Skills*. London: Deloitte LLP.

Donati, P. (2018). Transcending the human: Why, where, and how? In I. Al-Amoudi & J. Morgan (Eds.), *Realist Responses to Post-Human Society: Ex Machina*. London: Routledge.

Frey, C., & Osborne, M. (2013, September 17). *The Future of Employment: How Susceptible Are Jobs to Computerisation?* Paper, Machines and Employment Workshop.

Fullbrook, E. (2017). Unemployment: Misinformation in public discourse and its contribution to Trump's populist discourse. In E. Fullbrook & J. Morgan (Eds.), *Trumponomics: Causes and Consequences* (pp. 239–245). London: WEA Books.

George, D., Lehrach, W., Kansky, K., Lazaro-Gredilla, M., Laan, C., Marthi, B., ... Phoenix, D. (2017). A generative vision model that trains with high data efficiency and breaks text-based CAPTCHAs. *Science*, 358(6368).

Gu, C., Sun, C., Ross, D., Vondrick, C., Pantofaru, C., Li, Y., ... Malik, J. (2017). *AVA: A Video Dataset of Spatio-temporally Localized Atomic Visual Actions*. Open source at arXiv. Available online: https://arxiv.org/abs/1705.08421

Haldane, A. (2015, November 12). *Labour's Share*. Bank of England, Speech to Trade Union Congress, London.

Harari, Y. N. (2017). *Homo Deus*. London: Vintage.

IFR. (2017a, April). *The Impact of Robots on Productivity, Employment and Jobs*. Position Paper. Frankfurt: International Federation of Robotics.

IFR. (2017b). *Executive Summary, World Robotics 2017: Industrial Robots*. Frankfurt: International Federation of Robotics.

IFR. (2017c). *Executive Summary, World Robotics 2017: Service Robots*. Frankfurt: International Federation of Robotics.

Kalleberg, A. (2011). *Good Jobs, Bad Jobs: The Rise of Polarized and Precarious Job Systems in the United States 1970s-2000s*. New York, NY: Russell Foundation.

Lawrence, M., Roberts, C., & King, L. (2017, December). *Managing Automation: Employment, Inequality and Ethics in the Digital Age*. Discussion Paper, IPPR Commission on Economic Justice.

Lawson, T. (2003). *Reorienting Economics*. London: Routledge.

Lazega, E. (2015). Body captors and network profiles: A neo-structural note on digitalized social control and morphogenesis. In M. Archer (Ed.), *Generative Mechanisms: Transforming the Social Order* (pp. 113–133). London: Springer.

Maier, J. (2017). *Chair, Made Smarter Review 2017*. Department for Business, Energy and Industrial Strategy. London: HM Government.

Manyika, J., Chui, M., Madgavkar, A., & Lund, S. (2017b, January). *Technology, Jobs and the Future of Work*. San Francisco: McKinsey Global Institute.

Manyika, J., Chui, M., Miremadi, M., Bughin, J., George, K., Willmott, P., & Dewhurst, M. (2017a, January). *A Future That Works: Automation, Employment and Productivity*. San Francisco: McKinsey Global Institute.

Miriyev, A., Stack, K., & Lipson, H. (2017). Soft material for soft actuators. *Nature Communications*, 8(596): 1–7.

Moore, P. (2018). *The Quantified Self in Precarity: Work, Technology and What Counts*. London: Routledge.

Moore, P., & Piwek, L. (2017). Regulating wellbeing in the brave new quantified workplace. *Employee Relations*, 39(3): 308–316.

Morgan, J. (2013). Forward-looking contrast explanation, illustrated using the Great Moderation. *Cambridge Journal of Economics*, 37(4): 737–758.

Morgan, J. (2018). Yesterday's tomorrow today: Turing, Searle and the contested significance of Artificial Intelligence. In I. Al-Amoudi & J. Morgan (Eds.), *Realist Responses to Post-Humanist Society: Ex Machina*. London: Routledge.

Morgan, J., & Patomäki, H. (2017). Contrast explanation in economics: Its context, meaning, and potential. *Cambridge Journal of Economics*, 41(5): 1391–1418.

Naastepad, J., & Mulder, J. (2018). Robots and us: Towards an economics of the 'good life'. *Review of Social Economy*, 76(3): 302–334.

Porpora, D. V. (2018). Vulcans, Klingons, and humans: What does Humanism encompass? In I. Al-Amoudi & J. Morgan (Eds.), *Realist Responses to Post-Human Society: Ex Machina*. London: Routledge.

SCAI, House of Lords Select Committee on Artificial Intelligence. (2018, April). *AI in the UK: Ready Willing and Able*. Report of Session 2017–19. London: HM Government.

Schwab, K. (2016). *The Fourth Industrial Revolution*. Geneva: World Economic Forum.

Seabrooke, L., & Henrikson, L. (Eds.). (2017). *Transnational Networks in Transnational Governance*. Cambridge: Cambridge University Press.

Tegmark, M. (2017). *Life 3.0*. London: Allen Lane.

World Economic Forum. (2015). *Deep Shift: Technology Tipping Points and Societal Impact*. Geneva: World Economic Forum.

World Economic Forum. (2016). *The Future of Jobs: Employment, Skills and Workforce Strategy for the Fourth Industrial Revolution*. Geneva: World Economic Forum.

7 Anormative black boxes

Artificial intelligence and health policy

Ismael Al-Amoudi and John Latsis

Anyone reading the news in 2018 will be aware of the imminent arrival of artificial intelligence (AI) in everyday life. From the workplace (Boston Consulting Group, 2017) to the bedroom (Harari, 2016) and from the kitchen (Ibid.) to the local council (Ibid.), AI is expected to transform in depth the way we work, choose romantic partners, purchase and consume goods, and participate in public life.

Numerous reports on AI address, with differing levels of depth, the economic and social implications of AI. For instance, debates have emerged as to whether, and where, AI-driven automation is likely to create more jobs than it destroys (Frey & Osborne, 2013; for a discussion, see also International Federation or Robotics, 2017).

More recently, critical voices have highlighted the fact that AI cannot explain how it reaches decisions (AI Now, 2018). Whilst it already produces results that surpass human capacities in many fields, the specific process through which AI reaches each decision is often described as unaccountable. AI algorithms, while following relatively simple principles and using backward propagation, also generate remarkably lengthy and complex calculations that are extremely difficult to audit, discuss or criticise meaningfully (AI Now, 2018; but see also the nascent attempts at self-justifying algorithms by Park et al., 2016). Equally problematically, AI, as we know it in 2018, involves categorisations that are fundamentally disconnected from human sense-making. To all intents and purposes, AI operates as a black box: while we can know its inputs and its outputs, we cannot fully make sense of its internal workings.

The present chapter takes a lead from the previous reflections on AI, but it also asks a question that we have not come across elsewhere: How will the introduction of AI affect our communities' capacity to discuss, challenge and decide on the norms governing health policy?

We believe the question we ask is important for at least two reasons. Firstly, it matters to readers interested in the normative dimension of AI. Indeed, the black-boxing inherent to AI is all the more problematic whenever complex ethical questions are raised. As long as the role of artificial decision making is deemed to be instrumental, where the objective is to render an established process more efficient, then the adoption of an expert system such as AI can be relatively unproblematic and promote human welfare. The matter is different, however, when AI is employed to take decisions that involve complex normative considerations. Indeed, we know since Wittgenstein's *Philosophical Investigations* (Wittgenstein, 2000) that no set of rules, however extensively defined, can define the totality of cases in which those rules should be respected, or suspended, or superseded (see Latsis, 2005, on exemplars, and Al-Amoudi, 2010, on immanent rules). Normative decisions are therefore fundamentally open to (myriad) interpretations and yet, to be normatively binding, there must be some commonly agreed way of resolving differences of interpretation within the communities where they apply (Boltanski & Thevenot, 2006; Habermas, 1990; Rawls, 2001). The fact that AI operates as a normative black box generates a puzzle: how can AI reach normatively binding decisions if the latter cannot be discussed, justified, criticised and compromised upon by the people affected by its decisions? By addressing this question, we hope to make a contribution to the ethics of AI as we know it.

But our chapter is also of interest to readers preoccupied with the fairness of health policy. Rather than address the problem of normative black boxes in general, we have chosen to focus our discussion on AI developments likely to transform health policy. The latter is defined in broad terms. These include the direct provision of healthcare services by states through national organisations such as the British National Health Service (NHS); the regulation of mandatory health insurance; and the prioritisation of certain patient categories, drugs and treatments by supervisory bodies such as the British NICE (National Institute of Clinical Excellence) and the French HAS (Haute Autorité de Santé). But the expression 'health policy' also encompasses public health information campaigns on such topics as flu vaccination, smoking addiction, safe(r) sex, and so forth. Finally, though they are not strictly part of health policy, we also discuss the entwined strategies of for-profit actors such as private insurers determining optimal actuarial policy or pharmaceutical companies deciding which drugs they will produce and how they will market them.

Our chapter is structured as follows. We start by providing an overview of the basic processes through which AI operates. We then examine how the practices of health policy have started to be disrupted by the introduction of AI. Doing so allows us to identify and discuss the novel normative problems arising from AI's bearing on public health policy's practices. In the last section, we speculate on the future. To do so, we reflect on how current developments could lead, through gradual social morphogenesis, to an undesirable outcome; but we also identify strategic themes of struggle for those wishing to shape a different future.

Artificial intelligence, deep machine learning and neural networks

Since we are not computer scientists, we felt vulnerable to spectacular and ill-founded popular science claims about AI. One of us has therefore attempted to learn rudimentary deep machine learning by following step-by-step the operations of a programme that teaches a home computer how to recognise handwritten digits. In doing so, our purpose was both to clarify the internal operations of deep machine learning and to get a sounder grasp on what can, and cannot, be expected from AI as we currently know it.

The programme we have studied relies on principles that were developed about half a century ago. However, while deep machine learning has known many developments since then, the basic principles remain unchanged (3Blue1Brown, 2017). Most refinements since the pioneering theoretical works concern either the application of deep machine learning to novel applications (e.g. playing Go or recommending books) or improved processes of optimisation in contexts characterised by scarce examples and/or limited computing power. It is our understanding, however, that our example's architecture and basic principles remain unchanged in contemporary AI applications. We start our description with the first (input) layer of neurons. We then describe the last (output) layer of neurons, before describing the middle neural strata that connect the first and last layers.

The first layer of neurons: input vector

The deep machine learning programme we examine is structured as a neural network that consists of several layers of neurons. The latter are quite simply placeholders for a value typically comprised between 0 and 1. These placeholders are called neurons because, like biological neurons, they are connected to one another through connections that may be stronger or weaker and that evolve throughout the learning process.

AI programmers usually distinguish between three types of layers of neurons. In the programme that serves as an illustration in the present section, the machine is taught how to recognise a handwritten digit that was scanned on a 28*28 pixel cell. The information contained in the 28*28 pixel cell can be converted into an input vector of 784 values (28*28=784), each comprised of between 0 and 1. Each pixel on the scanned image corresponds to one and only one value in the input vector; the darker the pixel, the closer its associated value to 1.

The last layer of neurons: output classification

The last layer of neurons corresponds to the machine's output classification. Each neuron holds a value comprised of between 0 and 1, and each neuron corresponds to one of the possible classifications for the input vector. In our example, the last layer of neurons would thus consist of ten neurons corresponding to the numerals 0–9. At the end of the learning process, we want the programme to correctly qualify the input vector by assigning a value close to 1 to the neuron corresponding to the image's correct classification and values close to 0 for all other nine neurons.

At the start of the learning process, the machine generates random classifications. However, the point of the deep learning process is to gradually amend the connections between the first and the last layers of neurons so as to improve the programme's capacity to adequately qualify handwritten digits. To understand how this is achieved, we must first understand the structure of the mid-layers of neurons as well as the mechanism of backwards propagation through which the links between neural strata are improved as the machine 'learns'.

The middle neural strata: connecting input and output

The middle neural strata comprise several layers of neurons (six in our example). At the start of the learning process, the value of each neuron in every layer (except the first input vector) is calculated as a function of each neuron in the preceding layer. In simple informal terms, the idea is that the value of each neuron is calculated as a function of the values of preceding layers. However, not all neurons carry equal weight, and some neurons influence the values of the rest of the network more than others.

A more formal mathematical proceedure consists in creating and then refining a functional relation between each given neuron (after the first stratum) and all the neurons in the preceding stratum. So, if Vx,y designates the value of the xth neuron in the yth layer, and if Wx,y designates the weight attributed to that same neuron, then a typical functional relation could be: $Vx,y = \delta\ (\Sigma Wi,y - 1.Vi,y - 1)$

Note that we have used a sigmoid function because we wanted to keep all neurons' values between 0 and 1 while remaining able to perform basic calculus in the backward propagation phase that follows.

Note too that at the start of the learning process, the weights Wi,j are distributed randomly. However, as the neural network is trained, these weights will be gradually adjusted so as to generate increasingly reliable classifications in the last layer.

Backward propagation

On its first run, the machine is likely to generate a very unreliable classification. For instance, when shown a written "7" it might attribute relatively high values to the neurons in the last layer corresponding to "0" and "8" while attributing a relatively insignificant value to the neuron corresponding to "7". But it is possible to build on this erroneous classification to marginally enhance the network's classificatory ability, a process known as backward propagation.

To do so, the programme compares the machine's output with an ideal classification provided by a human agent. So, in the case of a handwritten "7", the ideal classification would be the vector [0,0,0,0,0,0,0,1,0,0].[1] Backward propagation consists in marginally modifying the weights associated with each layer of neurons in the mid-layers so as to reduce the difference between the computed and ideal solutions in the subsequent iteration.

To our surprise, backward propagation involved relatively simple mathematics (basic calculus, linear algebra, the sigma function) that we had covered while studying social and economic sciences many moons ago. Overall, through thousands of try/miss/correct iterations on thousands of handwritten digits, the simple

1 Following mathematical convention, we rank digits starting from zero: 0, 1, 2, 3, 4, 5, 6, 7, 8, 9.

programme that we followed can, according to its designers, reach a reliability rate of 95%, enough to make it useful for many an application.

General remarks on deep machine learning

Our illustrative example allows us to draw a number of important practical and philosophical remarks on deep machine learning. In practice, the programming of deep machine learning is less difficult to achieve than the provision of the thousands of adequately qualified exemplars that are used to compare and gradually improve the neural network's estimates.

It is for this reason that we could not ourselves test the claim by the programme's designers about the reliability rate of the programme we followed step-by-step. This shortcoming points to a more general practical challenge, as it is exceedingly difficult for third parties, especially individuals, to assess the claims made by AI manufacturers and providers.

It is also because providing exemplars can be costly that there exists a synergy between deep machine learning and big data. The latter supplies exemplary qualifications that can be collected from medical records (e.g. radiographies qualified by a competent pathologist), from Facebook accounts (remember the last time someone tagged you on a picture) and, more generally, from any form filled by the user and available to the data scientists.

Beyond the practical and contingent synergy with big data, we can also draw a number of philosophical considerations of import for our reflection on public health policy. Ontologically, the machine operates in a lifeworld composed of 10 digits. There is no room for pi, or even for a 12 or a 3.5. Moreover, the expressions 'intelligence' and 'learning' are at best loose metaphors and are more restricted than in everyday parlance.[2] If shown seven objects, the AI would be incapable, without further ad hoc programming, to infer a 7. All it can do is infer a digit (between 0 and 9) resembling somewhat the picture of the seven objects.

But even the notion of 'resemblance' is misleading because the way the programme qualifies images is radically different from human sense-making. For instance, a human being might recognise a handwritten "7" on the basis of the picture containing two lines forming an angle on the upper right corner. One may add that the upper line is short and horizontal while the lower line is longer and at an acute angle. The machine, however, 'recognises' a "7" because after many iterations, the network's weights are so fine-tuned as to associate a value close to 1 to the output neuron corresponding to "7" and values close to 0 to the nine other output neurons. While the machine simulates intelligence, it is not properly intelligent (for a full development of this point, see Morgan, 2018). Artificial

---

2 We do not contest that the human brain may work in a way that is physically and functionally similar to the neural net. However, even if this is the case, we cannot deduce similarity at the level of human thought from similarity at this functional level. For a discussion of the role of so-called 'qualia' in the philosophy of mind, see Chalmers (1996).

intelligence, as we know it, operates as a black box whose outputs can be known but never justified. This is so because the machine's operations, while painstakingly traceable, are disconnected from human sense-making. When confronted with a "7" wrongly qualified as a "1", we can't expect a justification of the kind: 'The upper line was very short and not quite horizontal while the lower line was quite vertical, so I read a one instead of a seven. Sorry!' At most, an external observer auditing the AI will be able to retrace how the initially arbitrary weights associated to each mid-layer in the neural network have been gradually modified. Yet, doing so tells us nothing about the cultural conventions according to which the categorisation can be justified within a human community.

Although AI is (currently) incapable of providing justifications that are understandable by human beings, the process of machine learning is highly dependent on human categorisation. In the case of digit recognition, the process necessitates a large library of handwritten digits associated with their ideal classification. The constitution of such a library necessitated as many acts of human classification as there are images, and this leads to the practical difficulties mentioned previously. But reliance on ex ante human labelling also raises a number of theoretical issues. The process of categorisation does not tolerate ambiguity: for every image, there must be one and only one suitable category into which it fits, independently of context. This technical limitation, we will argue in a later section, runs against phronetic conceptions of healthcare ethics. More fundamentally, the process of categorisation is dogmatic rather than dialectical. The human agent is deemed to know infallibly, and no room is left for a fusion of horizons of understanding (Gadamer, 1997). This limitation, we will argue in a later section, enshrines the values used in past decision making, which is very conservative, unreflective and risks reproducing unjustifiable societal prejudices. It also excludes machine-generated decisions from well-ordered public debate as it impedes justification, critique and compromise.

Normative black boxes

To recap, deep machine learning, as we know it, operates as a black box: we can know its inputs and outputs but if we ask how outputs are generated, we will not find justifications that would be acceptable or could even be discussed within a human community.

This is all the more problematic when AI's decisions bear on normative questions of justice rather than instrumental questions of expediency. When the sole purpose of AI is to improve expediency, it remains possible to compare the results achieved by the machine with results otherwise achieved by human decision making. We encounter a problem, however, when the decisions entrusted to AI involve normative considerations. Whenever AI operates as a normative black box, its decisions cannot be evaluated purely in terms of achieved efficiencies. AI's normative decisions must also be evaluated, through public discussion, on the face of its congruence with principles and values shared within the human community affected by its decisions. Unfortunately, our discussion so far indicates that AI's decisions are immune to public discussion, critique and compromise.

In the remainder of the chapter, we scrutinise how deep machine learning could transform health policy; and we anticipate the novel normative problems that can emerge as a consequence.

How deep machine learning transforms health policy

In this section, we take stock of how AI is transforming health policy. In particular, we examine how AI has already started to transform national health systems, but also public health campaigns and the practices of for-profit organisations.

How AI transforms national health systems

We have seen in the previous section that deep machine learning needs a large number of qualified examples. Since these are generally costly to generate, we can witness a contingent synergy with big data. The implementation of AI in national health systems follows a similar trend. In the UK where we are based, millions of British patient records are being analysed by Google's Deep Mind and IBM's Watson – the technologies behind the programmes that won spectacular victories against human Go and chess champions. Full medical records of millions of patients have been scanned, coded and added into an immense library destined to feed future AIs.

But what are future AIs expected to do with the millions of hospital records they have been fed? At the level of the hospital, a common expectation is that AI will provide an enormous range of cheaper solutions: from automated diagnosis to efficient bed allocation,[3] management of operating theatres, and even automated treatment for some conditions. AIs have already demonstrated their usefulness in the domain of medical imagery (Harari, 2016: 315–317). Two specific areas are the analysis of X-ray images, where AI programmes have rapidly become equivalent to or more accurate in terms of interpreting results than all but the best human radiologists (Jha & Topol, 2016); and skin cancer diagnosis, where Sebastian Thrun's AI programme developed at Stanford University outperformed the vast majority of dermatologists in correctly identifying malignant skin cancers from photographs (Esteva et al., 2017). Moreover, as we write, hospitals in the UK and in the USA are experimenting with entrusting the coordination of various specialists' interventions on each patient to AI expert systems (Miliard, 2018). Doing so seems all the more relevant in organisational contexts characterised by high pressure on rotating teams of health professionals. AI is expected to make coordination around a patient both more reliable and cheaper as bureaucracy is automated and interaction costs are minimised.

Finally, some medical practitioners are currently testing AI programmes that issue suggestions regarding plausible diagnoses, but also likely prognoses and

---

3 The seemingly technical problem of bed allocation supposes eminently normative decisions regarding the principles of allocation. E.g. first come first served vs. economic contribution to hospital vs. expected quality of life years ahead etc.

possible treatments (Burgess, 2018). This is a much more controversial area because of the crucial role of medical judgment in treatment decisions and the fact that many hospitals operate with standard treatment procedures (called protocols) that are linked to various regulatory and insurance-related considerations. As we write, the recommendations issued by AIs are not (yet) considered binding for medical practitioners and the legal issues that this would raise have not been faced.

What this brief discussion shows is that, where the adoption of AI has shown promise, it has been used as an 'expert system' which either coordinates logistically complex processes (hospital management), or checks results against a predefined and well-understood 'objective' criterion (imagery diagnosis). Here we return to our previous point about AI and big data: for AI to work in the medical field it seems that it requires a pre-existing standardised procedure, and a huge database of readily analysable information that is not likely to suffer from inherent human bias. To take the previous example of skin cancer diagnosis: the AI could be trained up on a database of patient data where the final diagnosis had been confirmed and the patients' health outcome was known. In this way, the system was able to 'learn' from the huge number of cases available (many more than any human doctor could see) and quickly attain a level of expertise that competed with the best professionals. This is what we mean by an expert system: one that renders more efficient and comprehensive a predefined process that has clear and relatively simple success criteria.

But the applications of AI within national health systems extend beyond the confines of clinics or hospitals. They can also bear on health policies affecting whole countries or economic zones (such as the European Union). In particular, we can reasonably expect AI to influence how public subsidies are distributed. For instance, AI might be able to help decide which treatment ought to be covered by the welfare state, and for which patients. Indeed, some elements of healthcare provision have already been semi-automated without the use of AI. To give a simple example: the use of Quality Adjusted Life Years or QALYs (see Batifoulier, Braddock, & Latsis, 2013) removes a key element of medical judgment by imposing a standardised limit on the amount of money that can be spent by the state to extend a human life. Embedded in the function used to calculate QALYs are various assumptions about the relative worth of human lives based on age, disability and underlying health conditions. This function will then have a direct impact on the treatment options available to patients in different categories, which might (and often do) differ from the treatment decisions that a doctor acting purely in accordance with the Hippocratic oath would normally apply.[4]

---

4 We are not asserting either the infallibility of doctors or that state resources are unlimited here. However, we are pointing out that the key role of medical judgment in the distribution of healthcare has already been attenuated, which makes its full replacement by an expert system much more capable of being envisaged.

How AI transforms public health campaigns

The influence of AI on public health is likely to extend beyond the provision of resources and services. The combination of AI and big data has already started to affect patients' practices, habits and even their tastes and personal choices.

Over the 20th century, propaganda has evolved from mass messages directed to a presumably uniform public to more targeted messages directed to segments of the population. Moreover, campaigns are also becoming more subtle and insidious. Thaler and Sunstein's 'nudge theory' (2009) provides both a historical testimony and an economic theorisation of this phenomenon. Their thesis is that people do not behave in a consistently rational way. Rather, people's decisions can be significantly influenced by nudging them. In Thaler and Sunstein's work, nudging consists of addressing light but well-tailored incentives to people so as to transform their behaviours, attitudes and even beliefs about a defined topic.

Nudging can take many forms and may act through a variety of psycho-social and technological mechanisms. For instance, successful nudging can be achieved by addressing messages tailored to potential patients' specific situation (one of the principal advocates of nudging in public policy and a former advisor to British Prime Minister David Cameron is the health economist Paul Dolan). For a low-tech example, think of anti-abortion posters hanging on sexual health clinics' walls.

But nudging can also be achieved by transforming people's choice architecture (Thaler & Sunstein, 2009). The latter refers to the breaking down and ordering of a large, complex, decision into smaller and seemingly simpler decisions. One of behavioural economics' key arguments since it began in the 1970s is that, while choice architecture is in principle irrelevant for perfectly rational agents, it is highly relevant for real people. Through smart organisation of the choice architecture proposed to people, it is possible to influence their choices without their realising it. As Thaler put it about organ donation campaigns:

> In the world of traditional economics, it shouldn't matter whether you use an opt-in or opt-out system. So long as the costs of registering as a donor or a nondonor are low, the results should be similar. But many findings of behavioral economics show that tiny disparities in such rules can make a big difference. By comparing the consent rates in European countries, the psychologists Eric Johnson and Dan Goldstein have shown that the choice of opting in or opting out is a major factor. Consider the difference in consent rates between two similar countries, Austria and Germany. In Germany, which uses an opt-in system, only 12 percent give their consent; in Austria, which uses opt-out, nearly everyone (99 percent) does.
>
> (Thaler, 2009)

But the combination of AI and big data now allows for an unprecedented level of personalisation. Both the choice architecture through which we make decisions and the nudging messages we receive could be fine-tuned for each of us by taking into account all the clues left by our use of internet navigation, but also by the messages we post on social media and our (digitised) health and administrative records.

How AI transforms corporate practices

The combination of AI and big data has also started to interest a number of for-profit actors in the health sector. In particular, private insurers have started to propose personalised plans to their customers on the condition that the latter exercise regularly. These plans allow customers to benefit from particularly attractive rates, but at the cost of intensified monitoring powered by AI and big data. Thus, some customers of the Swiss Insurer Helsana who want to benefit from a personalised plan's advantages agreed to accept to have their physical activity monitored by the insurer through a pedometer embedded in their mobile phones. This approach has been challenged in the Swiss federal courts on the basis that it could lead to variable pricing that discriminates against those who do not wish to share data, or to reduce insurance premiums for certain individuals below the legal minimum mandated by the state (Guillaume, 2017). There are also more general ethical concerns about the type and amount of personal data that could be used to single out individuals for special treatment.

The activity of customers on personalised plans can also be monitored and analysed through automated information exchange with the fitness clubs where they train on a regular basis (and which also avidly collect their data), or collaborations with the major internet companies, whose applications collect relevant data through health apps that are increasingly fitted as standard to new smartphones and smartwatches. In the future, we can expect these trends to intensify. As already mentioned, insurers could offer selected patients cheaper rates in exchange for fuller access to their medical records, but also their bank accounts (How many rounds in the pub?) and their email and Facebook accounts (Is their lifestyle healthy? Are they complaining of ailments?). The purpose of such monitoring is to build, automatically and in real time (and possibly without consent), a profile of customers' lifestyles and associated risks that can feed into actuarial estimates.

However, insurance companies are by no means the only type of for-profit actors interested in AI's public health applications. As of 2018, five of the world's largest firms (Amazon, Apple, Facebook, Google and IBM) own the lion's share of investments in AI and big data. They also dominate the scene regarding expected profits and influence over future AI developments. Yet there are a myriad of much smaller AI firms, often financially backed by venture capital and private equity, that are positioned at various stages of the 'medtech' and health technology value chain. While some of these actors develop highly specialised open-source modules, most are profit-driven and either act as subcontractors to larger firms, or try to build their business to a sufficient size to make it a takeover target. In business strategy terms, AI constitutes a relatively new high risk/high return market,[5] and

---

5 It might be objected that with well-developed databases investment in this area would be relatively low risk and high return. In reality, however, investment tends to be speculative and targets early stage companies. The quality of their databases and algorithms is extremely difficult to assess before they have been widely adopted. The expansion of the internet giants such as Apple and Google into healthcare is a much less risky endeavour, but this type of investment is generally done in-house.

there is a corresponding growth in the number of specialised funds that deploy private capital to buy AI-related start-ups, products and algorithms.

Our brief overview of how AI attracts commercial interest would be severely limited if we did not mention the growing influence of China in this area. While the firms we have mentioned so far are based in Europe and the USA, the Chinese government has announced its intent to lead the arms race to AI (Cyranoski, 2018). This declaration and others are substantiated by the gargantuan amounts of funding reserved to research in this domain and the advances of medtech firms in China itself. Such funding seems to have started to generate results, as in 2017 China has caught up with the USA in terms of AI-related patents applications (Huang, 2018). This rapid development is partly a function of the availability of data in a country where mobile (as opposed to laptop or desktop computer) penetration is very high, consumer trends tend to be technology-driven and individual concern for privacy is limited compared to Europe and the United States. However, the buoyancy of AI in countries that have feeble democratic traditions also indicates the potential for further normative problems. In the following section we move from discussing the challenge of AI at the highest level of generality to analysing the effects of AI in the specific case of health policy, where a number of serious normative problems arise.

Normative problems

We argued in the previous section that the combination of AI and big data has already started to transform key practices of significance to public health policy. However, such spectacular changes of practices also bring implicit and unspectacular, yet wide-ranging and potentially long-lasting, problems for the normative foundations on which public policy rests. We now identify normative problems concerning how AIs are trained, how their decisions are followed, and how the latter might be discussed within human communities.

When training the network obfuscates normative choices

As of spring 2018, the human element is still indispensable for deep learning. Human intervention is quite obvious in simple deep learning processes such as the one we followed in this chapter's first section. As we could see, each of the thousands of AI attempts at classification is compared and marginally improved through comparison with a classification performed by a human being. Less obvious, perhaps, are the normative assumptions that must be taken for granted for the whole process to be meaningful.

For instance, the anonymous human agent who completed the library of exemplars by performing and recording the initial categorisations is deemed to be perfectly (or at least reliably) competent. Yet, we typically know little about his/her training, his/her familiarity with the subject matter and his/her own ethical and cognitive prejudices. An obvious way around this problem is to use data sets that take the experiences of many individuals in diverse locations and of diverse backgrounds. But such data sets are rare and expensive to assemble, and the issue of data quality will always be raised. Even if a sufficiently comprehensive data set were available to the developers of an AI algorithm designed to replicate human judgment, they would still face a basic issue: their expert system will always carry an inherent conservative bias because AI algorithms are trained on historical data. Training implicitly assumes that the lessons of the past are a more or less accurate guide to the future. As we saw with the deployment of expert systems to identify skin cancers, this can work well if the data being judged is objective (a photo) and the final output (survival rate of the patient) is known. However, a larger part of health policy does not involve this type of data and has completely different objectives. In particular, the inherently normative elements of policy tend to be focussed on decisions about defining categories (Does patient x suffer from a long-term condition, illness or disability?); justifying and prioritising care (How long should a terminally ill or brain-dead patient be kept on life support?); or selecting between different treatment protocols (Should we always adopt cheaper protocols, or ones that work better with a wider array of cases?).

Moreover, as we noted in the first section, the process of exemplar categorisation excludes the possibility of ambiguity. In our example, for every handwritten digit, there is one and only one corresponding correct qualification. Yet, the world is replete with ambiguous objects that do not fit pristinely into a single category. Think for instance of a handwritten seven "7" that may seem exceedingly similar to a number one "1". Or, in the context of public health policy, think of people whose identity does not fit predefined bureaucratic categories, be these related to sex assignment (Butler, 2004) or migratory status (Zetter, 1991) or mental health (Kenny, Fotaki, & Scriver, 2018), and so on. Manipulating these categories has long been part of the strategy of corporations that sell products and treatments to healthcare providers and patients. It should be noted that the introduction and widespread use of AI could be used to bolster such manipulative strategies by giving them an additional (but undeserved) veneer of empirical reliability.

But the fact that classificatory categories are predefined, once and for all, before the start of the learning process is also problematic. The reflections of Roy Bhaskar (1978) and Tony Lawson (2009) on the progression of human knowledge can help us clarify this point. According to them, knowledge and the categories through which it is articulated progress dialectically rather than deductively or inductively. Contra deductive epistemologies, the categories we use do not remain static but are also transformed as our knowledge of any subject matter (including ethics and justice) progresses. But knowledge progression also differs from the assumptions of inductive epistemologies because knowledge and categories are not formed exclusively through astute analysis of empirical data but also depend on anterior knowledge and categories that existed prior to the discovery process.

A dialectical view of category formation supposes that at the start of the discovery process we are already equipped with (perfectible) theories and categories. The latter are refined, however, through their confrontation with inconvenient facts and arguments. This contradiction prompts in turn researchers to corroborate, amend and replace pre-existing categories and theories with novel categories and theories that provide a more consistent match with observed phenomena and convincing arguments. But while moral insights are thus formed through dialectical discussion, deep machine learning processes as we know them do not allow for continuous critique and refinement of the categories on which public policy's normative decisions are based. Human agents may accept or reject the normative decisions made by AI, but they cannot engage in discussions from which both parties learn and refine their own categories.

Our previous discussion is closely linked to the distinction between supervised and unsupervised learning in AI. Programmes that engage in supervised learning include our simple numerical example and what we have called expert systems previously: they have access to a data set of output variables that can 'teach' the algorithm to perfect itself. In stark contrast, unsupervised learning is used when an algorithm has access only to input data, but lacks corresponding output variables. The goal of this activity is to attempt to discover or model an underlying structure in data that does not appear to have any in the eyes of a human interpreter. Unlike in the case of supervised learning, this process lacks 'correct' answers and therefore lacks the 'teacher' element that is the key to supervised learning – algorithms are left 'unsupervised'. It seems clear that unsupervised learning of this sort is particularly poorly suited to problem solving with significant moral or normative content, since the machine learning algorithms lack all of the tools (empathy, experience, moral intuition amongst others) required to make qualitative judgments about the meaning and significance of patterns in the data.

When practical wisdom is eliminated

The normative problems raised by the use of AI for health policy extend beyond the neural network's training. One problem of particular significance is highlighted by the fact that health policy decisions involve a capacity for practical wisdom, aka *phronesis*, that is not trained by deep machine learning as we know it and that is therefore still lacking from AI.

Practical wisdom was succinctly characterised by Aristotle as 'a true and reasoned state of capacity to act with regard to the things that are good or bad for man' (Aristotle, 350BC: Book VI). Aristotle clarifies further the link between practical wisdom and decision making by adding that

> Pericles and men like him have practical wisdom, viz because they can see what is good for men in general; we consider that those who can do this are good at managing households or states.
>
> (Ibid.)

More recently, the importance of phronesis for sound decision making attracted the attention of management scholars. Indeed, Shotter and Tsoukas (2014) identified the value of entrusting major decisions to what they call 'phronetic leaders', that is

> people who, in their search for a way out of their difficulties, have developed a refined capacity to intuitively grasp salient features of ambiguous situations and to constitute a 'landscape' of possible paths of response, while driven by the pursuit of the notion of the common good.
>
> (Shotter & Tsoukas, 2014: 224)

Unfortunately, AI as we know it is incapable of practical reasoning of this type. Firstly, AI is endowed with a very limited capacity to contextualise data, to identify 'worthy' exceptions, and to analyse novel situations with few precedents, especially when the latter have not already been categorised as such.

Secondly, AI as we know it is also incapable of performing functions for which it has not been trained. Thus, the programme that taught itself to beat the Go world champion cannot learn to drive a car, and the programme that can drive a car cannot learn to translate human languages. This incapacity to perform functions for which the programme had not been designed is problematic when dealing with complex decisions – such as the design and implementation of health policy – that involve intertwined moral, economic, sociological and biological considerations.

Thirdly, AIs as we know them have no conception of the good. While we cannot exclude in principle the possibility of, some day, teaching a machine to simulate human notions like the common good, dignity, thriving or flourishing, this possibility still does not exist in 2018 and there are no signs that we should expect it in the foreseeable future.

Finally, notions such as 'dignity', 'the common good' and 'thriving' are open to contestation. Human communities may arrive at a shared understanding of moral principles, but the process of realising them in practice is one of critique, discussion and compromise. In human communities, this difficulty is partly alleviated by people's use of practical wisdom through which a person may invent novel ways of coping with unforeseen situations but without jettisoning the notions s/he recognises and the norms s/he respects.[6] However, although it is often necessary, the practical wisdom of individuals is usually insufficient to cope with disagreement on key notions and conventions. The process through which social activities and institutions are continuously qualified, criticised and requalified is eminently social. It entails social dynamics of justification, critique and compromise between members of the human community affected by the decisions being made

---

6 Think of the Judgment of Solomon, a proverbial example of practical wisdom in monotheistic civilisations. When two women quarrelled about a child, each one claiming to be the mother, Solomon issued a decision that surprised both contestants: he would himself cut the child in two and give a half of it to each mother. Upon hearing this, the younger woman cried that the child was the other's. Solomon (correctly) inferred that she must be the child's mother for favouring the child's life over winning the quarrel. It is still unclear whether and how deep learning processes can arrive at such an original solution in the face of such a dilemma for which there are no precedents and no formalised procedure of action.

(Boltanski & Thévenot, 2006). In health policy this has been vividly illustrated by the debate over how QALYs (Quality Adjusted Life Years) should be used in prioritisation policy, where commentators immediately pointed out the conflict between QALY-based prioritisation and many of our most basic intuitions about fairness (Nord, 1999). But can AI participate meaningfully in social processes of normative justification? This is the question we now address.

When critique and discussion are not possible between man and machine

Situations of normative conflict are an unavoidable feature of social life. Pacific solutions can more often than not be found through discussion among participants. It is key to note, however, that normative discussions involve more than mere exchange of data. They also require each discussant to accept opening their own world-view to that of others, a dialectical process studied by Gadamer (1997) and captured by his notion of a *fusion of horizons of understanding*. Other political theorists have developed their own models of the ethics of discussion (Habermas, 1990) or, more recently, of legitimate justification (Boltanski & Thévenot, 2006). In spite of differences, all share a common requirement that participants be capable of understanding one another, of amending their own views in light of others', and of holding some (perfectible) conception of the common good.

Yet the current state of AI does not allow machines to meet these requirements for democratic participation in normative debates. Humans cannot understand machines in the manner required, nor can machines understand humans. We argued in an earlier section that machine learning, as we know it, operates as a normative black box incapable of providing justifications that would be acceptable or that could even be discussed within a human community. It is so for pragmatic but also for ontological reasons. Pragmatically, the computational power needed to audit machine decisions is even greater than the already huge computational power needed to reach these decisions. This practical difficulty has been the topic of much writing on AIs as black boxes (AI Now, 2018; Park et al., 2016). But discussions between AIs and humans are also undermined by an ontological difficulty. The process of discussion supposes some 'thing' that participants discuss, in other words it presupposes a common referent. The latter may be a mind state, such as a toothache or the hope of recovery, held by at least one participant and (hermeneutically) interpreted and felt by others. In this case, the discussion process requires that all participants be capable of experiencing mind states of some kind, a condition that does not seem to be fulfilled for AI. Yet, as the illustrative example of digit recognition has shown, AIs learn to recognise digits without ever forming the concept of one. They can infer the least remote visual pattern to match the digit's shape, but they can't infer a seven from a picture of seven objects.[7]

---

7 It is of course possible to add, on an ad hoc basis, an additional programme that learns to recognise the number of discrete patterns on a picture. But even then, the machine has not learned what a digit

Three possible dynamics of justification in the face of AI decisions

As AIs are involved in health policy, new dynamics of classification and norma-tive discussion are likely to emerge. Prior to the appearance of AI, classifications were exclusively proposed by human beings, who subjected any act of classifica-tion to the possibility of critique and the imperative of justification and, whenever necessary, of compromise (Boltanski & Thévenot, 2006). However, the introduc-tion of AI acts as a game changer. AIs operate as agents who perform and propose classifications which are unjustifiable with regards to common conventions of justification. And this calls in turn for novel dynamics of categorisation. While it is historically too early to take stock (empirically) of the specific novel dynamics of categorisation that are emerging because of AI, we can nonetheless identify (speculatively) at least three possible dynamics. These dynamics are not necessar-ily exclusive of one another, and even when they are, they may coexist in different fields or in relation to different practices.

In the first dynamic, AIs are employed exclusively as heuristic devices whose input may be overwhelmed by human judgment without the need of justification. This is the role that is presently attributed to expert systems whose function is to assist decision making by making suggestions that the expert practitioner is free to ignore, and for which the AI does not provide any form of justification, other than its past track record of empirically verifiable successes. These dynamics are argu-ably the least normatively problematic of the three we can identify. But neither are they entirely unproblematic.

In practice AI often plays the role of a triage device, an efficiency measure, or both. Where the criteria for triage are clear and the data can be accurately meas-ured against those criteria, the task of the AI is simply to speed up the process of categorisation on the basis of empirically measurable standards. This leaves the human decision-maker to check and ratify the results (possibly by looking at a sample) and to deal with all the 'difficult' cases. Compliance is an area where this type of software already exists and can perform well whilst reducing the workload and cost of the legal departments of banks and financial service firms (for example). Another area where AI is beginning to be introduced is in the analysis of documentary evidence before a trial (Winick, 2017). Here the process is similar in that an appropriately trained AI can sift a much larger set of documents for relevant material than a team of humans, reducing a job that can take 360,000 man-hours to a few seconds with comparable if not better-quality results. Of course, once the documents have been searched and classified they are handed over to a human lawyer to argue the case. In both these cases, AI increases efficiency by restricting the data set and thereby narrowing the set of possible courses of action: this is essentially a power of suggestion, which one might view as relatively innocuous and always subject to human control.

---

is. It would not be capable of answering 'What digit comes after 6 and before 8?' unless another programme were added for this specific task, etc.

However, suggesting is an act of power akin to the 'nudging' identified by Thaler and Sunstein (2009).

As we have seen in our discussion of how neural networks are trained, the categorisations performed by AIs can be normatively significant, even if that is not one of the intentions of their designers. For instance, if an AI programme designed to identify skin cancer is trained on a database consisting exclusively of photographs of lesions in Caucasian patients, but is then deployed to serve a diverse population, we would not expect it to perform as well in identifying skin cancer in non-Caucasians. We could therefore expect that some of the categorisations routinely proposed by AIs qua expert systems will (and should) be contested by groups that disagree with AI classifications on grounds of unfairness or discrimination. While practitioners are free to ignore suggestions made by AI, the former remain subject to a form of agenda-setting power akin to the second face of power identified by Steven Lukes (1974). It would therefore not be surprising to witness normative conflicts between human groups who favour different AI programmes on the basis of the classifications they tend to produce. Think for instance of AI programmes that might recommend diets that are incompatible with the religious beliefs of some minority. It is easy to envisage that members of such minority groups would prefer if health decisions concerning them could be suggested instead by AIs who are guaranteed to provide suggestions congruent with their own practices and beliefs.

A second dynamic may, at least in theory, emerge from the first. As AI categorisations become more common and more familiar in many aspects of everyday life, it can reasonably be expected that AI categorisation might become a source of worth in its own sake. Thus, as health policy relies on AI, some molecules or some protocols may be more prone to a favourable classification by AI than others. If this happens, then a process similar to the development of new labels and standards might occur (Sainte-Marie et al., 1995). Not only would favourable AI classification become part of the worth of medical objects and persons, but also traits reputed to be conducive to favourable AI classification may be regarded as signs of worth. Consider our earlier example of AI-powered medical diagnostics: it is perfectly feasible to imagine an insurer in a private insurance-based healthcare system requiring that a particular diagnostic algorithm 'must' have been used in order to justify reimbursement for subsequent treatment; or similarly that a particular treatment protocol must have been endorsed by an algorithm rather than a human doctor. Indeed, it is our opinion that such a move would be quite easy to justify through evidence-based arguments that invoke the past success of the relevant algorithms. Our theoretical point is that the introduction of AI may create a world of worth of its own, a world in which favourable classification by AI operates both as higher common principle and test of worth. While it is too early to speculate on the objects that are likely to populate such an AI world of worth, we can reasonably expect to find in it algorithms; machine training; consensual versus contested classifications; libraries of examples; AI expert versus lay users; AI trainers; AI certification firms (that certify that the basic algorithms operate as advertised); and so on. This world of worth, if it ever emerges, would constitute the renewed space in which normative discussions relative to AI classifications would be organised.

But while the two dynamics we have identified so far subject AI qualifications to justification and critique by human actors, we can also imagine a third dynamic. In the latter, AI classifications are deemed so superior to human judgment that justification and critique are deemed superfluous or inappropriate. This dynamic may emerge in situations in which the normativity of AI qualifications is less evident or in situations in which AI is reputed to outperform human classification by a large margin. In this situation, human judgment would be subordinated to AI classification. Normative discussions would not necessarily be eradicated; however, they would take AI's classifications as a non-renegotiable given.

To recap, the imminent introduction of AI into health policy generates a number of actual or potential normative problems. The way neural networks are trained obfuscates some normative choices while the way AI qualifications are used may downplay or inhibit the practical wisdom of medical practitioners, patients and policy-makers. While AIs as we currently know them are not capable of participating in normative discussions as discussants, we can expect their outputs to become increasingly often the objects of normative discussions between human groups. But so far, our analysis has remained speculative as we examined possibilities suggested by our understanding of AI against the background of our understanding of basic mechanisms of normative conflicts and resolutions. We are left with the question of what likely future may lie ahead.

A bleak future scenario

We have identified previously three possible dynamics of normative discussion relative to AI inputs on health policy. But these dynamics do not yet exist. Moreover, since societies are open systems, we have little certainty about whether and how these dynamics will historically come into play. However, the observations and reflections gathered in the previous sections of this chapter allow us to delineate plausible, though bleak, future developments. Fortunately, our discussion so far also allows us to identify areas where action and/or resistance could lead to a different future.

Our future scenario is best presented in two historical phases. While the first phase has already started, the second phase will commence once the role and legitimacy of AI's influence over health policy is stabilised across society.

In the first phase, AI is initially adopted by for-profit organisations such as private insurance companies. The latter gradually adopt AI for two main reasons. Firstly, they employ AI as a tool to reduce information asymmetry with customers who know better than any other agent how risky their personal situation is and how much they are ready to pay for an insurance policy. We have seen that insurance companies such as Helsana have already started to offer schemes specially designed for customers who agree to share their information systematically and thus reinforce the firm's AI and big data capacities. Secondly, and equally importantly, the introduction of AI allows healthcare providers to shift legal responsibility from persons and organisational procedures to AI black boxes. As we write, the responsibility of human actors relying on AI decisions still presents a juridical vacuum (Greenemeier, 2018) and it is not clear whether responsibility lies with the individual operator, with the AI manufacturer or with the AI considered as a legal person (Čerkaa, Grigienėa, & Sirbikytėb, 2017).

During the first phase, it is not in the interest of everyone to participate in AI-related developments in healthcare. Patients may fear that disclosing their data might lead private organisations to increase the risks associated with their insurance covers and hence either ask for higher premiums or refuse to provide coverage altogether in less regulated healthcare markets where universal coverage is not compulsory. Others may object to sharing their data for ethical reasons if they suspect that by doing so they create the conditions for a police state. In spite of this, we can reasonably expect that, however, enough people will be willing to share their data so as to constitute a viable market segment for AI-reliant schemes. Prima facie, the individuals most interested in sharing their data with few restrictions are likely to be younger people who are more used to technological intermediation and believe that their health and habits are 'superior' to older segments of the population and therefore conducive to lower insurance premiums.

Preventative healthcare campaigns may also rely increasingly on AI during the first phase, and they have already begun doing so. We can think, for instance, of messages communicated via social platforms such as Facebook on which users have already waived their privacy. As we indicated earlier in this chapter, governments, nongovernmental organisations (NGOs) and economic lobbies may use the combination of AI and big data to nudge users via tailor-made messages. Personalised nudging messages about, say, birth control, may be prompted by the user's specific situation (e.g. if they mentioned 'having a date tonight' in a Facebook post), or through their personal profile (e.g. if AI deduces from posts that the user is likely to be a heterosexual woman aged 15–45), or even through personal triggers computed by the AI under the supervision of a specialist team (e.g. whenever a user posts a message that correlates with fear of pregnancy).

As we have pointed out, medical practitioners have already started to rely on the advice of expert systems. The latter combine AI and big data to provide advice on possible diagnoses, prognoses and even suggestions of appropriate treatments and associated side effects. For now, practitioners are careful to use AI only for 'decision support' as opposed to decision making (Weintraub, 2018). However, the use of AI is fast spreading across medical disciplines, from oncology to dermatology, and from cardiology to gerontology.

While the first phase of development of AI in health policy has already started, it is still ongoing. The association of AI with health and other forms of policy is still subject to caution from experts, and debates around the legitimate uses of AI are beginning. But if these debates are inconclusive, or if they are silenced by powerful actors, we can expect the use of AI to be legitimised gradually over time. If the previously mentioned commercial and public health usages of AI become routinely accepted, we may reasonably expect to enter a second phase of AI development.

The second phase of AI usage for health policy will start if the use of AI becomes generalised to the point of becoming familiar, and if the discussions surrounding AI fail to produce binding conventions around its usage. In this second phase, the commercial use of AI has become almost unquestionably legitimate. In such a normative context, we can envisage that for-profit organisations will be tempted, and may eventually succeed, to push the use of AI one step further and to penalise those customers who refuse to provide personalised real-time data. Customers' refusal to provide information would then be interpreted (perhaps as a matter of law) as a signal that they are attempting to hide facts that would, if disclosed, negatively affect the risk associated with their patronage or insurance premiums. In the second phase, a large proportion of users of health insurance who avoided joining AI-driven schemes are likely to subscribe, as the penalties for not doing so overwhelm the cost of disclosing one's personal data on a continuous basis. While such foreseeable problems concern, strictly speaking, big data rather than AI, the use of the latter justifies, intensifies and accelerates reliance on the former, and vice versa.

At the level of hospitals, the banalisation of AI and its increased legitimation are likely to shift the role of AI from decision support to decision making, effectively stripping human doctors of their authority and responsibility. While it is not possible to propose a date for this revolution of medical practice, it may be possible to indicate a plausible tipping point: that is, the day when a doctor will be successfully sued for having acted against the advice of an AI. After such a legal precedent, it is likely that most medical professionals will prefer to defer to AI judgment rather than bear the additional responsibility of acting against AI's advice.

Public health campaigns and health policy are also likely to take a different direction if the pervasive usage of AI is accepted. While public health campaigns were characterised in the first phase by tailored messages, the second phase might also include systematic tracking and reporting of individuals whose personal data indicates they may be neglecting or otherwise harming their health. This move from public campaigns that inform to campaigns that track and report citizens may evolve in synergy with a personalisation of health policy for each citizen.

Beyond health campaigns, the legitimation of pervasive AI usage in phase 2 may eliminate 'public' health altogether. Indeed, it might become possible to develop, at the level of welfare states, health policies that rely on AI and big data to decide for each citizen whether they deserve such or such treatment with regards to their medical profile but also their practices as revealed through the data they generate. This would effectively personalise healthcare provision to an extent that is currently difficult to imagine and would render most of today's public health measures – which are targeted at specific groups and segments of the population, or occasionally at the population as a whole – redundant. This would probably only be possible in an illiberal political system because such policies divorce healthcare provision from citizenship and violate the principle of common humanity. However, an AI-induced healthcare dystopia remains a plausible outcome of recent technological developments.

Concluding remarks: protective organisations and conventions

As can be seen throughout this chapter, the combination of AI and big data generates unprecedented problems for the normative discussions surrounding health policy. Unless citizens and governments engage in appropriate collective action, we can reasonably expect to witness over the next decade dystopian developments akin to the ones we have delineated previously. But current times are also a pivotal period during which citizens and governments can still attempt to avoid, or at least mitigate, the problems that are otherwise likely to enter the scene. On a more general level, politicians, regulators, NGOs must acquire a better understanding of the AI strategies of the dominant internet companies and the connections between them. As the main developers of algorithms and the owners of the largest and most valuable databases, companies such as Google, Apple or Amazon are in a position that allows them to shape policy in numerous areas. Yet regulation has failed to track their current strategies or anticipate the risks that they present for future societies. They may do so, we propose, by creating organisations and conventions that will limit and harness the use of AI in public health and other areas. Our discussion of the introduction of AI in health policy allows us to make the following suggestions.

Firstly, we need independent think tanks, watchdogs and forums of discussion in which the normative problems raised by reliance on AI and big data are thoroughly and continuously discussed. Unless such organisations are created, discussions about the future of AI are likely to be monopolised by powerful profit-oriented actors such as Google, Amazon, Facebook and Apple, but also large pharmaceutical and insurance companies. In the absence of such investment from governments and NGOs, both their technical expertise and their capacity to criticise AI developments on normative grounds are likely to melt in comparison with the capacities of for-profit actors. Indeed, a strategic objective for the organisations we call for may be to maintain room for arguments borrowed from civic and domestic polities (Boltanski & Thévenot, 2006). When discussing how reliance on AI generates novel dynamics of justification, we identified the possibility of a novel world of worth relative to persons and objects subjected to AI classification. If human normativity is to be safeguarded, it is vital that the novel world of worth contain not only elements of the industrial and commercial polities, but also elements from the civic and domestic ones.

Secondly, we need adequate systems of protection for individuals unwilling to continuously share information that will feed into big data. Existing legislation covers individuals' right to access and rectify information concerning them. But little effort has been spent, to our knowledge, on empowering individuals to control how their information is stored, how it circulates and how it is used by third parties. While the European Union has recently issued an ambitious General Data Protection Regulation, it remains unclear whether it will act as an efficient deterrent for the abuses we have identified in the present chapter (Brandom, 2018).

Thirdly, while AI is currently employed by medical practitioners as a tool of assistance in decision making, the distinction between assistance and effective decision making may tend to blur over time. In particular, practitioners' vulnerability to legal action may incite them to delegate responsibility, and authority, to AI. One way around this imminent problem may consist in legislating that AI input cannot be used as evidence in legal trials relative to medical malpractice. At the time of writing, we are unsure whether it might already be too late for this measure, as machines providing diagnostic information (e.g. scanners) already rely on AI. It might therefore be exceedingly difficult to disambiguate AI-reliant from non-AI-reliant medical tools.

Fourthly, and lastly, our discussion of public campaigns in a world populated with AI and big data calls for novel organisations and conventions. These could take several forms which need not be exclusive of one another: computer programmes that block nudging messages; commissions on the model of France's Conseil supérieur de l'audiovisuel that take legal action whenever a breach is noticed; legislation regarding the use of personalised nudging on the internet; and, at the cultural level, a shared understanding that nudging is a very efficient form of power whose efficiency depends precisely on its apparent innocuousness.

References

3Blue1Brown. (2017). But what *is* a neural network? *Video Tutorial*. Available online: www.3blue1brown.com/videos/ (accessed June 2018).

AI Now. (2018). *Algorithmic Impact Assessments: A Practical Framework for Public Agency Accountability*. Available online: https://ainowinstitute.org/aiareport2018.pdf (accessed June 2018).

Al-Amoudi, I. (2010). Immanent non-algorithmic rules: An ontological study of social rules. *Journal for the Theory of Social Behaviour*, 40(3): 289–313.

Aristotle. (350BC). *Nicomachean Ethics*. Available online: http://classics.mit.edu/Aristotle/nicomachaen.html (accessed June 2018).

Batifoulier, P., Braddock, L., & Latsis, J. (2013). Priority setting in health care: From arbitrariness to societal values. *Journal of Institutional Economics*, 9(1): 61–80.

Bhaskar, R. (1978). *A Realist Theory of Science* (2nd ed.). Hassocks, Sussex: Harvester Press.

Boltanski, L., & Thévenot, L. (2006). *On Justification: Economies of Worth*. Princeton, NJ: Princeton University Press.

Boston Consulting Group. (2017). *Putting Artificial Intelligence to Work*. Available online: www.bcg.com/publications/2017/technology-digital-strategy-putting-artificial-intelligence-work.aspx (accessed June 2018).

Brandom, R. (2018, May). Facebook and Google hit with $8.8 billion in lawsuits on day one of GDPR. *The Verge*. Available online: www.theverge.com/2018/5/25/17393766/facebook-google-gdpr-lawsuit-max-schrems-europe (accessed June 2018).

Burgess, M. (2018, April). Stop Googling your symptoms – The smartphone doctor is here to help. *Wired Magazine*. Available online: www.wired.co.uk/article/ada-smartphone-doctor-nhs-gp-video-appointment (accessed June 2018).

Butler, J. (2004). *Undoing Gender*. London: Routledge.

Čerkaa, P., Grigienėa, J., & Sirbikytėb, G. (2017). Is it possible to grant legal personality to artificial intelligence software systems? *Computer Law and Security Review*, 33(5): 685–699.

Chalmers, D. (1996). *The Conscious Mind*. Oxford: Oxford University Press.

Cyranoski, D. (2018, January). China enters the battle for AI talent. *Nature*. Available online: www.nature.com/articles/d41586-018-00604-6 (accessed June 2018).

Esteva, A., Kuprel, B., Novoa, R. A., Ko, J., Swetter, S. M., Blau, H. M., & Thrun, S. (2017). Dermatologist-level classification of skin cancer with deep neural networks. *Nature*, 542(7639): 115.

Frey, C. B., & Osborne, M. A. (2013). *The Future of Employment: How Susceptible Are Jobs to Computerisation?* Oxford: Oxford Martin Programme on Technology and Employment.

Gadamer, H-G. (1997). *Truth and Method*. New York, NY: Continuum.

Greenemeier, L. (2018). Intelligent to a fault: When AI screws up, you might still be to blame. *Scientific American*. March 15, 2018. Available online: https://www.scientific american.com/article/intelligent-to-a-fault-when-ai-screws-up-you-might-still-be-to-blame1/ (accessed July 2019).

Guillaume, M. (2017, November). L'application santé d'Helsana fait l'objet d'une enquête. *Le Temps*. Available online: www.letemps.ch/suisse/2017/10/31/lapplication-sante-dhelsana-lobjet-dune-enquete (accessed June 2018).

Habermas, J. (1990). *Moral Consciousness and Communicative Action*. Cambridge: Polity Press.

Harari, Y. N. (2016). *Homo Deus: A Brief History of Tomorrow*. London: Harvill Secker.

Huang, E. (2018). China has shot far ahead of the US on deep-learning patents. *Quartz*. Available online: https://qz.com/1217798/china-has-shot-far-ahead-of-the-us-on-ai-patents/ (accessed June 2018).

International Federation or Robotics. (2017). *The Impact of Robots on Productivity, Employment and Jobs*. Available online: https://ifr.org/img/office/IFR_The_Impact_of_Robots_on_Employment.pdf (accessed June 2018).

Jha, S., & Topol, E. J. (2016). Adapting to artificial intelligence: Radiologists and pathologists as information specialists. *Journal of American Medical Association*, 316(22): 2353–2354. DOI: 10.1001/jama.2016.17438

Kenny, K., Fotaki, M., & Scriver, S. (2018). Mental health as a weapon: Whistleblower retaliation and normative violence. *Journal of Business Ethics*. Available online: https://doi.org/10.1007/s10551-018-3868-4 (accessed June 2018).

Latsis, J. (2005). Is there redemption for conventions? *Cambridge Journal of Economics*, 29(5): 709–727.

Lawson, T. (2009). Applied economics, contrast explanation and asymmetric information. *Cambridge Journal of Economics*, 33(3): 405–419.

Lukes, S. (1974). *Power: A Radical View*. London: Macmillan Press.

Miliard, M. (2018, May). How AI command centers are helping hospitals harness analytics to manage operations. *Healthcare IT News*. Available online: www.healthcareitnews.com/news/how-ai-command-centers-are-helping-hospitals-harness-analytics-manage-operations (accessed June 2018).

Morgan, J. (2018). Yesterday's tomorrow today: Turing, Searle and the contested significance of artificial intelligence. In I. Al-Amoudi & J. Morgan (Eds.), *Realist Responses to Post-Human Society: Ex Machina*. London: Routledge.

Nord, E. (1999). *Cost-value Analysis in Health Care: Making Sense out of QALYs*. Cambridge: Cambridge University Press.

Park, D. H., Hendricks, L. A., Akata, Z., Schiele, B., Darrell, T., & Rohrbach, M. (2016). *Attentive Explanations: Justifying Decisions and Pointing to the Evidence*. Proceedings of the IEEE Conference on Computer Vision and Pattern Recognition.

Rawls, J. (2001). *Justice as Fairness: A Restatement*. Cambridge, MA; and London: Harvard University Press.

Sainte-Marie, C., Prost, J-A., Casabianca, F., & Casalta, E. (1995). La construction sociale de la qualité: enjeux autour de l'appellation d'origine contrôlée 'Brocciu Corse'. In N. Valceschini (Ed.), *Agroalimentaire: Une économie de la qualité* (pp. 185–208). Paris: INRA.

Shotter, J., & Tsoukas, H. (2014). In search of Phronesis: Leadership and the art of judgment. *Academy of Management Learning & Education*, 13(2): 224–243.

Thaler, R. H. (2009, September). Opting in vs. opting out. *The New York Times*. Available online: www.nytimes.com/2009/09/27/business/economy/27view.html (accessed June 2018).

Thaler, R. H., & Sunstein, C. R. (2009). *Nudge Improving Decisions About Health, Wealth, and Happiness*. New York, NY: Penguin Books.

Weintraub, A. (2018, March). Artificial intelligence is infiltrating medicine – But is it ethical? *Forbes*.

Winick, E. (2017). Lawyer-bots are shaking up jobs. *MIT Technology Review*. Available online: www.technologyreview.com/s/609556/lawyer-bots-are-shaking-up-jobs/ (accessed July 2018).

Wittgenstein, L. (2000). *Philosophical Investigations*. Oxford: Blackwell Publishers.

Zetter, R. (1991). Labelling refugees: Forming and transforming a bureaucratic identity. *Journal of Refugee Studies*, 4(1): 39–62.

8 Swarm-teams with digital exoskeleton

On new military templates for the organizational society

Emmanuel Lazega[1]

Inside out: social digitalization as further bureaucratization

War and Society, a recent book by Centeno and Enriquez (2016), shows how wars and preparation for war transform societies. Organization of war shapes political and social structures, especially organization of total war far away from the 'gentlemen's war'. The line between soldiers in the battlefield and civilians behind them is blurred (81). War has become a war between peoples, not only between soldiers (82). It leads efforts to master new technologies (for example, transport, communication or weaponry), from which efficiency in battle can be gleaned. Dynamics of war can lead to organized and depersonalized genocides and to the physical and 'social death' of entire peoples. Strangest of all is the 'mutual agreement and understanding [between enemies] required to maintain the system' (114): 'nuclear arms, for example, requiring that the adversaries be in constant communication, mutually assuring each other of intentions and safeguards' (115), and often increasing similarities between them. The authors add: 'What we do not know yet is how these changes in war will change the nature of society in the decades to come' (172). If the impact of the military on societies is as extensive as they think, if the organization of war shapes political and social structures, our social change can be anticipated, at least in part, by the evolution of the contemporary military. For example, military institutions today, protected by secrecy, make pharaonic investments in the digitalization of their organizations and the battlefield. Digitalization of war promotes radical technological innovations for military objectives, but these innovations will probably become part of a broader process of 'social digitalization'.

Social digitalization, as an indicator and substantive part of contemporary social morphogenesis (Archer, 2014), takes complex forms. Part of this social change can be called 'organizational morphogenesis' – that is, co-constitution and co-evolution of two ideal-typical models of organization, bureaucracy and collegiality (Lazega, 2001; 2017), in multilevel, organized collective agency. These forms of co-constitution and co-evolution are particularly useful to understand

1 I am grateful to Ismael Al-Amoudi and Margaret Archer, as well as to all the authors in this edited volume, for stimulating comments.

social change because contemporary society has become an increasingly bureaucratized organizational society. In a simplified way, bureaucracy can be ideal-typically defined as a form of organization based on routine tasks, hierarchy and impersonal interactions between members. Collegiality can be ideal-typically defined as a form of endogenous organization based on non-routine and innovative tasks, carried out by peers who seek various forms of agreements to coordinate, and use personalized relationships to do so. In theory, we tend to see this co-constitution as a problematic, multilevel struggle without optimal equilibrium (Lazega, 2015a). But the technological revolution brought about by the creation of digitalization, with its capacity to invent new kinds of routines, strengthens the centuries-old process of bureaucratization theorized by Max Weber as the 'polar night of icy darkness'. With the new industrial revolution driven by digitalization, bureaucracy and social Darwinism are increasingly taking over again (Rosenblat, 2018).

This chapter explores a specific dimension of organizational morphogenesis by looking at how meso-level institutions – here the military – use this digitalization to try to reorganize and further routinize work and collective action by some of its members – here soldiers in the battlefield.[2] In this case in point, social digitalization appears to strengthen two processes: firstly, the already deep control of the world by these institutions and their capacity to reinvent bureaucratization – an increase of control traditionally brought about by wars (Centeno, 2002); and secondly, the capacity of these institutions to invent models of organization of work that are likely to spread later on in the organizational society at large, and to shape more mundane, everyday practices. This exploration focuses on the example of the digitalization of the battlefield, especially the remote control of teams of soldiers on the ground. Team building, team behavior and team management have long been a focus of attention in military organizations, not only with the purpose of increasing their efficiency, but also to neutralize their capacity to build oppositional solidarities, whether between *compagnons de feu* (Shils & Janowitz, 1948; Stouffer et al., 1949) or between disqualified or demoralized soldiers (Shibutani, 1978). This is equivalent to saying that, with such digitalization, large bureaucratic organizations could finally be in a position to collect and exploit, in real time, data on soldiers' behavior, exchanges, interactions and relationships, not only to guide their actions as in a digital straightjacket, but also to weaken or neutralize group 'bottom up collegiality' (Lazega & Wattebled, 2011) by transforming personalized relationships among soldiers into more routinized interactions (Lazega, 2017; Duran & Lazega, 2015).

This process of further digitalization and bureaucratization in the military can be found in its fascination with swarms. Beyond its biblical connotations (flies

---

2   This exploration is based on observations made as an expert embarked on a three-day 'Board of Visitors' of a contemporary Army Research Office, referred to as ARO-BoV in this text. None of the materials accessed during this visit were classified. Such visits are organized to try to attract scientists towards military-funded research. They are dominated by displays of research and its use of mathematical models of social phenomena developed for the military by academics, computer scientists and engineers. Among the models on display were the particularly visible models of swarms. In this chapter I use quotes for the military language that was used during the three days.

as the fourth plague, Exodus 8:24), in the military definition swarms are self-organizing systems. They are made of 'resilient, high performance teams assembled from heterogeneous networks, aligned on common mental maps and emotional reactions' (ARO-BoV). Military fascination with swarms leads to a representation of war as fight between self-organized (and to some extent unpredictable) teams scaling up linearly to entire battalions adapting flexibly, almost organically, to battleground tasks. Digitalization focuses on engineering and steering these teams and battalions with support from artificial intelligence that brings together and analyses big data and social network data in and around the battlefield in real time. Here the 'transformational capacity' of these technologies appears to be associated with, indeed often driven by, mathematical models of swarms as normative metaphors for collective action of teams and between teams.

Knowledge of swarms borrows from animal life (Van der Vaart et al., 2019). Reynolds (1987), and many others ever since, for example Hildenbrandt, Carere, and Hemelrijk (2010), reduce models of relative fixed speed (fear-based) movement of bird behaviour in flocks to three simple rules: Separation – avoid crowding neighbours (short-range repulsion based on ability to sense pheromone); Alignment on changing leaders – steer towards the average heading of neighbours; Cohesion – coordinate with a limited number of interaction neighbours (five for real starlings) and steer towards average position of neighbours (long-range attraction). The swarms of birds work by trying to keep a distance constant with five birds (in the front, on the left, on the right, above, below). There is a leader, but birds rotate in this position. A swarm can avoid and challenge a predator. Swarms are thus both vertically and horizontally structured forms of semi-autonomous common action. Given the rotation in the front position, they are a mix of both. Rules of positioning with distances completely standardized are enough to build coordination in to impersonal interaction. A swarm is meant to be self-organized and resilient. This has given rise to mathematical modelling of the work and behaviour of teams (for example Aggarwal et al., 2015; Bogdanov et al., 2013; Jones, Friedkin, & Singh, 2017; Lungeanu, Huang, & Contractor, 2014; Woolley, Aggarwal, & Malone, 2015) that is used for modelling behaviour of soldiers on the ground. Indeed, one of the reasons why this comparison seemed possible is that, in the contemporary military, soldiers are often trained to replace their superiors up to two ranks above their own, in case these superiors fall in combat: like birds, soldiers could lead the flock one after the other. Such replacements are called battlefield promotion (or 'field promotion', or 'jump-step' promotion as advancements from current rank to a rank above the next higher one), and they can occur only while deployed in combat. In theory, each soldier can thus be prepared to take the lead of the group/swarm. This potential for multilevel positioning introduces the possibility of a modicum of formal 'top down collegiality'[3] (Lazega & Wattebled, 2011) in military teamwork. It pictures soldiers locking

---

3 Multilevel positioning protects formal collegial pockets as recreated by the bureaucratic ruler. This is different from protecting basic, bottom-up collegiality (Lazega, forthcoming).

themselves in the swarm, taking turns for its lead, relying on digital equipment to steer the group as a single entity, and nevertheless free to break away at any time, at their own risk.[4]

From a broader organizational perspective, mathematical models of teams as parts of swarms are also fascinating for the military because they promote a model of cooperation that gets rid of traditional forms of internal contestations and oppositional solidarities. Indeed there are at least three ways in which we find bureaucracy and collegiality together in the same organizations (Lazega, 2017). At the top of bureaucracies, collegial oligarchies can be found, for example in the executive suite or in boards of directors. The top of organizations is always collegial because work at that level is rarely routine, always political. Even autocrats have around them a system of peers that controls the bureaucratic organization below (Lazega & Wattebled, 2011). Further below, we find two kinds of collegial pockets: either professional departments, such as R&D departments, in which expert members consider each other as peers; or further down the hierarchy, groups of members, for example at the shop floor level, who together build forms of 'autonomous regulation' (Reynaud, 1989) or oppositional solidarity (Shibutani, 1978; Wittek & Van de Bunt, 2004). One of the managers' tasks is to monitor and sanction oppositional solidarity in the lower levels.

The argument here is that if digitalization of the battlefield is explored by military management using the swarm template, among many purposes, to build and control efficient teams/platoons of soldiers[5] as they operate in the messy battlefield, the same templates could be used in the future to redefine collegial settings/pockets within bureaucratic organizations. This template becomes an example of how a new digital bureaucratization can be used by organizations and institutions to invent/explore new forms of collective action for society at large. The swarm template is a model for cohesion in action but also for neutralizing collegiality (and its built-in oppositional solidarity) that survives at the bottom of bureaucratic contexts. Teams are meant to keep the *esprit de corps* (they motivate, give courage, give the impression to individual soldiers that they are understood by their

---

4 Soldiers endure enormous physical and psychological pressures, from fear of ambushes to "blunders" costing lives, and often break down or revolt. They know that if they step aside in action, do not follow instructions (whether or not derived from mathematical models), there are consequences for their careers – at best their pension or invalidity insurance will be reduced by military bureaucracy. The same mindset applies with AI measurements and models, except that robotized individuals' behaviour and performances are then evaluated based on highly precise digital tools and comparisons with abstract models.

5 A rich body of research looks at finding ways of creating the most efficient teams of soldiers based on knowledge about them, who they are, how they react, etc. But we do not know a great deal about how teams are currently built in the military based on combined AI, Computational Social Science and Social Network Analysis. For example, do they last a few weeks, months, years? Much of this body of knowledge that is also public seems to be based on network statistical models of 'team assembly' and reshuffling derived from adolescent online war games (Contractor, 2013) that address the basic managerial dilemma raised by military teams – but in a gamified way. The data on applications on the ground we do not get to see.

peers), and at the same time to shed their capacity to create oppositional solidarity, to erase doubts about the purpose of the war, to not get out of control and start doing things that the military hierarchy does not want them to do.

This chapter first looks at how this digitalization is meant to exercise that influence on teams on the ground, beginning with soldiers' work and the mechanics of this digitalization, its meaning in organizational terms, its extension to society at large and the consequences in terms of reinventing specific forms of collective responsibility. It is indeed suggested that, in a creepy way, through this process of digitalization as bureaucratization of the battlefield and neutralization of team-based oppositional solidarities by remote-controlled task performance, social actors potentially become subjected to new forms of punitive collective responsibility.

In the specific example used here, i.e., military research on designing and using high performance teams, swarm fantasies are developed by mathematicians and engineers combining artificial intelligence (AI) and big data, including social network analysis (SNA) reducing relationships between soldiers to impersonal interactions at the "right" physical and social distance. In many ways, if combinations of AI and SNA provide military management with tools that build efficient teams while neutralizing oppositional solidarity, they are able to transform and bureaucratize collegiality as defined here. They want to turn relationships that are personalized into interactions that are impersonal, and still be able to retransform interactions into relationships when the *esprit de corps* is needed again. This can be called the 'inside out' effect (Lazega, forthcoming). In this model, collegiality is neutralized and steered towards alignment. Bureaucratic management has been dreaming of this magic formula for more than a century. The question raised by this combination of AI, SNA and CSS is whether or not the meeting of this mathematical template with this dream will have an effect on society through social digitalization and the emergence of a new form of collective responsibility as a result.

Military work in the battlefield: 'fire-and-forget swarms'

The next sections look at how the military wants to use AI algorithms applied to big data, including social network data, to make armies work in ways armies have never worked in history. AI is changing what it means to be a soldier on the ground. In the battlefield, soldiers are first becoming data-gathering informants-sensors for data discovery and analytics. The military discusses this under 'revolutionizing the soldier's equipment for situational awareness' (ARO-BoV). Soldiers' 'situational awareness' is meant to complement digital information systems available to officers. The soldiers' job is first to be there, describe into their microphone what they see, focus their cameras on anything that might be of interest, 'automatically discovering knowledge', providing information that helps their hierarchy deal with uncertain data and make decisions in a context where officers would rely on access to 'knowledge repositories' (databases, satellite observation, intelligence etc.). Information collected by the soldiers on the ground is recorded to augment a dedicated database processed mechanically using deep learning algorithms under the surveillance of the battalion's ICT analyst, who, in turn, is 'communicating with knowledge systems'.

From all of this, the battalion analyst watches AI algorithms process mountains of data, combining this military intelligence and surveillance systems with these observations made in real time by soldiers on the ground – thus helping officers make specific combat-related decisions (whom to target, how to get out of there etc.). This analyst communicates with officers who rely on AI output as the basis for such decisions and further instructions. In this work, soldiers as highly parametrized sensors and battlefield workers are remote-controlled and steered by these officers relying on AI platform recommendations. Soldiers help officers make 'trade-offs in accuracy and efficiency of algorithms', meaning that these help officers make sense of information, of analyses and of recommendations that they receive from AI machine learning algorithms. Without these sensors on the ground, the army recognizes that 'communication between humans and knowledge repositories is fraught with ambiguity and lack of trust (on part of the human), and the problem of mediating information exchange is open' (ARO-BoV).

Soldiers' work is thus redefined to serve sophisticated digital equipment carried on the battleground and communicating live with databases and AI algorithms that process this data and filter it towards scripted recommendations. Their tasks are partly parametrized to feed the database and to guide their swarm towards their targets. Compare this for example with discourse on swarms of robots. Parallel to the trend described here, there is another trend of deploying swarms of cheap robots networked together in a single 'swarmanoid' that can bring greater mass, coordination, intelligence and speed. The military use an interesting comparison with swarms of soldiers: 'Such machines do not get bored, tired, angry or frightened. They work out the best way to carry out their mission as it unfolds' (ARO-BoV). One important fact must be taken into account to understand the promotion of swarms as templates. Military digitalized/digitalizing bureaucracy is already infused with swarm thinking, assuming the possibility of diverse mechanisms: decentralized movement of self-organizing, autonomous systems ('*Fire-and-Forget Swarms*'), performing collective tasks with no intervention; interactions between individuals based on midge sensing being assumed automatically to scale up to produce the macroscopic state of the large swarm; mechanisms producing resilient networks that are robust towards cascading failures and that can be engineered. This digitalization is thus equivalent to routinization and bureaucratization of usually highly chaotic situations that often fail to produce collective action.

New intelligence, surveillance and reconnaissance methods, space-based communication and stealth technology are part of long-term trends in warfare. Autonomous systems must observe, orient, decide and act ('OODA'). They perceive the world through their sensors, including those worn by humans. The horizon is that of designing algorithms that will power and coordinate truly autonomous machines and teams. This digitalization and bureaucratization of the battleground drives the military to focus on autonomous learning systems, human-machine collaborative decision making, assisted human operations networked with autonomous weapons. Such human-machine collaboration in combat is meant to help humans make better decisions more quickly. AI algorithms become important in big data analytics managing unprecedented amounts of data, including video, generated by surveillance drones and the monitoring of social media posts by enemy groups. AI will combine all the information brought up by microphones, cameras, and so forth, analyse it and provide maps updated in real time, a description of the situation, and recommendations derived from analyses of similar situations recorded in the past. We do not know the extent to which this is actually used by officers to make decisions and manoeuvre through the battlefield.

Combat may speed up so much that humans can no longer keep up (Scharre, 2018), and therefore it is apparently hard for these soldiers to trust their digital assistants, i.e., systems they do not understand; but also to trust their officers who make decisions based on data that may not be accurate (missing information) and on norms/patterns that they may not share or even understand (see Al-Amoudi & Latsis, present volume). The information that is collected is heavily framed in graph-theoretic terms both for social network analysis (who is observed as interacting with whom in the 'host population', for example) and for semantic network analysis (which words recur in the soldiers' descriptions), and finally for the co-evolution of both social networks and semantic networks. The 'Army Impact' of this technology, that is, the more specific goals, is described using the following terminology: 'discovering information about social structures in a host population'; 'community detection in interaction diagrams'; 'processing neural network structures for functionality'; 'hidden structure detection: de-emphasizing strong communities to identify weak, hidden communities'; and finally 'finding hidden communities in large graphs for detection of adversarial groups embedded in host populations' (ARO-BoV).

A digital group exoskeleton against collegial/oppositional solidarity

In order to understand this focus on 'team assembly', it is useful to recall that teams have always raised problems for the hierarchical and bureaucratic military organization. Indeed, they represent both forms of motivation and secondary socialization, making it possible for soldiers to maintain high morale while behaving in ways unimaginable in civil life. Many studies (from Stouffer et al., 1949, to Shibutani, 1978) have confirmed the importance of small local units for morale among soldiers who understand each other as human beings. But also, a form of oppositional solidarity and informal norms are created by the same soldiers once they no longer feel that they understand, believe in or support the project behind the war. That is, when they are no longer willing to risk their lives for a war that does not make sense to them, or when they disobey orders coming from a hierarchy that is losing control.[6] Early and classical sociological work by

---

6 A Shibutani-inspired research project would notice that no information is available in the literature about potential resistance to swarm-teams. As shown by Scharre (2018), interactions between

Shils and Janowitz (1948) shows how important personalized relationships, group cohesion, esteem, affection, knowledge of expectations and protection of immediate associates, as well as a complex rapport to authority, were to Wehrmacht soldiers during WWII, not so much dedication to Nazi ideology (that characterized Waffen-SS troops much more).

When considered together with parallel research on 'team science', that is, team composition, the mathematical and normative template for team mobilization acquires a new meaning. The purpose of change in team management is expressed in military technocratic terms: 'Reducing Mission Planning and Execution' with a '25% decrease in planning and execution time'; with '50% reduction in gel time for squads, platoons, staffs, and joint combat operation teams'; and with '20% faster deployment of units' (ARO-BoV). The army benefits from high morale created by group solidarity but fears the disaffection of groups of soldiers once the latter start developing demoralized oppositional solidarity. Combined AI, CSS and SNA have raised military hierarchy expectations from social engineering in team management techniques that would prevent demoralization and solve problems more easily.

It is thus meant to leverage an assumed 'swarm intelligence' of the group. This would be equivalent to providing/imposing, with battlefield AI-driven equipment, what could be called a digital group exoskeleton for the group and its capacity for collective action. A sophisticated bureaucratic framework wants to compute and use an impersonal, interactional dynamic invariant around which the personalized relational infrastructure of the group can adjust. The managerial purpose is thus both to streamline the social energy and value of the group and leverage the capacity to coordinate that can be found in its nascent collegiality, and at the same time neutralize the potential for oppositional solidarity that it could generate simultaneously, and this by making soldiers more zombie-like than they have ever been. Pre-socialization to swarm-teams for these future soldiers, but also for future workers and citizens, might be provided by first-person shooter (FPS) video games (such as *Counter-Strike, Borderlands, Call of Duty, Gears of War*, etc.). These video games start by immersing the players into a situation in which they have a gun, a minimap and in which they receive real-time instructions about objectives to collectively clarify using this 'swarm intelligence'.

Zooming in, zooming out: extension to teams in society at large

This case of military use of AI, CSS and SNA deserves attention, in spite of all the questions that can be raised about this reasoning, because society is actually

---

humans and new technologies both excite and disturb the military establishments. This might be true of soldiers on the ground as well. Elite soldiers, for example, might dislike the deskilling entailed, and perhaps even sabotage manoeuvres by ignoring the voice in the mike, or by keeping the camera muddy.

ready for the transfer of the swarm template from the battleground to the work-place. Social scientists may interpret this fascination for swarms and mathematics as pure rhetoric and dismiss the underlying hyperbolic vision as laughable, as a vision in which no real-life chain of command believes a word. It could emerge from agency competition or corruption (companies selling technology to the military cost a fortune to taxpayers) even if a subgoal of this project is for many actors to line their own pockets, make sure their budget stays the same size, insure their buddy down the corridor does not get more than they do, and so forth. Part of this is a dream of replacing soft diplomatic expertise with hard military expertise based on science and other kinds of analysis within intelligence agencies. This is also what would drive this hyperbolic tone. Nevertheless, the reality is that society seems ready for these models and templates.

Rapid advances in AI and deep learning affect the ways wars are fought as much as how ordinary business is conducted in society (Mazzucato, 2015). The objective of swarms as a project is control and a new form of social discipline based on specific uses of technology that creates a new interaction between human and machine. This transition from military to civil life has been accelerating since 11 September 2001. If AI, machine learning, robotics, big data analytics, and theories of management of human groups in swarms transform military work on the ground and change warfare, it is important to look at how military competition and the unstoppable arms race for AI dominance might influence societal change. Trends in warfare will change society because they create new and overwhelming problems when the human is out of the loop.

Temptation to let the machine take over may itself become overwhelming,[7] and temptation actually to use the human group as a machine will be even more overwhelming. If, based on Centeno and Enriquez (2016), this becomes a template or model for widespread reorganization of work in society, then we may be witnessing a new form of bureaucratization, one that heralds the last days of collegiality at the ground level, on battlefields as much as on the shop floor or in everyday civilian projects. 'Swarming project management' might become a management tool for coordination in organizations. Beyond the buzzword, swarming might become a specific project management practice. Organizations and institutions beyond the military might be ready to follow this ideology and and use the technology. The datasets are available. They are not just owned by private Big Tech hegemonic platforms specialized in social and organizational networks.[8]

---

7 We were not provided with information about how this system might be implemented, adopted and criticized by the top brass of the military as well as from the rank-and-file soldiers, for example in terms of military efficiency (ratio of number of enemy destroyed per dollar spent; loss of a number of relational goods such as camaraderie, respect for the human element, respect for their own trade (being a (wo)man of war) or for their elite troop status (as opposed to just a drone with a human body), including collateral damage).

8 For example, the controversial decision taken by the U.S. Administration in March 2012 to allow the National Counter-Terrorism Center (NCTC), one of the agencies that was created in the aftermath of 9/11, to collect and merge into one database all the information the US government has

Relations between public authorities (in the US) and Big Tech companies are well known, and 'big surveillance' now extends not only to individuals but also to social and organizational networks and to the links between those networks. However, beyond the surveillance of individuals, whose private life and right to privacy are obviously threatened, if not disappearing, such organizations are able to piece together, and even anticipate, the development of different forms of social mobilization and collective action in civil society. This includes knowing the leaders and the members, their organization and the techniques they use to circulate information on social media, the structural and semantic characteristics of those movements, their coordination, their capacities to mobilize and their collective resources, including the content of their projects.

AI algorithms are also one of the specificities of CSS and complexity sciences in the analysis of such very large and rich network datasets (sociodigital media like the blogosphere, groups or lists of collective actors who 'follow' each other in real time and communicate in new sociotechnical environments, etc.) combined with big surveillance. Given the gigantic scale of those databases in which the private, for-profit study of social behaviour is increasingly grounded, the methods used in such approaches will for example result in the mechanical detection of 'communities' and their dynamics. Just as practitioners of targeted marketing look for specific niches and really central prescribers-intermediaries between those niches, the analysis and detection of communities allows for the zooming in and zooming out that institutions such as the NCTC practice.

Until recently, the very big digital social networks that were studied were made up of a very high number of entities on which very little was known. Relations between those entities were also usually written in a very simplified way: the 'data' was considered at a very high level of generality, which was enough to identify those 'communities' but rarely to specify, for example, their different forms of collective action. Action theories on which those approaches relied, when they existed, were minimal (see Barabási's (2003: 11) punchline: 'Think of yourself as a dreaming robot on autopilot, and you will be much closer to the truth'). Generalized competition, increasingly flexible labour markets and mobilizations of civil society lead actors to look for or create new tools to manage their economic and social interdependencies. The development of personal and organizational digital online networks, together with platforms organizing them, created a context where interdependencies can be managed as relational capital by the

---

on any US citizen, whether suspected, or linked to, a specific procedure of investigation by public authorities, was a news item, like so many others, that was put into the 'big surveillance' category. Now the NCTC can conduct any analysis of individuals and their behaviours, organized activities or networks based on the data the US public authorities have (in the financial, economic, educational, police, health, relational etc. domains). It can also share and exchange information with foreign governments when necessary. According to the American media, that political decision, though disputed within the Administration, did not meet with much resistance from the public, although half the Administration team in charge of the project left in protest. On that topic see: A Comparison of the 2008 and 2012 NCTC Guidelines: www.fas.org/sgp/othergov/intel/nctc_guidelines.pdf

individual or as social capital for the organization, which could sometimes have virtuous effects and sometimes disastrous ones. The forms of social discipline that citizens accept as legitimate has evolved with technological changes (Lazega, 2015b). Techniques of control of individual behaviour through the manipulation of sensitive reactions and emotions (in military ARO-BoV jargon: 'angry mood manipulations') have reached a degree of refinement which allows bureaucracies to directly and unobtrusively intervene on those behaviours.

AI is already increasingly used by administration, public or private, to forecast demand, hire workers and deal with customers, helping managers exercise extraordinary control over their employees. Badges already track employees around the office and reveal how they interact with colleagues, spreading ubiquitous surveillance. With merged data from badges and from employees' calendars and e-mails, for example, algorithms will decide whether or not employees are team players, monitor how they are collaborating, send feedback on their work in real time, and provide instructions on how to do better. The choice in some jobs will be between being replaced by a robot or being treated like one. This oppressive and Orwellian surveillance in the workplace is presented as creating trade-offs between privacy and performance, dehumanizing employees (Morgan, in this volume).

If the data is available for civil institutions to start fantasizing about the use of the swarm template, online social network data already falls in this category of big data and AI is already at the heart of how online social network platforms manage this network data. AI as a set of 'machine learning' or 'deep learning' algorithms are inherently secretive and normative black boxes. Their working can be next to impossible to understand for outsiders. They format, homogenize, analyse, classify and diagnose the phenomenal amounts of information that they have on billions of actors (persons, organizations, governments) and their behavior and interdependencies. Algorithms are programmed to filter and analyse these massive datasets that are updated sometimes in real time. These algorithms find statistical regularities in the data, and then associate these regularities with patterns and norms to identify solutions to problems by recommending content (news, thoughts, knowledge), contacts, jobs, behavior/action/moves, or products (marketing) in a personalized and mechanical way. Since data (about context – including context as social network and characteristics of one's contacts – behavior, relationships, etc.) changes continuously based on input by pervasive technologies, norms and solutions may change and be updated too. AI no longer uses fixed and rigid scripts to find 'solutions'. How these algorithms work, how they build this reflexivity, is proprietary and unknown to the public, with many arbitrary sub-decisions (related for example to thresholds, significance levels, etc.). Platform engineers are said to understand what the algorithms that they programmed do. But post-learning connections between new information cannot be predicted ex ante without running the algorithm first. Contemporary examples show that this digital infrastructure is used for directly political purposes, such as monitoring, intoxicating and paralyzing opposition. One can wonder through which specific processes Big Tech influences AI. How do they choose when the algorithms need refining and when they are fit enough for purpose? For instance, false results affecting rich, white, politically active people might prompt fine-tuning the algorithms even if this is costly; on the other hand, false results affecting poor, brown, politically neutralized people might be safer to ignore.

Struggles for the control of this technology by powerful actors is likely to be violent, providing new tools for political influence and socio-economic control of individual behaviour and societies and their institutions, for example through personalized 'filter bubbles' (Roth & Cointet, 2010). This transition is hyper-centralized, in the making, and based on mainly private research – public academic research being largely shut out and left behind. Perhaps swarm-teams were born in the military because it is an institution in which the organization of work leaves little room for normative discussions in the first place. In the army, situations are often urgent and hierarchy is usually clear and inflexible. As shown by Al-Amoudi and Latsis (this volume), AI is not capable of justifying normative decisions to human beings. In the context of the military, AI's incapacity to provide normative justification might perhaps explain how swarm-teams spread: first in the army, then at work, then in everyday life.

Broader social and cultural conditions of possibility for the spread of the swarm-teams template might include the more general weakening of collegial pockets below the executive suite in organizations, especially unions at the shop floor level and the professions in more expert departments. It will be difficult for soldiers (and after them perhaps for medical doctors, for lawyers and for academics) to criticize swarm-teams on the basis of their professional group's values. An additional cultural condition can be identified in the exclusion of morals from public reasoning that Porpora (this volume) wrote extensively about. So a soldier may criticize swarm-teams on the basis that they are not as efficient as they pretend to be. However, it might be difficult to criticize them on the basis that they undermine the honour of combatants (see Edelmann, 2018, for an extension of this argument).

Swarm templates as reinventions of collective responsibility

During my visit, the Board of Visitors was staffed with mathematicians advising about a more general mathematization and social digitalization of military work. Swarms as mathematical collective action templates show a vision of collegiality as shaped by bureaucracy, that is, that has been transformed inside out, as in stigmergic interactions. In this template, swarms are a top-down organizational process that is also meant to co-opt bottom-up processes such as oppositional solidarity. One may argue that if these are attempts to find mathematical laws that will lead to ways to control people and 'help' them govern society, they are bound to fail. However, the problem is that the assumptions and rules that are derived from these swarms end up framing decisions. Just because a goal is unattainable does not mean that pursuing it is without consequences.

Although this chapter does not provide an in-depth look at the military organization of teamwork in battlefields, the point is to understand the direction in which the military institution using AI is potentially steering social change with digitalization. The military swarm template signals that the large bureaucracies of the world want to neutralize collegiality 'below' in the hierarchy using AI. One of the few kinds of collegiality left in a bureaucratized world is in workgroups, in teams on the ground. Such collegial pockets/settings have always been closely monitored (and often targeted for dissolution) by the wider bureaucratic organizations of which they are part, because they are crucial to carrying out tasks but also tend to develop oppositional forms of solidarity, even if they are also innovative (Courpasson, 2000). This oppositional solidarity can be further dissolved, used and transformed by digitalization, but this time used and transformed inside out to become forms of solidarity that are no longer threatening to the bureaucratic organization as a whole.

Digitalization is the latest avatar of bureaucratization, a special avatar, one that has turned on collegiality itself, that is, innovative work that needs coordinated human relationships to be carried out, trying to routinize what had always resisted routinization. It does this by trying to reduce relationships to digitalized interactions. Thus what swarm templates represent or illustrate is a generic attempt at uniformization of cooperation and innovation emerging from relationships, relational infrastructures and social processes in society. There is something dystopian and profoundly socially destructive in this social trend: the idea that AI technology will finally succeed in doing, unobtrusively, what bureaucracy was never able to achieve up to now: controlling the residual part of action that needs appropriateness judgments, endogenization of structure, relational infrastructure and reflexive commitment to the whole – not just to five flock neighbours.

More public knowledge is needed about criteria for team assembly (Contractor, 2013). Team composition may be important to answer the question of whether it is really possible to eliminate oppositional solidarity and at the same time make a team effective. Solidarity is an element of effectiveness, which emerges from experience and questions the possibility of achieving both goals simultaneously. This is where criteria of team assembly are important. Common experience sometimes erases the salience of differences between team members. Teams sometimes begin as very unsettled and then emerge as very effective groups thanks to experience.

The military institution invests massively in mathematical research and digital technology of collective action that is meant to redesign its ways of war. And yet social scientists are sceptical, not just because coordination among humans cannot be perfect, but because the very uncertain nature of many of their tasks requires personalized relational work that is not just a series of impersonal interactions that can be remote controlled systematically (Duran & Lazega, 2015). But the military has long been a source of inspiration for management, from leadership vision, organizational preparation, planning, evaluation of tactics against broader strategy, and avoidance of mission creep, all considered as requisites to winning battles. This includes for example principles of commando training: clear communication and alignment; definition of a team's goals and missions; recruitment of people who want to be part of a team and are willing to be good followers; clear definition of team members' roles and responsibilities, of everyone's action plans in uncertain and changing environments; autonomy and the ability to take decisive action; capacity to assume the roles of superiors at a moment's notice; giving and receiving support.

As presented everywhere today in the mass media, artificial intelligence is one of the most powerful technologies developed by humankind. AI prospects and pumps and centralizes unprecedented quantities of data, non-stop, from the internet, open or closed access, public or private, confidential or intimate, on all digital online devices, in all its forms, written, images, audio, video. Then it analyses, classifies, aggregates, and updates in real time. This technology is transforming almost every industry, including the medical, finance and banking industries. Due to its potential, there are enormous financial investments into AI. Every time one of the users of online hegemonic platforms opens an application, a personalization algorithm sorts through all the posts that a person could theoretically see and dishes up the fraction it thinks she or he would like to see first. The system weighs hundreds of frequently updated signals. Without AI, many of these signals would be impossible to include in statistical analysis, but analysis nevertheless is never neutral.

Combined with the efficiency of AI described previously, these management devices will change the workplace. The overall argument is that bureaucratization is well positioned to win through AI which will help eliminate at least one form of collegiality in bureaucracy, that is, bottom up with oppositional solidarity, as Human Relations Management has been trying to do for a century. One critique of this argument is that if AI is giving good, effective information then armies based on this digital and social technology will fail by creating precisely the oppositional structure that they are trying to avoid.[9] So the question of how clear it is that the technology is succeeding or failing needs further attention. Indeed, failure and success are very relative in this area. Digital technology might just provide a more efficient killing machinery, a more efficient form of destruction that just spreads the illusion of efficiency and perfect organization by simply hiding certain forms of inefficiency. From this perspective, it is impossible not to mention, for example, journalistic information that the 'U.S.-led coalition in Iraq is killing far more Iraqi civilians than previously acknowledged in its "precision" air campaign against the Islamic State – 31 times more, in fact.'[10] This might be the cost of using AI and the swarm template to target enemy networks. The swarm-and-forget approach did indeed forget to measure the collateral damage of this military strategy. Social digitalization thus converges towards imposing on people's destiny a social script derived from such data by computer scientists, engineers and bureaucrats. Whether well intended or not, this trend can only reinforce physical and symbolic violence in a society already very unequal (Elias, 1984 edition; Delzescaux, 2016; Varman & Al-Amoudi, 2016). This imposition is nothing new,

---

9   Something very similar takes place in universities. Top management sees many adavantages in bureaucratization. Collegial units are monitored for their precise objectives and quantified performance outcomes, which generates further oppositional structure and mindset.

10   A.Khan and A.Gopal, "The Uncounted", *New York Times*, 16 November 2017.

but its systematization can only decrease social cohesion at a time when this cohesion is needed for more justice, more resilience in the ecological transition and more sharing of new ideas for institutional entrepreneurship.

Prospects of its extension to civil society may be linked to the fact that, in many ways, this swarm template requires a form of collective responsibility that might also be useful to governments in the management of future transitions. The lesson from the military swarm template might be that new forms of collective responsibility, based on transforming human beings into 'dreaming robots on auto-pilot', to use again Barabási's (2003) expression, reduce relationships to interactions. This is part of controlling and dehumanizing people, which is also what the military does, as historians have recently shown about manipulations of emotions by the massive distribution of alcohol in WWI trenches. With the swarm template and digital exoskeleton, social actors might be subjected to new forms of punitive collective responsibility as part of a now irreversible process of the digitalization of society.

Punitive collective responsibility has always been a reality. Recall Hannah Arendt's observations on collective responsibility in *The Origins of Totalitarianism* (1951):

> The Okhrana, the Czarist predecessor of the GPU, is reported to have invented a filing system in which every suspect was noted on a large card in the center of which his name was surrounded by a red circle; his political friends were designated by smaller red circles and his nonpolitical acquaintances by green ones; brown circles indicated persons in contact with friends of the suspect but not known to him personally; cross-relationships between the suspect's friends, political and nonpolitical, and the friends of his friends were indicated by lines between the respective circles. Obviously, the limitations of this method are set only by the size of the filing cards, and, theoretically, a gigantic single sheet could show the relations and cross-relationships of the entire population. And this is the utopian goal of the totalitarian secret police: a look at the gigantic map on the office wall should suffice at any given moment to establish, not who is who or who thinks what, but who is related to whom and in what degree or kind of intimacy. The totalitarian ruler knows that it is dangerous to send a person to a concentration camp and leave his family and particular milieu untouched; [It is a common practice in Soviet Russia to arrest whole families; Hitler's 'Health Bill' also foresaw the elimination of all families in which one member was found to be afflicted with a disease.] the map on the wall would enable him to eradicate people without leaving any traces of them – or almost none. Total abolition of legality is safe only under the condition of perfect information, or at least a degree of knowledge of private and intimate details which evokes the illusion of perfection.
>
> (Arendt, 1951/1973 edition: 432)

Arendt's early lucidity suggests that a new form of punitive collective responsibility is in the making in society where AI is organizing collective action based on the swarm template.

These trends represent vital challenges for sociology. This transformation of one of the last forms of bottom-up collegiality as an organizational form into bureaucratically remote-controlled processes may have more effects than we currently anticipate and deserves more attention. In current environmental and societal crises, the number of complex and extreme situations that citizens must face, experience and act upon is increasing. In this context, different kinds of social networks, physical and digital in particular, are building blocks of new forms of collective action. Sociologists should look more at how citizens use relational and network thinking and new (particularly digital) technologies to build new forms of social discipline that they (the citizens) consider to be legitimate, and that they (the citizens) hope will help them manage the dilemmas of their individual and collective actions in such complex and extreme situations. One requirement for facing this challenge is to build public knowledge of how social network analyses help citizens approach the generic processes of their own social life at the local level: forms of social solidarity, inequalities and exclusions (for sharing all sorts of resources, including cultural, economic, emotional); collective learning and forms of socialization; social control and conflict resolution; regulation and institutionalization of new norms and practices; and so forth. The recursive feedbacks between such processes on the one hand, the creation of new and specific digital technologies or web-based social networks on the other hand, are among the frontiers of current knowledge in the social sciences.

Are we bound to witness and participate in this bureaucratization through AI digitalization based on this swarm template? Since this might kill innovation as well as people, facing this challenge requires finding alternatives. A recent explosion of collegial organizations harnessing the potential of collegial networks online and in real life is associated with peer-to-peer (P2P) networks (Pazaitis, Kostakis, & Bauwens, 2017; Bauwens & Kostakis, 2017): control of these technologies could be shared at least by open science, preventing monopolistic hegemons from acquiring the power over knowledge that the military has over physical strength and violence. Technology will not facilitate the good society if it is hoarded and monopolized. Other uses of data and applications may make bottom-up collegiality easier and easier to afford and operate, as in P2P self-organization by coworking groups or cooperatives. The latter may solve difficult and costly problems associated with collegiality, building consensus for example, by relying on P2P technology, cloud computing and information available to all on the internet (with or without internet neutrality).

Indeed, such alternatives might help resist the privatization of knowledge and privatization of social sciences by private web giants increasingly monopolizing data about individuals, relationships and societies, reshaping economies and politics through platform reorganization, concentrating power to compete with public authorities and build institutions, and dismantling checks and balances to the point of threatening already fragile democracies. The new technology is not necessarily violent in the sense of physical brutality. It is violent in the sense that it undermines alternative forms of collective action based on the commons, including the knowledge commons, and alternative conceptions of the public interest. A credible regulation of such giants remains to be designed and enforced.

Swarm templates mobilize belief in 'laws'[11] derived from heavy-duty mathematics and are a symbol of further bureaucratization of warfare and of military-driven social morphogenesis. The public at large does not know exactly what the algorithms of AI are and what they do. They are private and secret. Big Tech companies build their competitive advantage and monopoly powers on this secrecy. But AI models will be 'efficient' as long as their assumptions hold. If society follows that path, this new kind of bureaucratic and symbolic violence will allow those in power to decide who will be able to coordinate and pool resources (material goods, intelligence, effort, time etc.) to act collectively. This struggle has always been part of democracy, but the latter's future is again at stake in the new ways in which this further struggle takes place between digitalized bureaucracy and collegiality turned inside out.

References

Aggarwal, I., Woolley, A. W., Chabris, C. F., & Malone, T. W. (2015). Cognitive diversity, collective intelligence, and learning in teams. *Proceedings of Collective Intelligence*, 1(3.1): 3–3.

Archer, M. S. (Ed.). (2014). *Late Modernity: Trajectories Towards Morphogenic Society*. Berlin and Heidelberg: Springer Science & Business Media.

Arendt, H. (Ed.). (1951/1973). *The Origins of Totalitarianism*. Boston, MA: Houghton Mifflin Harcourt.

Barabási, A. L. (2003). *Linked: How Everything Is Connected to Everything Else and What It Means for Business, Sciences, and Everyday Life*. New York, NY: Plume.

Bauwens, M., & Kostakis, V. (2017). *Manifeste pour une véritable économie collaborative: vers une société des communs*. Paris: ECLM.

Bogdanov, P., Baumer, B., Basu, P., Bar-Noy, A., & Singh, A. K. (2013, September). As strong as the weakest link: Mining diverse cliques in weighted graphs. In *Joint European Conference on Machine Learning and Knowledge Discovery in Databases* (pp. 525–540). Berlin and Heidelberg: Springer.

Centeno, M. A. (2002). *Blood and Debt: War and the Nation-State in Latin America*. University Park, PA: Penn State Press.

Centeno, M. A., & Enriquez, E. (2016). *War and Society*. Cambridge: Polity Press.

Contractor, N. (2013). Some assembly required: Leveraging Web science to understand and enable team assembly. *Philosophical Transactions of the Royal Society A*, 371(1987): 20120385.

Courpasson, D. (2000). Managerial strategies of domination: Power in soft bureaucracies. *Organization Studies*, 21(1): 141–161.

Delzescaux, S. (2016). *Norbert Elias: Distinction, Conscience et Violence*. Paris: Armand Colin.

Duran, P., & Lazega, E. (Eds.). (2015). *Les figures de la coordination*. Special issue of *L'Année Sociologique*. Paris: PUF.

Edelmann, A. (2018). Culturally meaningful networks: On the transition from military to civilian life in the United Kingdom. *Theory and Society*, 47(3): 327–380.

---

11 "Laws" that echo George Orwell's "Sooner or later a false belief bumps up against solid reality, usually on a battlefield" (*In Front of Your Nose*).

Elias, N. (1984). *What Is Sociology?* New York, NY: Columbia University Press.

Hildenbrandt, H., Carere, C., & Hemelrijk, C. K. (2010). Self-organized aerial displays of thousands of starlings: A model. *Behavioral Ecology*, 21(6): 1349–1359.

Jones, A. T., Friedkin, N. E., & Singh, A. K. (2017, November). Modeling the co-evolution of committee formation and awareness networks in organizations. In *International Workshop on Complex Networks and Their Applications* (pp. 881–894). Cham, Switzerland: Springer.

Lazega, E. (2001). *The Collegial Phenomenon: The Social Mechanisms of Cooperation Among Peers in a Corporate Law Partnership*. Oxford: Oxford University Press.

Lazega, E. (2015a). Synchronization costs in the organizational society: Intermediary relational infrastructures in the dynamics of multilevel networks. In E. Lazega & T. Snijders (Eds.), *Multilevel Network Analysis: Theory, Methods and Applications*. Dordrecht: Springer.

Lazega, E. (2015b). Body captors and network profiles: A neo-structural note on digitalized social control and morphogenesis. In M. S. Archer (Ed.), *Generative Mechanisms Transforming the Social Order* (pp. 113–133). Dordrecht: Springer.

Lazega, E. (2017). Networks and commons: Bureaucracy, collegiality and organizational morphogenesis in the struggles to shape collective responsibility in new sharing institutions. In M. S. Archer (Ed.), *Morphogenesis and Human Flourishing* (Vol. V, pp. 211–237). Dordrecht: Springer

Lazega, E. (forthcoming). Bottom-up collegiality, top-down collegiality, or inside-out collegiality? Research on joint regulation in multi-level relational infrastructures as laboratories for social change. In G. Ragozini & M.-P. Vitale (Eds.), *Challenges in Social Network Research*, Dordrecht, Springer.

Lazega, E., & Wattebled, O. (2011, November). Two definitions of collegiality and their inter-relation: The case of a Roman Catholic diocese. *Sociologie du Travail*, 53(1): e57-e77. Available online: http://sociologiedutravail.org/spip.php?article34

Lungeanu, A., Huang, Y., & Contractor, N. S. (2014). Understanding the assembly of interdisciplinary teams and its impact on performance. *Journal of Informetrics*, 8(1): 59–70.

Mazzucato, M. (2015). *The Entrepreneurial State: Debunking Public vs. Private Sector Myths*. London: Anthem Press.

Pazaitis, A., Kostakis, V., & Bauwens, M. (2017). Digital economy and the rise of open cooperativism: The case of the Enspiral Network. *Transfer: European Review of Labour and Research*, 23(2): 177–192.

Reynaud, J-D. (1989). *Les Règles du jeu: L'action collective et la régulation sociale*. Paris: Armand Colin.

Reynolds, C. W. (1987). Flocks, herds and schools: A distributed behavioral model. *ACM SIGGRAPH Computer Graphics*, 21: 25–34.

Rosenblat, A. (2018). *Uberland: How Algorithms Are Rewriting the Rules of Work*. Berkeley, CA: University of California Press.

Roth, C., & Cointet, J. P. (2010). Social and semantic coevolution in knowledge networks. *Social Networks*, 32(1): 16–29.

Scharre, P. (2018). *Army of None: Autonomous Weapons and the Future of War*. New York, NY: WW Norton & Company.

Shibutani, T. (1978). *The Derelicts of Company K: A Sociological Study of Demoralization*. Berkeley, CA: University of California Press.

Shils, E. A., & Janowitz, M. (1948). Cohesion and disintegration in the Wehrmacht in World War II. *Public Opinion Quarterly*, 12(2): 280–315.

Stouffer, S. A., Lumsdaine, A. A., Lumsdaine, M. H., Williams Jr, R. M., Smith, M. B., Janis, I. L., & Cottrell Jr, L. S. (1949). *The American Soldier: Combat and Its Aftermath: Studies in Social Psychology in World War II*, Vol. 2.

Van der Vaart, K., Sinhuber, M., Reynolds, A. M., & Ouellette, N. T. (2019). Mechanical spectroscopy of insect swarms. Science Advances, 5(7), eaaw9305.

Varman, R., & Al-Amoudi, I. (2016). Accumulation through derealization: How corporate violence remains unchecked. *Human Relations*, 69(10): 1909–1935.

Wittek, R., & Van de Bunt, G. G. (2004). Post-bureaucratic governance, informal networks and oppositional solidarity in organizations. *The Netherlands' Journal of Social Sciences*, 40(3): 295–319.

Woolley, A. W., Aggarwal, I., & Malone, T. W. (2015). Collective intelligence and group performance. *Current Directions in Psychological Science*, 24(6): 420–424.

Subject index

Printed in the United States
by Baker & Taylor Publisher Services

Printed in the United States
by Baker & Taylor Publisher Services